FROM PALACE TO PRISON

T0306313

From Palace to Prison

Inside the Iranian Revolution

EHSAN NARAGHI

Translated from the French by Nilou Mobasser

Chicago Ivan R. Dee *1994*

FROM PALACE TO PRISON. Copyright © 1991 by Éditions Balland as *Des Palais du Chah aux Prisons de la Révolution*. English translation copyright © 1994 by Ivan R. Dee, Inc. All rights reserved, including the right to reproduce this book or portions thereof in any form. For information, address: Ivan R. Dee, Publisher, 1332 North Halsted Street, Chicago 60622. Manufactured in the United States of America and printed on acid-free paper.

www.ivanrdee.com

The paperback edition of this book carries the ISBN 1-56663-767-8.

Library of Congress Cataloging-in-Publication Data:
Narāqī, Iḥsān, 1926–
[Des palais du chah aux prisons de la Révolution. English]
From palace to prison: inside the Iranian Revolution / Ehsan Naraghi; translated from the French by Nilou Mobasser.
p. cm.
Includes index.
ISBN 1-56663-033-9
1. Narāqī, Iḥsān, 1926– 2. Politicians—Iran—Biography.
3. Prisoners, Political—Iran—Biography. I. Title.
DS316.9.N37A3 1994
955.05'3'092—dc20 93-13873
[B]

In memory of my mother,
to my wife, and, through them,
to all the wives and mothers of prisoners,
wherever they may be found

Preface

On September 28, 1978, I was summoned to the Saadabad Palace for the first of eight audiences with the Shah spread over the last hundred days of his reign. During these meetings the monarch, anxious to understand the growing revolutionary crisis in Iran and if possible to find a way out, questioned me closely about my views of the situation. The result was a series of conversations, reconstructed in the first part of this book, which touched on issues ranging from the historical and ideological origins of the revolutionary movement to the significance of the day-to-day events of those turbulent months.

I was not someone whom the Shah would normally have met in this way. As director of the Institute of Planning and Research for Science and Higher Education, I had in the 1970s sat on various state councils dealing with educational matters, and on several occasions I had advised the queen on cultural affairs; but my work was not of a kind that brought me into direct contact with the Shah. Furthermore, he had a robust scorn for intellectuals in general and a particular reason to be cautious of me. For, as he must have known from a hostile report in my file with Savak, the Shah's security police (a file which I later learned about when I was interrogated at Evin Prison after the revolution), my associations were suspect. When I was director of Tehran University's Institute for Social Studies and Research, I had kept under my wing a number of young scholars who were vehement opponents of the regime. I was not myself an active member of the opposition, but my independent political outlook, evident from my books, and my professional contact and personal friendships with open dissenters would in normal circumstances have excluded me from the Shah's circle of advisers.

But as the political situation deteriorated in 1978 the Shah began to bypass his usual channels of information—the security police and various courtiers—and to seek independent counsel. This was because, as I explain in the pages that follow, he felt himself isolated and abandoned. Many of the people who surrounded and flattered him in the good days had already fled the country, and the obvious discrepancy between official Savak reports and daily events on the streets had left him disenchanted with the organization. At the same time he was desperate to find a way out of the crisis that engulfed him, especially after the Jaleh Square massacre of September 1978, and had begun to consider meeting some of the demands of the moderate opposition. But neither he nor any of his usual advisers had connections with leading moderates or any knowledge (save through the prism of Savak reports) of how such people viewed the world, his regime, and the political crisis. For the very reason that, only months earlier, I would have been regarded with suspicion, I suddenly became someone with whom it might be useful to discuss events.

I began to write this memoir soon after the Shah left Iran on February 11, 1979, two days after my last conversation with him. My intention was to record my impressions of a man who for several decades had been one of the world's most powerful leaders and whose reaction to the disintegration of that power I had witnessed at close quarters. I have tried to make my testimony as accurate and authentic as possible. My main source is the notes I wrote immediately after my audiences with the Shah, while our conversation remained fresh in my mind. But I have also drawn on additional notes I prepared *before* the audiences, for after the first conversation the Shah told me I should feel free to raise whatever issues I felt were important. To supplement my own record I have used the notebooks put at my disposal by Abdollah Entezam and Gholam-Hossein Sadighi, both highly respected independent politicians to whom the Shah turned for advice in the last months of his reign. My conversations with the former prime minister Ali Amini, who saw the Shah regularly during this period, and with Aslan Afshar, who was chief of protocol and the Shah's constant companion throughout the revolutionary crisis, have also been of great help. Finally, Michel Poniatowski, who was sent to Iran by Giscard d'Estaing to ascertain the Shah's thinking and mood on the eve of the Guadeloupe summit of January 5–6, 1979, kindly provided me with an account of his long interview with the Shah on December 26, 1978. I am deeply indebted to all these people.

I more or less completed the first part of my memoir toward the end of 1979 and planned to publish it the following year. But in December 1979 I was arrested at Tehran airport as I was about to board a plane to Paris. When I was released four months later I began to add the notes I had taken in prison, and I made up my mind to delay publication. Later events justified my decision, for I was arrested again in June 1981 and imprisoned until September 1983. By the time I was free to write again I had such rich material on prison life—material which I felt threw important light on the experience of the revolution and the nature of Iranian society—that I decided to give myself time for reflection and put together in the same work my conversations with the Shah and my prison experiences.

In both sections of my memoir I have tried to report the facts as I saw them and to draw accurate and truthful portraits of the people involved. Whether writing about the Shah, a revolutionary activist about to be executed, or a prison guard, I have tried to capture individuals as they were, "as human beings who come into the world to suffer and to die." In reconstructing my conversations with the Shah, Queen Farah, and many of the people I encountered in prison, I have chosen to present them in the form of a dialogue. These dialogues do not of course represent verbatim accounts of our exchanges—particularly with the men I met in prison where I could not keep a diary; but I have made every effort to keep closely to the authentic tone and substance. If I have not been entirely successful, I hope the reader will forgive me, for no human being is without faults or shortcomings.

E. N.

Paris
August 1993

Contents

In golden letters 'tis written in a crystalline sky:
Good deeds will live, all else will die.

—HAFEZ (1320–1389)

FROM PALACE TO PRISON

PALACE

From Dreams to Awakening
(First Conversation with the Shah)

Monday, September 23, 1978, 3:30 p.m.

My first audience with the Shah took place at his summer palace of Saadabad in the Alborz foothills in northern Tehran. He had been intending to see me since March, but the meeting had been postponed several times because, I believe, deep down the Shah was reluctant to receive me. In this he was undoubtedly influenced by reports prepared by the head of Savak, the secret police, about the Institute for Social Studies and Research during the 1960s. Nonetheless, when the chamberlain led me to his office, the Shah, who was adept at hiding his feelings, received me very amicably, standing in the middle of the room. He politely shook my hand and invited me to sit in a chair facing his own. I knew immediately that the crisis had brought about a change in him, for in normal times whenever he received Iranian subjects he would remain standing, and if the discussion went on for some time he would pace up and down the room while the visitor was expected to remain still with his eyes always turned toward the monarch.

Before me sat a man profoundly shaken by recent events, who had lost the self-assurance he had displayed not long ago in the official meetings I had sometimes attended. He said in a friendly manner, as if to excuse himself, "My responsibilities prevented me from seeing you sooner. What are you doing now, and what is your assessment of the situation?"

I gave a quick resumé of my activities over the previous twenty years, emphasizing the fact that Savak's hostility to the Institute of Social Research had compelled me to leave the country in 1969.[1] Through the books I had published, my articles, and my interventions in the media, I had tried to explain to the technocrats in power that the path they were following would not lead us to the "great civilization" desired by the Shah but instead to a chaotic upheaval. I believed that their policy would split the nation in two, with a modernist minority on one side and a large traditionalist majority on the other. Our national unity would be undermined, and we would be exposed to a totally unprecedented cultural conflict. To back up my assertions, I offered the monarch a copy of my book entitled *Raw Greed*, in which I had tried to show that this method of achieving progress would result only in catastrophe.

After this preamble, the Shah said, "I'd like to hear your analysis of the current situation in Iran. Where does this rebellion and spreading agitation originate? Who is instigating it? Who is sustaining this protest? Who triggered this religious movement?"

"You yourself, Majesty," I replied.

He looked at me, at once surprised and horrified, and cried, "Me?"

He had obviously been hoping that I would find a scapegoat of some kind. Anyone would do: the Palestinians, the communists, Qaddafi, Khomeini, the Americans, and heaven knows who else.

"Why me?" he persisted.

"Fifteen years ago, in 1962, you paid a visit with Arsanjani[2] to the holy shrine at Qom. There you openly attacked the religious leaders, describing their opposition to agricultural reform and the right of women to stand as candidates for parliament as a sign of their reactionary position. You were so abrasive and even abusive that Moiniyan, who was at the time head of radio and television, was forced to censor your remarks. . . . Indeed, your position was so

1. I accepted an offer from Rene Maheu, director general of UNESCO, to go to Paris to work as director of the organization's youth division.

2. Arsanjani was minister of agriculture in 1962. He had radical ideas and was the architect of a thoroughgoing land reform.

extreme that the next day I remarked to a group of acquaintances: 'We must not forget this historic day when His Majesty set off an immense Islamic movement in the country against himself.' When my colleagues asked me to explain myself, I said, 'From now on, the religious leaders will be forced to step into the political arena to refute the charge of conservatism and to prove that their rejection of agricultural reform is not based on an attachment to an archaic social order. By relying on the enormous resources of Shi'ism, they will show that they are more revolutionary than His Majesty and his White Revolution.' "[3]

The urgency of this situation did indeed force religious leaders to return to Shi'i history and to retrieve all its revolutionary elements. They were even led to studying other civilizations—as was demonstrated, for example, by their sudden interest in foreign languages. I reminded the Shah that it was easy for a Shi'i mullah (a quasi-clerical Muslim) to fight all political powers—which are judged illegitimate until the return of the Hidden Imam:[4]

"As you know, since the assassination of Imam Ali, who ruled as caliph for barely five years, the Shi'a have regarded all caliphs as usurpers, and this suspicion has extended to all political powers. Furthermore, symbols play a very powerful part in our religion. I recently attended a funeral at which the preacher spoke about several illegitimate Sunni caliphs, stressing the immorality of their ways. When he came to the subject of one of these, he described in great detail the depravity of his family and the people around him. The congregation, about two thousand in all, knew he was referring to Your Majesty's court. But the allusion was based on vivid symbols so deeply embedded in everyone's mind that no one could take offense at what he was saying, even the highly experienced Savak officer who was observing the meeting. Another feature of Shi'ism, which lends

3. The "White Revolution" was a series of reforms carried out by the Shah in 1962–1963, the most important of which was the land reform. The Shah wanted to use the reform program to provoke a confrontation with the Shi'i clergy in order to show the Kennedy administration and Iran's modernist elites that his main enemies were reactionary mullahs.

4. For the Shi'a, the Hidden Imam or the "Mahdi" is the eleventh descendant of Ali (600–661), cousin and son-in-law of the prophet Mohammed. The Mahdi mysteriously disappeared, while still young, in Samarra twelve centuries ago. He is said to have concealed himself, awaiting the day when he will return to establish the reign of order and justice on earth.

the religious movement exceptional vitality and sustains a constant sense of hope in believers, is its belief in the eventual reappearance of the Hidden Imam. Perhaps you have noticed that the prayer of lamentation has been said much more frequently in recent years."

The Shah seemed to be unaware of the significance of the prayer. No doubt he had never concerned himself with the political interpretation his subjects could attach to religion. He asked, "What is the prayer of lamentation?"

"It's a relatively long prayer, recited after the morning prayer on Fridays. It is, at one and the same time, an expression of grief at the injustices of this world and a supplication to God for the reappearance of the Hidden Imam."

At this point I said jokingly to the Shah, "You see, Sire, you are trapped on both sides: behind you there is Ali, the model of a just ruler, entirely beyond reproach; and in front of you there is the Twelfth Imam, whose return is considered to be imminent by believers."

The Shah replied with an air of helplessness, "Must we call everything into question then? What is to be done? What I don't understand is why young people are drawn to these religious and traditional ideas which used to interest only older people."

"Religious leaders realized that they had to attract the young," I answered. "Their associations have worked to increase the number of publications available to the young, and in the mosques they use simple words to catch their interest. Ali Shariati[5] played an extremely influential role in all this. On the one hand he strengthened the idea of eternal struggle, inherent to Shi'ism, and on the other he used a lyrical language which combined utopian politics with spiritual symbols and completely captivated the young."

"As far as I know," the Shah said pointedly, "the religious leaders do not agree with Shariati's interpretation of religious principles. I was told that at one point they described him as a Wahhabi.[6] If my

5. Ali Shariati was an Iranian political theoretician who died in London in 1977 on the eve of the Islamic revolution. Shariati tried to build a bridge between Muslim traditionalism and militant third worldism.

6. Wahhabism is a form of Sunni Islamic fundamentalism which originated in Arabia where it has been the official religion for almost two centuries under the Saudi dynasty.

memory serves me correctly, some of them even considered him to be a heretic."

"Your memory serves you well, Your Majesty. Religious leaders do not agree with his interpretation of the Koran and the sayings of the Prophet. But these same leaders stopped criticizing him when they realized his movement was gaining ground. They realized that Shariati was renewing the language of Shi'i Islam by drawing on Muslim anticolonialist movements in different parts of the world. In particular, by speaking of the struggles of the Algerian and Palestinian peoples, he succeeded in giving Islam a much more attractive image than in the past. Shariati was inspired by the ideas of Franz Fanon. The magic of his poetic language, with its biting formulas opposing, for example, Safavid Shi'ism, which represented all that was contrived and illegitimate in the religion, to Alawite Shi'ism, which represented all that was pure and true, was also very potent.[7] The language of religion, previously regarded as old-fashioned, became a source of inspiration for the young. In this new form it promised the attainment of such ideals as justice and equality. The clergy gradually allowed themselves to be carried along by this movement and finally found themselves in a position directly opposed to you, Your Majesty."

Involuntarily reaching out to me with both hands, the Shah said in a confiding tone: "You must know that I am a deeply religious man. I have nothing against religion, but, as we both know, in the past our clergy have exploited the superstition and ignorance of the illiterate: they have always tried to incite mass fanaticism for their own political ends. They have tried to bring religion into everything in order to gain power for themselves and in practice to drag the country backward. They have no interest in the progress and development of this country."

"Sire, our country's constitution is based on three pillars: the clergy, the monarchy, and the national will as expressed in truly free elections. Now that the Parliament has been discredited, you must place greater reliance on the clergy."

7. The Safavid dynasty ruled Iran from the sixteenth to the eighteenth century and made Shi'ism the official religion of the country. The term Alawite Shi'ism denoted the religion of Imam Ali. Shariati's argument about the contrast between the two types of religion does not stand the test of historical analysis. Nevertheless, his ideas enthralled the young.

"An understanding between the clergy and the monarchy existed until the death of Ayatollah Borujerdi.[8] We even postponed agricultural reform during his lifetime because he disapproved of it."

"But Your Majesty, that disapproval was not aimed at protecting the interests of the big landowners. The clergy simply felt that the reforms went against certain principles of Islamic law. Islam respects private property within certain limits. That is the essential difference between it and communism."

"And yet the religious camp is marching shoulder to shoulder with the communists in demonstrations against the regime. It is not even clear which of them is instigating the demonstrations. In my opinion, what brings them together is their common desire to destroy our national achievements, particularly in the economy."

"It is possible that they find themselves united in their struggle against your system. At heart, however, they have profound differences. But to return to the question of the land reform. In 1962 I met Ayatollah Milani of Mashad who in the course of our conversation remarked: 'The charge that we clerics are opposed to the land reform and equal electoral rights for women is unfounded. The government makes us out to be reactionary and backward. On the contrary, we are prepared to find religious justification for any reform which His Majesty may wish to initiate. But on one condition: he must recognize the limits of his prerogatives. He must also be mindful of our rights and obligations and of the constraints which we face in our dealings with the people; he must not impose his reforms on us by force.'"

"What have I imposed on them?" the Shah retorted in his candid way. "Like other countries, we too wanted to have our land reform: we wanted to end a situation in which a single landlord could own ninety villages; we wanted peasants to own a piece of land. You are a sociologist. I am sure you have been to villages where you could see for yourself that the reform restored dignity to the peasants."

"In the eyes of the clergy, Your Majesty's objective was to win over the peasantry from them, because you had been let down politically in the towns. The clergy claim that if they had been consulted they would have found a solution that would have taken into account the

8. Ayatollah Borujerdi, who became supreme leader of the Iranian Shi'a after World War II, died in Qom in 1961.

interests of the rural population without infringing any religious principles. In sum, if you wanted to exercise your rights as a monarch, you ought at the same time to have respected their rights as clergy."

The Shah looked as though he was waking from a dream: "Before 1962 one never heard any mention of Khomeini. It was only later that people began to speak of him. Where was he? Why does he have so many followers all of a sudden? Where do they come from? What makes him different from all the other religious leaders?"

"For many years Ayatollah Khomeini taught philosophy and mysticism in Qom. He trained many students and he was able to maintain strong links with them. His strength comes from the fact that he kept his distance from the grand ayatollahs by accusing them of conservatism and of subservience to you, Your Majesty. He therefore drew countless young members of the clergy who were feeling frustrated and seeking a new path. In the end he used the 1961 law giving Americans immunity from prosecution—the capitulations—as a platform from which to attack the government. That was the beginning of his movement."

"It was not a question of capitulations in the usual sense. We had established an agreement with Washington whereby American civil and military personnel could benefit from a certain degree of diplomatic immunity in Iran. Similar agreements exist between the United States and some European countries, such as Germany. The 1961 law concerned only minor offenses—violations of the highway code, for example. The issue was blown out of all proportion by the clergy."

"Majesty, after the fall of Mosaddeq[9] in 1953, hatred of the Americans ran so deep that it was easy for Khomeini to unleash an anti-American movement in response to the law. Or put it another way: when Mosaddeq's nationalist aims were defeated, they were adopted by religious opposition. That was why the younger clergy, who were in search of purpose, threw themselves into the arms of Khomeini, thus forcing the hands of other ayatollahs. What lent

9. Mohammed Mosaddeq (1881–1967) was prime minister from 1951 to 1953. He challenged both the Shah's absolutism, in the name of liberal democracy, and foreign, particularly British, interests in Iran. By nationalizing the Anglo-Persian Oil Company he alienated the British and was subsequently deposed in an Anglo-American coup. Thereafter the Shah became the undisputed center of power in Iran, but he remained traumatized by the Mosaddeq experience.

Khomeini strength was the fact that he said openly what the others felt secretly. Bear in mind, too, that Khomeini lived in exile from 1964,[10] which meant that he could speak more freely than the other ayatollahs who remained in Iran."

The Shah seemed irritated. "If I understand you correctly, then, Khomeini is no longer a religious leader. He has become a politician, an agitator who incites the young and fanatical clergy to rebel against the West and modern civilization? He intends to drag the country back hundreds of years and use religion to destabilize the state and the government."

"But Sire, Shi'ism is a totally political religion, and Shi'i religious leaders claim the right to intervene in affairs of the state."

"How can the clergy survive without the monarchy?" he sneered. "If the monarchy ceases to exist, the communists will do away with them."

"For the time being the clergy think they can manage without the monarchy. They also believe they are strong enough to get rid of the communists at the appropriate time."

"Khomeini is the only ayatollah who opposes the monarchy. We have evidence bearing this out. Other ayatollahs have let it be known discreetly that they don't share his point of view."

"As you yourself say, Majesty, they have to let you know discreetly, but they don't dare contradict Khomeini openly. They're forced to keep their opinions to themselves and to behave as if they are on his side for fear they might otherwise alienate the masses from whom they draw their strength."

"What about foreign agitators? Don't you think they too have played a part in all this? We have reports indicating that the regime's detractors are receiving financial help from abroad."

"That, unfortunately, is the kind of argument used by those people around you who insist on ignoring the realities facing them. The Islamists who are opposing you have no need for foreign money: one of the characteristics of Shi'ism is that it has no difficulty obtaining the resources it requires. The bazaar merchants are in a position to respond to the financial needs of the religious leaders because, as you yourself are well aware, a pious Shi'i must donate up to a fifth of his

10. Khomeini spent most of his long exile (from 1964 to 1969) in Iraq.

income, depending on the instructions of the religious leader he chooses to follow."

"But the bazaar merchants have been major beneficiaries of the economic development we brought about. Why have they joined this movement? What do they have to complain about? Why are they taking part in this movement of destabilization?"

"First of all, because you excluded them from the decision-making process. You simply favored a small elite who with state support now control the country's industry. As a result, the bazaaris, who receive the crumbs—albeit big crumbs—are not happy. They are not helped by your system. Next, by virtue of their way of life, the bazaar people depend completely on religious personalities, whose support and approbation raises their standing and helps their business affairs. As for the Shi'i clergy, unlike the Sunni they do not depend on the state because they live off the contributions of believers. Your policies in recent years have, if anything, brought the two groups, the clergy and bazaaris, closer together. They now complement and mutually support each other. But to go back to the question of foreign assistance, my impression is that even if it exists, it is negligible in comparison with the help the militants can get at home. At any rate, the militants' argument is a simple one: since your regime has benefited from all kinds of foreign assistance, why shouldn't they do the same? I should also say that the increasingly close ties between your government and Israel have pushed the religious movement into forging ties with militant Palestinians and preaching Islamic nationalism."

"Do other Muslim countries, the Arab ones in particular, always agree with our militant Islamists? According to our information, there are countries which have their eyes on our richest province, Khuzestan."[11] (The Shah was referring to Iraq without naming it.)

"That's true enough, but Your Majesty's nationalism was not strong enough to attract the militants; and your excessively close relations with Israel sowed the seeds of doubt among them. In brief, Iranian nationalists do not believe you can be a symbol of authentic nationalism while at the same time being a defender of Western interests, an unconditional ally of the United States, and a friend of Israel."

11. A region situated along the Iran-Iraq border where part of the population speaks Arabic. Outside Iran it is sometimes called "Arabestan."

"Our economy and military achievements have turned us into a force which the superpowers must reckon with in the Persian Gulf. We have succeeded in extending our influence as far as the Indian Ocean.[12] We had every intention of becoming an immense power in the region. We planned to extend our security range to the 10th parallel, south of India and north of Ceylon. How can patriots fail to understand this?"

"They call you the *gendarme* of the Persian Gulf."

"The term 'gendarme' was first used by the great powers, especially the British, because they could not stand to see their place being taken by one of the countries of the region. I proposed a military pact to all the coastal countries of the Indian Ocean, with the aim of neutralizing it, that is, eliminating Soviet and American military personnel."

Looking directly into my eyes and raising his voice, he said, "Aren't those who call us the gendarme of the Persian Gulf adding grist to the mill of Western powers who oppose any local political and military influence in the region? Are you aware of what the Iraqis and Saudi Arabians are doing in the Persian Gulf? Do you realize that their military expenditures are much higher than ours?"

"Sire, regardless of your desire for independence and your patriotic sentiments, your extremely close links with Israel and the United States offend the nationalist and Muslim sensibilities of Iranians. That is a weak point in your policies, and your opponents have wasted no time exploiting it. But, diplomacy aside, what has strengthened your adversaries' position is without a doubt a combination of three factors. First, the inequalities in the country's living standards: the rapid enrichment of a recently created class which has benefited from oil revenue and which does not even have the relative appearance of dignity possessed by the feudal class you weakened. Next, the economic and financial nepotism practiced by your entourage and especially by your . . . family. Finally, the brutality of Savak, the secret police, which prevents the expression of even the slightest criticism. All this engenders a host of grievances which trickle into a river, swollen by numerous small streams of discontent, and finally overflow into an ocean of bitterness."

12. The Shah wanted to turn the port of Chah-Bahar, in the southeastern corner of Iran, into the Indian Ocean's largest air and naval base.

"How was it that such a river went unnoticed by all the people in positions of power? It is not something which suddenly sprang up overnight?"

"The political class did not see the rising tide. The technocrats who put you in power were incapable of hearing the cry of reality."

"But we selected them from the ranks of graduates from the best European and American universities. How could all these engineers and doctors who studied at the most prestigious Western universities fail to warn me about what was to come?"

"It has to do with our system more than anything else. We have a pyramidlike system in which even the prime minister is not concerned about anything other than orders from above. No one considers himself politically responsible because all that matters is what comes from you. Since decision-making is your exclusive prerogative, the elite believes it is doing you a service by informing you of only those things which fit in with your policies. The elite lays its intelligence and knowledge on the altar of obedience to you, and consequently it prevents you from seeing things the way they are. You wished to put the technocrats everywhere. The technocrat is a machine which responds only to the questions put to it. It does not pose its own questions."

"Are you saying that everything must be changed? That all those in positions of responsibility must be replaced? Tell me what you are saying!"

"I believe they should be replaced for two reasons. First, because they are incapable of facing the current situation and give every impression of being overwhelmed. Second, because the society itself is expecting change. When religion seeps into every aspect of political life, the society moves toward a kind of puritanism and citizens become very demanding of the people governing them. They expect them to be guardians of faith, to be saints. In the face of these demands the political class must adopt a new life-style and avoid ostentatious luxuries. Its actions and demeanor will be subjected to public scrutiny. It will become impossible to keep public and private life apart as they do in the West. That is why, if officials wish to benefit from a good moral standing, they would do well to declare their assets publicly. It might even be conceivable that you yourself, Majesty, may decide to turn over your two palaces to charitable works and live instead, with the Queen and your children, in a simple house, as Nasser did in Egypt."

"What you are asking me and my family to do is, in effect, to play at being poor. Would they not accuse me of hypocrisy and demagoguery?"

"Not at all! It would be useful if you were to set an example for a ruling class which has become exceedingly arrogant, extravagant, and contemptuous of the people. You must try to show that it is possible to rule a big country while at the same time living simply. I hope Your Majesty has realized that our country is sliding toward a revolutionary explosion. The enormous economic and cultural gap between the residents of northern Tehran and the masses in the south of the city will simply fan the fires of revolution. In the course of the demonstrations during the month of Ramadan,[13] it was possible to see for the first time crowds of militants, including women in black chadors, marching through Tehran's northern quarters. When foreign journalists asked me what was happening, I said, 'For the first time today the South has occupied the North,' and I believe, Your Majesty, that this 'occupation' will continue. Let me give you an example: As we were on our way to the palace, my driver, who is an employee of the Ministry of Higher Education, said to me, 'Do you think His Majesty is aware that I earn only 1,500 tomans[14] after twenty years of service?' He begged me to show you his pay slip."

I rose from my seat and held out the pay slip to him. The Shah was clearly reluctant to hold it in his hand. I practically forced him to take it, and, sitting down again, I watched him closely as he examined it. At that moment he seemed totally pathetic to me. It was obvious he had never seen a pay slip before in his life, and he could not even begin to imagine what 1,500 tomans meant. To relieve him of his embarrassment, I spelled it out for him.

"You wouldn't be able to rent the smallest house with this sum, even in the south of the city. It is true that I pay him almost double overtime, but I'm doing it against all the rules. What I'm trying to say is that hundreds of thousands of public employees have the greatest difficulty in making ends meet."

13. The first big popular demonstration which really shook the ruling class took place on the holiday marking the end of the fasting month of Ramadan in 1978, a few days before my first conversation with the Shah.

14. The equivalent in purchasing power of £200 sterling, or about $350.

The Shah put the pay slip on the table and regained his composure.

"So people think that if Khomeini comes to power, they will be any better off? What economic program is Khomeini going to carry out to improve their lives? I'm certain they will lose even what little they have. Have you noticed the slightest concern for people's economic welfare in his proclamations? I really fail to understand these people. It is as if they have completely taken leave of their senses. Khomeini has bewitched them. They're rushing to their doom and can no longer see where their interests lie. I find it heartbreaking."

He suddenly fell silent again. Lowering his eyes, he gazed dejectedly at the flowers on the huge Persian carpet. In order to break the silence and, acting as if I had before me a schoolboy to whom one must explain, report card in hand, the reasons for his failure, I tried as gently as I could to make him understand what had given rise to the grumbling which grew louder every day.

"As far as the economy is concerned, Majesty, you're quite right. These people will gain nothing. But, as the saying goes, 'An injustice well shared is already justice.' They believe that by following Khomeini they will move toward a more egalitarian society and that there will no longer be any differences between people—not, at any rate, in terms of living standards. They look at the way the religious people live and compare its austerity and simplicity with the life-style of the Westernized class with its extravagance and ostentation. Foreign journalists, who visit religious heads in the holy city of Qom, unfailingly attest to their austere living conditions. They asked me about it the other day and I said in reply, 'That is the nub of the matter; the confrontation between the simplicity of Qom and the excesses of Tehran.' That's why I was telling you that the ruling classes will find themselves in a difficult position from now on. Their private as well as their public lives will be scrutinized with a magnifying glass. They must understand that the party is over."

The Shah seemed unconvinced: "Where are these saints you are telling me about? You would be doing the country a great service if you introduced them to me. I would immediately ask them to form a new government."

He pressed his point with an almost naive stubbornness: "Well, where are they? Give me a few names. I will be most indebted to you."

Knowing full well he would not be pleased, I complied, nonetheless: "Mosaddeq's friends and the nationalists, for example."

Cut to the quick, he cried: "You consider Mosaddeq and his friends to be patriots, to be nationalists?"

"Certainly. In any case, for the Iranians, Mosaddeq's name conjures up a will to be free, directed at the indomitable British. To be perfectly honest with you, one of the reasons behind the people's unhappiness since the fall of Mosaddeq has been your disparaging remarks about him."

From the moment I first mentioned Mosaddeq's name, the sovereign had become visibly irritated. He was on the verge of launching into a tirade against the former prime minister. I tried to calm him down by saying, "I'll tell you an anecdote. A few days before Mosaddeq's death in 1967, two young nationalists who worked at my institute brought me a message. Mosaddeq's family wanted me to go to Hoveida[15] to tell him Mosaddeq was dying and persuade him to ask Your Majesty to allow the minister of court to announce an official memorial service for him, if only to honor his first year in office when he nationalized Iran's oil. You had always given the impression that you agreed with Mosaddeq on this point."[16]

Suddenly very interested, the monarch pressed me on. "So, what did you do?"

"I of course went to see Hoveida."

"And what did he say?"

Despite the Shah's impatience, I took my time over the reply and chose my words carefully. "I remember it vividly. I was sitting face to face with Hoveida, who was smoking his pipe. Looking directly into my eyes, he said, 'It's an excellent idea, but you must be mad if you think His Majesty could allow such a thing!' But I persisted: 'My dear Amir-Abbas, if you are persuaded that such a gesture on the part of His Majesty could prove to be a useful step, if it can soothe and heal wounds, why can't you follow the young people's suggestion? Why can't you throw yourself at the King's feet and wrench an agreement

15. Hoveida was at the time prime minister. I had been on friendly terms with him since the early 1950s when I was a student in Geneva and he was a young functionary at the High Commission for Refugees.

16. At heart the Shah would himself have liked to nationalize the oil industry but felt that, given Britain's overwhelming power in the region after World War II, the task was impossible.

out of him, as the great chancellors of the past would have done?' Hoveida replied, 'You're no doubt thinking of Qa'em Maqam and Amir Kabir?'[17] I had to smile and say, 'In view of the two statesmen's tragic end, I don't think I should pursue the matter any further.' "

I did not feel sufficiently at ease with the Shah to be able to tell him the rest of the story. Despite his reservation Hoveida had said to me, "The Shah always harbors suspicions about people. That's why if I suggest to him that he organize a memorial service for Mosaddeq, he may put his own interpretation on the request. I'd advise you to go and see Ardeshir Zahedi [the Shah's son-in-law and then foreign minister]. The Shah is more at ease with him than with me, because he collaborated with Zahedi's father when Mosaddeq was deposed." I followed his advice. Zahedi's reaction was very positive. He thought the idea was ingenious and politically opportune. He went so far as to say that the Shah, and he himself, had always admired, if not approved of, the first period of Mosaddeq's government during which he nationalized the oil. "But," he continued, "knowing His Majesty, I'm afraid he won't accept your suggestion. Nevertheless, I'll broach the subject with him tomorrow in our usual morning meeting at eleven o'clock. Come and see me at one o'clock tomorrow afternoon." The next day, as he approached me, Zahedi shouted, "Professor Naraghi, the task of acting as your messenger earned me a few insults and profanity this morning. But don't be discouraged. You must continue your efforts toward reconciliation. You have my full sympathy." The matter rested there.

The Shah was now feeling uncomfortable at the idea that he had missed a possible opportunity for national reconciliation and tried to defend himself by justifying his animosity toward the former head of government. "I believe Mosaddeq initially came to power with the consent of the British. Rapidly thereafter his demagoguery and obstinacy brought him to a string of defeats. He then adopted a new political platform in which his principal objective was to oppose me. And yet at the beginning of my reign I liked him a great deal and always defended him. When all is said and done, if we had let him have his way, Mosaddeq would have completely destroyed this country."

17. Two nineteenth-century statesman famous for their integrity and their bold programs of reform, both were victims of court intrigue and were assassinated by royal command.

"But Majesty, it was precisely his obstinacy—or what you describe as his obstinacy—which forced the British to leave Iran. Everyone knows that the British and their friends, both inside the country and out, did everything they possibly could to sabotage Mosaddeq's program, and it was in fact thanks to London's agents that your disagreement with him intensified."

The Shah pursued his own line of thought: "You could not possibly imagine a more stubborn and obtuse man. He irritated me constantly."

"Majesty, how could we have shaken free of Britain, which was then the most formidable world power, without Mosaddeq's stubbornness? It is thanks to him that the battle against the British was won."

For the first time in the course of the discussion, after more than two hours during which he had remained calm, the Shah seemed close to losing his self-control. If the country had not been in such a state of crisis he would undoubtedly have asked me to leave, but in the circumstances he tried to master himself and to make an effort to convince me.

"Listen, the reason I dismissed Mosaddeq was that the economy had become paralyzed by the end of his term of government. The Abadan refinery had been lying idle for nearly two years. Fifty thousand oil workers had to be paid for doing nothing, and in the meantime our debts were mounting. The communists were infiltrating everywhere, even the army, the backbone of our national security and independence. More than six hundred officers were members of a communist organization—in other words, they received their orders from Moscow. That's what Mosaddeq achieved with his demagoguery and irresponsibility! And that's precisely why in the end the grand ayatollahs sided with me and against him."

I allowed myself to retort: "Your Majesty should see Mosaddeq's achievements in a different light!"

The Shah was annoyed and said sarcastically, "In what light? Please tell me. In what light? In the light of rebellion and anarchy?"

"In the light of national dignity. Here too the people's heroes are like heroes everywhere. They are not always the builders of dams and factories. What did Gandhi, Nehru, or de Gaulle do for their countries? At a crucial moment in the history of their people, they fulfilled a great national dream: driving the British out of India, driving the

Germans out of France. Throughout my childhood I heard tales about the selfishness of the British. People spoke, often with great bitterness, about the way they hindered the development of Iran for several generations. In the end it was Mosaddeq who made the people's dream come true, who drove the British out of our country and did away with their influence! That is what makes him so popular—and that is why it is so regrettable that Your Majesty has refused to allow Mosaddeq's epic a place in the nationalism Your Majesty has been proclaiming since the start of our conversation."

The Shah, who despite my outburst wanted to show that he was following my line of argument, especially insofar as it related to the prevailing situation, continued: "Let's assume that what you're saying is true! The fact remains that at the moment Mosaddeq's followers have virtually no power. It's not the nationalists who attract the crowds. It's not their leaders who are mobilizing the demonstrators. If anything, they are the followers."

"Your Majesty is right," I replied. "The masters of the streets are the religious leaders and the supporters of Khomeini. But Mosaddeq's political discourse has been essential to the success of the religious movement. The imprisonment and house arrest which you imposed on Mosaddeq turned him into a martyr—hence he has become a source of inspiration to the current movement. His friends can still play an important role, even today. With a little show of goodwill on your part they can form an alternative and can act as mediators between Your Majesty and the religious leaders."

The Shah seemed intrigued. "How? In what context? What do they want?"

"Yesterday evening, when my old friend Dariush Forouhar,[18] spokesman for the National Front, learned that you were to receive me, he asked me to convey the following message to you, in the strictest confidence: 'Notwithstanding the fact that we have traveled a long way with the revolutionaries, both religious and secular, a considerable part of the National Front is prepared, despite everything, to support your regime or even that of your son, on condition that you

18. Forouhar was an ardent and militant supporter of Mosaddeq who spent a total of more than twelve years in jail under the Shah. In June 1977 he was one of three signatories of an open letter to the Shah demanding that the constitution be observed and political liberties guaranteed.

very clearly acknowledge the rights of the people as they are defined in our constitution.' Since you will be opening the new session of the Parliament in ten days' time, you will have an excellent opportunity to state in your role as guarantor of the constitution: 'I acknowledge that the constitution has been gravely infringed, especially with respect to the rights of the people, occasioning the crisis and protests now gripping our society. I hereby pledge to do my utmost to make good the damage and to ensure future adherence to the constitution.' My friends stressed that if you give such assurance you could seize the very last chance for a reconciliation with them; otherwise they will find themselves irredeemably distanced from you and compelled to fight the monarchy."

The message seemed to perplex the Shah. As I prepared to leave his office I kept expecting him to say something or ask me at least to convey a note to his secretary—Forouhar's message having been of the utmost importance. But I was granted no more than an "Oh well, we'll see!" I understood then that he had yet to grasp the extreme precariousness of his position.[19]

Before leaving I nevertheless felt it necessary to mention in some way the royal family's excessive interference in economic affairs. He seemed surprised. "What are you suggesting? Isn't my family allowed to engage in business activities like everyone else? Is it fair to victimize them just because they're my relatives?"

'They are not like everyone else, Majesty. They enjoy so many privileges and advantages that it wouldn't be unreasonable to deprive them of some."

"I know of no other royal family in the entire world—even in Europe—which is expected to forgo such rights. I would even hazard a guess that the Queen of England is the richest person in her country."

"Yes, but because of the role played by Parliament, the judicial system, and the media in Britain, nepotism and the abuse of power hardly exist there. That's not the case in our country. You saw how Prince Bernhard, the husband of Queen Juliana of the Netherlands, was recently stripped of his rights for his involvement in the Lock-

19. Ten days later, in an address to Parliament, the Shah referred to the constitutional system, but what he had to say fell far short of the expectations of Forouhar and his colleagues.

heed bribery scandal. Since we cannot apply the same methods here, it would be highly desirable if the royal family kept strictly out of all business affairs."

I did not press the point and moved instead to another matter. "I wanted to suggest that you receive a number of intellectuals who have devoted a great deal of time and study to the issues I touched on today."

"In view of the present circumstances, I don't think it would be a good idea for me to receive them. It could easily give rise to rumors about imminent changes and weakening the government's position. Since the appointment of Sharif-Emami as prime minister, I've decided to stick to the letter of the constitution [by which he meant the king would not meddle in affairs of state over the prime minister's head]. I'd prefer it if you kept in touch with those people and conveyed their suggestions to me instead. I also hope you'll go to see the prime minister and describe to him the same picture you painted for me today."

"Sharif-Emami is unfortunately not the man for the job. He is not up to the task of rescuing the country from its present crisis; as a former president of the senate and the outgoing president of the Pahlavi Foundation, he is one of the targets of opposition. With your permission, I'll just go to see him to discuss the question of political prisoners and to ask him to release those who have not committed serious offenses."

With an air of near resignation the Shah replied, "Fine, fine."

I also told him I was going to Senegal to attend a meeting at the invitation of President Senghor, before going on to Paris to take part in the UNESCO General Conference, and that consequently I would be away for several weeks.

"Very well, come and see me as soon as you're back," he returned.

Before leaving the room, I turned and said, "Majesty, what shall I do with the books I brought you?"

"Give them to my principal private secretary," he began by saying, but suddenly added, "I forgot! You were going to tell me about your book on greed. Here, give it to me."

He bid me a warm farewell. I saw the chamberlain, who drew attention to the fact that the conversation had lasted two hours and forty-five minutes.

From Persepolis to Jean-Paul Sartre

(Second Conversation with the Shah)

Tuesday, November 13, 1978, 10 a.m.

This time I was received by the Shah in his large office in the Niavaran Palace, overlooking the city. A week earlier, following demonstrations which had degenerated into arson attacks on cinemas and banks, there had been a change of government. To show his determination to liberalize the regime, the Shah had dismissed the cabinet of Sharif-Emami which he had appointed at the end of August 1978 in response to the growing wave of popular protests, and created a military government. At the same time he had appealed to the people, saying, "I understand your revolution!"

I was in Paris when the change was announced, and on French television's Antenne 2 that evening I spoke openly about the meaning of the revolution and the mistakes of the Shah and the ruling class. *Le Monde* had also invited me to offer an analysis of the unfolding events in an "open column," and there I had stated that the only solution for Iran was a return to the 1905 constitution.

While I waited to see the Shah, the chief of protocol informed me that he was aware both of my television interview and my article.

"So much the better," I said. "I'll be able to speak more freely, since he knows exactly what I think."

When I entered his office the Shah gave me a warm welcome. Inviting me to take the chair opposite his, he asked in a very relaxed manner, "Where did you go? What's new?"

"I first went to Dakar for a symposium on dialogue between civilizations, organized by Leopold Sedar Senghor, and then I went on to Paris to take part in the UNESCO General Conference."

"Were you able to see Senghor himself?"

"Yes, I went to see him in his villa near Dakar one Saturday afternoon."

"I imagine you spoke about what's happening in Iran. I'm interested to know what he thinks."

"In view of the recent developments in relationships between Iran and Senegal, President Senghor seemed anxious about the regime's ability to survive in the face of an increasingly strong opposition.[1] He could not hide his concern about Iran's and Your Majesty's future. He also criticized the attitude of the French government, particularly that of President Giscard d'Estaing, for allowing Ayatollah Khomeini to reside in Paris and giving him media coverage which could not fail to weaken your regime. He was clearly very disturbed by the situation: he could not understand how a political movement of such magnitude could be religiously inspired in this day and age."

Without wishing to be malicious in any way, but with more than a hint of sarcasm in his voice, as if the situation did not really concern him personally, the Shah remarked, "I expect you gave him a full explanation."

I answered in the same vein and said that President Senghor had been completely unaware of the revolutionary potential of Shi'i Islam. I also told the Shah that I had run into Prince Hugh de Bourbon-Parme at the symposium.[2]

"You mean the red Prince. I know him well. We have received him

1. An accord on technical, scientific, and cultural cooperation had been signed between the two countries in 1974. Iran had also started helping Senegal with the domestic distribution of refined oil products and was about to begin the construction of a refinery there.

2. Charles-Hugh de Bourbon-Parme was then the head of the Carlist movement and pretender to the Spanish throne. During Franco's reign he lived in exile in France, and his movement gradually inclined to socialism. After Franco's death and the accession of Juan Carlos he renounced his claim in recognition of the new king's democratic role, and he returned to Spain.

here several times. His revolutionary ideas apart, he's an extremely cultured man. What does he think about the situation?"

"He was very skeptical. He and his wife felt there was no way out for the regime and that the revolution would prevail."

"You mean they could not see any solution to the current crisis."

"Yes, precisely that; they cannot see any solution. They believe the current crisis began sometime ago, though they did not foresee it would take a religious turn. According to them it all started with the celebrations in Persepolis, marking the country's 2,500th anniversary."

"I don't understand why even the people of royal descent criticize the Persepolis ceremonies. After all, we celebrated one of the great monarchies of the world! It's especially incomprehensible bearing in mind that we brought together an unprecedented gathering of heads of state—many from communist countries."

"That's precisely the problem. The Princess de Bourbon-Parme's criticism mentioned the resentful reaction of Europe's crowned families which I had never heard before. What she said might be summed up as follows: The French Revolution, culminating in the beheading of Louis XVI, and the Russian Revolution, followed by the assassination of Nicholas II, dramatically shook the monarchical system of Europe. The ending of this system in many eastern and southern European countries (Italy and more recently Greece) made remaining European monarchies extremely vulnerable. That's why they have increasingly put aside pomp and ceremony and live more discreetly. They believe that the publicity surrounding events such as the Persepolis celebrations revives old animosities against kings. That's why, Majesty, you could not count the Queen of England or the Queen of Holland among your guests, despite your expectations and despite the concerted pressure exerted through your embassies. As for the presence of five heads of communist states, the democrats of the world today do not see it as a matter of any political significance but rather as a manifestation of those regimes' Machiavellian policies."

"But we made a point of emphasizing Cyrus the Great's[3] role as a

3. Cyrus the Great (died 528 B.C.E.) conquered Lydia, Asia Minor, Arabia, and finally Chaldea, capturing Babylon and liberating the Jews. On his death the Persian Empire was one of the largest known to the ancient world.

liberator. We commemorated his proclamation on the rights of the people, which was the first instance of the assertion of human rights in history."

"That's true enough, Majesty, but the celebrations had two flaws which undid all their charm: one of substance, the other of form. The problem of form was that examples such as Cyrus the Great, liberator of the people, are relatively rare in our history; kings who built minarets with the heads of the people who had the courage to resist them were much more common, as were kings who blinded and castrated all the male children in their family in order to deter any possible pretenders to the throne. As far as substance is concerned, how could the enormous expenditure on the enterprise possibly be justified in the light of your people's poverty?"

The Persepolis celebrations did not correspond to any national aspiration. Rather, they were seen in Iran as a manifestation of the megalomania and whim of a man who never showed a deep understanding of the country's history. For one thing, Iranian historians generally consider the origin of monarchy as predating the Achaemenid dynasty—if the Medes are taken into account. For another, Iranians have never unreservedly sung the praises of the monarchy. If there are one or two royal personalities who enjoy great favor with the people, they owe it in part to their wisdom in the administration of the country, but even more to their heroism in the face of foreign invaders. The many kings who were famous for their avarice and cruelty invite nothing but contempt and disdain. Indeed, the pantheon of historical figures who are revered by the people includes rather more accomplished chancellors and statesmen, driven from power or assassinated because of court intrigues, than well-respected kings.

The idea of the celebration dates back to 1961 when the Israelis invited Iranian historians to a scholarly symposium to mark the liberation of the Jewish people from their captivity in Babylon by Cyrus the Great, who seized the city in 539 B.C.E. and led the captives back to Jerusalem where he ordered that their temples be rebuilt. On hearing of the Israeli symposium, the court's cultural adviser, who was familiar with the Shah's megalomania, went to see the monarch in the company of a gifted historian (a learned man but unfortunately biddable and of not very strong character) who put forward the following argument: instead of letting the Israelis monopolize the commemoration of the liberation of the Jews from Babylon, why not use the occasion to throw the spotlight on all the merits of Cyrus the Great, the Achaemenian King, to demonstrate that the monarchy had a noble and ancient origin in Iran?

To the Shah, who still had not fully recovered from his struggle against Mosaddeq, this was a very attractive proposition. Here was a way in which he could legitimize his one-man rule on the basis of a monarchy dating far back into history. In response to demands for democracy and human rights, he could invoke the protection of minorities by Cyrus the Great and his original "declaration of the rights of man." He could, moreover, follow his father's footsteps down the path of anti-Arab and anti-Islamic nationalism and separate even further the fate of the Iranian people from the fate of the Islamic world as a whole.

Thus, from 1957, when the idea was first raised, until 1971, when the commemoration was held on a scale unprecedented in contemporary history, God only knows what exorbitant sums were spent and what hitherto extravagant contracts were signed with architects, decorators, joiners, jewelers, and caterers, who, to crown it all, were mostly French! The outlandish expenditure and propaganda shocked the majority of Iranians, including some members of the political establishment. It also provided an ideal opportunity for Khomeini to challenge the Shah's authority from his ultra-modest house in Najaf. Khomeini had lived fairly discreetly since his expulsion from Iran in 1964, but in 1971 he came once more into public view, attacking the Shah as a megalomaniac and mindless autocrat and launching a serious attack on the very institution of monarchy the Shah wished to exalt. It goes without saying that the criticism fell on receptive ears and reverberated throughout the country.

To make matters worse, the Persepolis celebrations had hardly ended when preparations were begun for the celebration of the fiftieth anniversary of the accession of the Pahlavis to the throne in 1975. Although a number of government officials managed, with considerable dexterity, to give this occasion an aura of commemoration rather than of pomp and ceremony, the two spectacles combined left a negative impact on the Iranian people. Above all they damaged all hope of presenting the Shah in the traditional ideal image of a just and wise king who embodied the collective conscience and oversaw the protection of national interests with care and discretion.

Up to then the people had held an austere and almost mystical view of their monarch. But extravagant celebrations transmitted on television screens throughout the world completely shattered that image. Television transformed an almost supernatural and invisible quality into a mere banality, and it failed to replace the lost image with a vision of a democratic and modern figure. For in official ceremonies the Shah simply came across as the personification of extreme haughtiness. Because of his shyness (well known among his own circle) he appeared to be distant and cold. But ordinary Iranians knew nothing of his shyness and imagined his behavior to be a manifestation of his arrogance and contempt, although, to those who knew him personally, he was not lacking in human kindness and warmth.

Another move, which caused the Shah the greatest harm, was the changing of the calendar. In 1976 he antagonized the clergy yet again by replacing the official Islamic calendar with the "imperial calendar" which, instead of beginning on the day the Prophet left Mecca for Medina—known as the *hejira*—calculated the date from the foundation of the Achaemenian dynasty. Again he wanted to emphasize Iran's non-Islamic past and to identify himself with Cyrus the Great, seeking thereby to make a distinction between Iranian and Arab history and to diminish the influence of Islam on the Iranian people.

"What's happening in France?" the sovereign asked. "The French press seems to have completely abandoned itself to Khomeini. You would think they had found a new Gandhi! Why this infatuation with someone they scarcely know? I must confess I don't understand the French. When it comes to dealing with the political life of other countries, they seem to have no scruples; they're incapable of exercising any restraint. Can you explain this to me?"

I answered lightheartedly, "Perhaps they're trying to settle their accounts with you, Majesty. In 1974, when the price of petrol quadrupled, you became very condescending toward Europeans. You described them as decadent and denounced the permissiveness of their society. At the time they needed your oil; they had to grin and bear it. Now they're taking their revenge."

"But," he persisted, "a paper like *Le Monde* has always criticized us. How many times have I read articles about the political situation in Iran, with such references to Savak excesses and political prisoners that I have been forced to demand verification. On examination the paper's statements have often turned out to be inexact or exaggerated. I discussed the problem with the French ambassador once. I showed him that *Le Monde* had added several zeros to the number of political prisoners. The ambassador assured me that he would demand an explanation from *Le Monde* and keep me informed. I never heard anything more about it. We could in fact ask him again, but," he added with resignation, "it's not worth the bother! Forget it. When people are dishonest, there's nothing to be done. In any case, it's not just *Le Monde*. French intellectuals don't like us either. Take Jean-Paul Sartre, for example. He's manipulated by a group of agitators in Paris and makes absurd statements on the political situation in Iran."

"Sire, I must tell you something Sartre said. In 1975 I was still working for UNESCO and I used to see René Maheu fairly frequently, even though he was no longer the organization's director-general. One evening he invited me to dinner, and I found myself in the company of Sartre and Simone de Beauvoir, who were old friends of his because they had been fellow students at the École Normale Superieure before World War II. When René Maheu introduced me as an Iranian friend, Sartre said to me, "Listen, I have a message for your Shah. He was surprised, during a press conference, to find that Monsieur Sartre, a great philosopher, showed an interest in the problems of prisons and torture in Iran. I would therefore be grateful if you could tell him that taking an interest in the difficulties of people in prison and under torture is precisely what a philosopher is meant to do!"

Exasperated, the Shah exclaimed, "Does Monsieur Sartre also take an interest in concentration camps in the Soviet Union and other communist countries—in Cambodia, for example!"

"Sire, Sartre has not hesitated to condemn repression under communist regimes. He was in fact the first to denounce the injustices committed against the Cambodian and Vietnamese people."

"You don't need to be a great philosopher to understand that the Khmer Rouge are barbarians. What I'm trying to say is that Sartre and other French intellectuals, who have always been the ideological mentors of our left-wing opposition, have said nothing about the Soviet Union for a long time. It was Khrushchev—who was, in my opinion, a courageous man despite his tendency to go to extremes—who first spoke about Stalin's crimes, and after him Solzhenitsyn described the suffering of millions of people. Those other gentlemen, who spend their time lecturing the world, were silent about this particular matter for thirty or forty years. Do you know why? Because the Sartres of this world can see such regimes only through their ideological glasses. They never bother to understand the realities of the countries about which they speak. There are regimes which they like and regimes which they don't; that's all there is to it. They've never liked our regime, for example. Exclusively critical, they've refused to see the improvements in the people's living conditions. And yet they claim to be interested in the fate of the people."

"Maybe that's the price we have to pay for the fact that they hold the Iranian people in high esteem. It is precisely because of our achievements that they've been shocked by excesses in recent years."

"Why don't they criticize the human rights situation in Saudi Arabia or the brutality of the security forces in Iraq, for example. There's no shortage of things that can be said."

"For the simple reason, Sire, that those countries do not lay claims to becoming the world's fifth largest military power or to moving toward a 'great civilization,' as you yourself have done. Do not forget either that our country boasts a brilliant past, that it is the proud possessor of countless cultural treasures, and that it also has to its credit the democratic revolution of 1906 and, in 1951, the first example of nationalization of oil—an event which had repercussions throughout the world. All these things make us a special case. It may even be that they are interested in us solely because we surprise them: Mosaddeq in his pyjamas, Khomeini, with his inscrutable gaze, sitting under an apple tree in Neauphle-le-Chateau. Bear in mind also that after their secular and antireligious revolution the French have now suddenly discovered a people who want to have a religious revolution."

"That's just what I don't understand. This revolution has nothing to do with the democratic and secular ideals which the French people wished to spread throughout the world. It has even less to do with the Marxist materialist ideas of left-wing intellectuals like Sartre."

"Majesty, it's because the situation baffles them that they find it interesting. They're filled with admiration for a man like Khomeini, who has been able to mobilize, not to say hypnotize, a people against a regime as powerful as yours without any kind of organization or political party and while remaining outside the country the entire time. For them it's a new and wholly unprecedented event."

"Very well. What you're saying may well hold true for left-wingers and intellectuals, but what about government and business circles? I know that a man like François Mitterand backs my opponents—which is to say, he doesn't like us.[4] Big French companies have benefited considerably from our industrialization, much more so than other industrialized countries. We signed so many contracts with them that they ended up saying they couldn't honor them all. If the circumstances in our country change, they will no longer enjoy such benefits."

"But you must also accept, Majesty, that business and government circles often must bow to public opinion. Besides, if they've come to the conclusion that the regime is tottering, they'll naturally tend to favor the future regime."

"Is what I hear true, that Giscard d'Estaing is banking on Khomeini's success? And yet, when Khomeini arrived in Paris they assured us that he would not be allowed to engage in political activities in France."

"I've heard it said that you yourself gave consent to the French for Khomeini to be allowed to remain there."

"Yes, that was our wish. But they gave assurances that it would not

4. I had known for quite some time that François Mitterand had no great liking for the Shah. It had become clear to me in the early 1970s when I lived in Paris. At the house of a great Parisian lawyer, François Sarda, I became acquainted with Edgar Pisani and Jacques Delors. They both made a great impression on me. A few months after my return to Iran in 1975 I invited them, in my capacity as the director of the Institute for Research and Planning on Science and Education, to come to Tehran as advisers for several weeks. Being familiar with the characters of the two men and their tendency to frankness, I hoped they would tell the Shah a few truths, things he would unfortunately not hear from his own subjects or even from other foreigners who, because of their own interests, preferred to flatter the king. They indicated their acceptance in principle, and M. Pisani's trip had already been arranged when Mitterand, whose opinion they had solicited, intervened and advised them against visiting Iran. He felt that because of the Shah their trip would be a wasted effort.

result in any destabilizing activities in France against the Iranian regime."

"Who gave you those assurances?"

"Our ambassador sent us a telegram stating that the Elysée Palace had—through the intermediary of Jean-François Poncet, its secretary general—conveyed a message to him from the president, who was on a visit to Brazil. According to the message, Khomeini had been allowed into France as a tourist and was not engaging in political activities there.[5] On the following day Bahrami informed the Elysée that Giscard's message had reached its destination and that Iran accepted the position France had adopted with regard to Khomeini. Our ambassador also stated that the Iranian authorities had nothing more to say on the subject."[6]

The Shah went on: "Now we find that the Ayatollah is using all the official French media to transmit his calls to subversion and even to murder, and that he has turned his residence into a revolutionary headquarters without anyone saying so much as a word."

"You must also bear in mind the constraints under which the French authorities have to operate, Majesty. It's true that their main radio station and their television channels belong to the state, but the fact is that they're actually run by the journalists, and journalists follow developments and make their decisions on the basis of what the public wants to know. I'm sure Giscard himself is quite embarrassed. Caught between his close ties with you on the one hand, and the pressure of public opinion and its fascination with Khomeini on the other, he probably doesn't know which way to turn."

The Shah, at once bemused and resigned, responded, "Oh, these Western politicians! One never knows what they really think."

5. Jacques Wahl, assistant secretary general at the Elysée Palace, called Mr. Bahrami, the Iranian ambassador, to say that the president had tried in vain to speak to the Shah from Brazil. He had the following message to transmit to His Majesty: "I learned through the media that Ayatollah Khomeini had arrived in Paris with a valid Iranian passport [at the time there were no visa requirements between France and Iran]. He was therefore allowed to remain in France for three months as a tourist without a visa. He was, naturally, not to engage in political activity. Please convey our assurance to this effect to Tehran."

6. Iran's ambassador in Kabul, Mr. Davoudi, told me how the French ambassador in Afghanistan had gone to see him to convey the same message. When he asked why he was being used as an intermediary, he was told it was because Paris was using different methods to ensure that the message was received by the Shah.

In reality the Shah found himself in a very awkward position on this question and was at a loss as to what to do. After pressing the Iraqis to expel Khomeini and after putting pressure on Britain and other friendly countries (notably on neighboring Kuwait) to refuse him entry if and when the occasion arose, he was pleased at last to see Khomeini land in Paris.[7] Since Khomeini's movements had already aroused passions in Iran, the Shah was afraid he would provoke an even stronger reaction if he asked France to send him elsewhere. Giscard had let him know, through his ambassador, that he was prepared to expel Khomeini, but only on the condition that the expulsion be specifically demanded by the Iranian authorities. This the Shah was reluctant to do.

The Shah suddenly uncrossed his legs and said, "Well then, let's change the subject. What else have you heard?"

"I ran into an old friend, Mehdi Alawi, who had just returned from Baghdad, and he told me something very interesting. He is a Moroccan socialist activist who has lived in Paris for a long time and has worked with Ben Barka and the Socialist International. The organization has been planning to hold a congress of socialist parties in Vancouver in 1978, and it sent Mehdi Alawi to the Middle East to find out about the political situation in the countries of the region. In Iraq he met a number of leading politicians, including President Hasan al-Bakr and Michel Aflaq, the Ba'th party theoretician, who told him they were very glad to see the back of Khomeini because he would no longer be able to exercise an influence on Iraqi Muslims (especially Shi'as, who form the majority in Iraq)—an influence which had posed a growing threat to the Ba'th party. But what my friend found paradoxical was that Iraq's leaders have succeeded in convincing public opinion that Khomeini's departure was at the request of the Iranian authorities during a meeting between the two countries' foreign ministers on the fringes of the UN General Assembly in September 1972.[8] If I understood Alawi correctly, the vice-president, Saddam Hussein, and his friends have managed to rid themselves of

7. General Gharabaghi, *Verite sur la crise Iranienne* (La Pensee Universalle, 1985), p. 42.

8. A secret mission was also sent to Iraq toward the end of summer 1978, at a time of increasing disturbances in Iran, to ask the Iraq authorities to expel Khomeini from the country.

Khomeini's destabilizing influence and at the same time to make the Iranians appear solely responsible for his expulsion. They are, Alawi suggested, even capable of obtaining a few concessions from the Iranians in return."

The Shah, as if he'd suddenly been wounded, said, "We've known for a long time that the Ba'thist regime had reached the end of its tether as far as Khomeini was concerned. Until 1975, that is, just up to the Algiers Accord,[9] the Ba'thists were, in effect, trying to turn Iraq into a base for all the different Iranian opposition groups. They were thus hoping to force us to halt our assistance to Iraqi Kurds. When Mustafa Barzani and his men decided to stop their battle against the Iraqi regime and when we granted them asylum in Iran, Saddam no longer had any reason to house opponents of our regime, especially since Khomeini's militant Islamic stand threatened his own undeniably secular state."

"Sire, you have to acknowledge, nonetheless, that due to his relentless pride—if you're reluctant to call it patriotism—Khomeini never allowed himself to be manipulated by the Ba'thist regime, even when relations were at their lowest ebb between the two countries. I know from people close to him that he had systematically rejected their demands. That's why Saddam now has it in for him, and that's why he expelled him at the first opportunity."

The Shah nodded. "Yes, I agree with you. He may have put up with Saddam, but he never fell into step with him."

Both Iranian and Iraqi leaders feared Khomeini because of his influence in their respective countries. In September 1978 they agreed jointly to remove him from Najaf, in Iraq, at any cost. At the same time the two governments did everything possible to conceal their decision for fear of public opinion in both countries. The Iranian authorities, who did not have a clear understanding of the Ayatollah's channels of influence within the country, were convinced that they were largely rooted in Najaf. What lay behind their belief was the fact that, for Shi'i Muslims, Najaf is the holiest place after Mecca, because

9. An accord between Iran and Iraq, signed under the auspices of Algeria, settling the question of the border between the two countries along the Shatt al-Arab. In 1980 Baghdad announced the unilateral annulment of the accord. After the invasion of Kuwait in 1990 Iraq changed its mind and declared that it would respect the Algiers Accord.

Ali, the Prophet's cousin and son-in-law and the Shi'a's first Imam, is buried there. In the last few centuries, moreover, Iran's grand ayatollahs had received their theological training in Najaf or had taught there, and it was from Najaf that, in the late nineteenth century, they promulgated their anathemas against colonial powers and "cursed" sovereigns.[10]

The game of hide-and-seek between the two governments, recounted to me by Mehdi Alawi, finally ended to the Shah's disadvantage because of Saddam's skill.[11] All the more so because the Ayatollah's media success in Paris was a complete surprise to both the Iranian and the French authorities; it was, indeed, even a surprise to Khomeini's entourage. Khomeini had not intended to travel to Paris after leaving Baghdad. When he was driven to the Iraq-Kuwait border, he considered instead the possibility of going to Syria or Algeria. The only European country which he could have favored was the Federal Republic of Germany, where in Hamburg Europe's sole Shi'i mosque was to be found. Nevertheless, after the Kuwaitis' refusal to let him into their country and in view of the Iraqis' unyielding determination to make him leave, he chose to go to Paris—at first temporarily because of the presence there of a small core of sympathizers, and then on a more permanent basis because of the facilities accorded to him by the media.

What happened next was without precedent: bypassing a state—Iran—and its censor, the foreign media, particularly foreign radio,

10. During the 1906 constitutional revolution Iranian ayatollahs living in Najaf, then under Ottoman rule, played an important role in the popular uprising against the despotic rule of the Qajar shahs.

11. On October 11, 1978, a few days after the Ayatollah's arrival in Paris, Mr. Aleyassin, Iraq's ambassador to Iran, requested an urgent meeting with the foreign minister in Tehran. He was received by Mr. Zellu, the deputy minister for political affairs. The ambassador had come to protest to the Iranian authorities about the insinuations in the Iranian press suggesting it had been the Iraqi government on its own initiative that had forced Khomeini to leave Iraq; the Iraqis maintained that Khomeini's expulsion had been in response to an Iranian demand. The Iranian deputy foreign minister tried to calm the ambassador by saying that in the turbulent climate of the time, the expulsion had in any case been in the interest of both countries. But the ambassador insisted that behind the press reports there lay a political will to place the blame for the Ayatollah's expulsion on Baghdad, and that this was totally unacceptable as the rumor could have dangerous repercussions in Iraq, which has a predominantly Shi'i population.

transmitted Khomeini's message to an entire nation. And so began another game of pass-the-buck (it wasn't me, it's you), this time between the Shah and Giscard. As soon as Khomeini had managed to gain a prominent place for himself in the French press, the Shah was not prepared to give his opponents another pretext for agitation by having Khomeini expelled from France or by asking the French authorities to curb his access to the media. Indeed, he was hoping to be able to send emissaries to Paris in order to reach an understanding with the Ayatollah. To this end he had held discussions with King Hussein of Jordan and had later suggested that Ali Amini, a former prime minister, go to Paris. But Khomeini had rejected all offers of negotiation. The king had also been counting on the Americans to talk to Khomeini and calm him down.

Banking on his good personal relations with Giscard, the sovereign had hoped that the French president would keep Khomeini on a tight leash and prevent him from playing a destabilizing role in Tehran. Giscard, for his part, valued his relations with Iran, and not having thought of Khomeini's arrival in France as a matter of great political import, he had tried initially to control him and to keep him away from political activity. As the days went by, however, things began to change. He began receiving reports from his ambassador in Iran predicting the regime's decline. As a result, he was less and less inclined to limit the Ayatollah's media exposure. In the end Giscard came to the conclusion that it was not in France's interest to check Khomeini's activities in Neauphle-le-Chateau, where groups of French-speaking Iranian intellectuals were organizing his contacts with journalists—something which may have led Giscard and his advisers to believe that the future Iranian regime would move away from the United States and establish closer ties with France.

The Shah, who already mistrusted the Americans and the British, also started having doubts about Giscard. In this way he became increasingly convinced that he was the victim of a conspiracy hatched by the great powers. That is why he tended to jump whenever I mentioned Giscard; he felt he had already been partially betrayed. He had been thinking that if his "friend" President Giscard proved unable to silence Khomeini, he would at least try to begin a dialogue with him in order to appease him. In reality, however, Giscard's attitude was: if the imperial government specifically asked France,

Khomeini would be expelled; but while he was in France, the French authorities really had no way of muzzling him.

The Shah asked me, as if he did not know already, "So who are the people around Khomeini? They say he's created a revolutionary headquarters around himself, that he's working with a team, and that they come running from all over Europe to see him. Do you know the people close to him?"

"I know of two of them, since I was the one who sent them to France on scholarships. Now, they've turned into his lieutenants."

"How and when did they become Khomeinists?"

"The two men I'm speaking about, Abolhassan Bani-Sadr and Hassan Habibi, were among the more moderate of Mosaddeq's supporters, and although they always had Islamic tendencies, neither are fanatics. They studied at the Institute for Sociological Research before leaving for France. Habibi has already translated the works of Gurvich and Bergson into Persian."[12]

The Shah was clearly surprised. "How is it possible that with a background in modern sociology they became Khomeinists? What do they want, progress or regression?"

"Majesty, let me explain to you why all these young people who were dissatisfied with the regime moved toward Khomeini—whether they lived inside or outside the country. A whole generation has been prevented from expressing its grievances through political leaders who share its ideals. Mosaddeq's allies enjoy obvious esteem and have maintained their distance from your regime throughout the past twenty-five years. But your policies have meant that these liberal nationalists have not been in a position to create a political movement. As a result, members of the younger generation have been attracted either by Marxist tendencies or, if they are religiously inclined, by Islamic ones. The latter group formed 'Islamic associations' in the United States and Europe which at first were not taken seriously, either by the regime or by the Marxists. They did not really come into the forefront of things until the 1970s. Then they slowly moved closer to Khomeini, and since 1977, when the religiously motivated protests acquired real significance within the country, they completely accepted his authority."

12. Bani-Sadr became the first president of the Islamic Republic in 1980. Hassan Habibi is, as I write, the Islamic Republic's vice-president.

"What happened during Sanjabi's visit to Paris? It seems his negotiations achieved nothing other than the complete abandonment of his position and his unconditional defection to Khomeini."

Karim Sanjabi, a professor of law who studied in Paris before World War II, was a loyal supporter of Mosaddeq. A year before my conversations with the monarch he had published an "open letter to the Shah" also signed by two other Mosaddeq followers, Shahpour Bakhtiar and Dariush Forouhar, warning him against his contempt for the constitution and his abuse of personal power. Sanjabi succeeded to a certain extent in reviving the old nationalist movement and in presenting it as a viable alternative which could operate within the framework of the constitution (including the recognition of the king's prerogatives). In its turn, although it still distrusted Mosaddeq's followers, the Shah's regime felt compelled—in the face of ever-increasing dangers and uncertainty—to invite them to take part in the government. By that time, however, the nationalists were not prepared to accept such an invitation unless they had Khomeini's support—which is why the entire ruling class, particularly the technocrats who favored some kind of political liberalization, invested a great deal of hope in Sanjabi's trip to Paris.

The nationalists, for their part, were hoping that Sanjabi would return to Iran with some kind of understanding which could be transformed into a charter accepted by the different opposition forces, whether secular or religious, defining their common methods and objectives. But Sanjabi had neither the time nor the audacity to discuss the ins and outs of such a program with the intransigent religious leader who suspected that the purpose of the delegation was to make him acquiesce in the establishment of a government which would ultimately fall under the Shah's command. In any case, Khomeini was not prepared either to legitimize the 1906 constitution or to turn the country over to the nationalists.

Sanjabi had imagined that Khomeini was like the other ayatollahs he had met previously and would content himself with delineating a few general political and religious priorities, leaving it to secular leaders to work out the means to carry them out. What he found instead in Neauphle-le-Chateau was a man with an unrelenting and inflexible will to overthrow the monarchy, who also held very definite ideas—without wishing to express them—about the kind of regime he wanted to install.

"I have the impression, Your Majesty, that Sanjabi believed he would succeed in his talks with the Ayatollah, where Bazargan[13]—who had been to Paris a few days earlier—had failed."

"Bazargan is one of them. I'm sure he has no differences with Khomeini. In any case, the Ayatollah owes him a great deal. It was Bazargan, after all, who introduced political Islam to universities. He had always been fanatical and intractable."

"They have misrepresented him to you, Sire. He is neither of those things."

"Do you know him well enough personally to be able to say that?"

"Yes, Majesty, I know him well. I can tell you that despite his Islamic inclinations and his respect for the Ayatollah, the differences between the two of them are much greater than the differences between Khomeini and Sanjabi. In the first place, he went to Paris to discuss fundamental questions, such as the army's future and the country's new political and administrative system. As he says himself, he would like to see a 'step-by-step' approach in order to protect the country from the damaging consequences of sudden drastic change. I can, moreover, assure you that if the present regime showed a degree of tolerance and flexibility toward the liberal opposition, Bazargan and his friends would be prepared to play a part in government and to tackle some of the problems you currently face in such dramatic fashion."

In order to hide his regret over a lost opportunity to collaborate with a man like Bazargan, the Shah continued ironically: "Nowadays we even hear that they're on good terms with the Americans. The Americans are protecting them!"

"That's because you yourself did not protect them, Majesty! And because Savak was forever after them. You also have to admit that the regime never hid its liking for the Americans. . . . Today Bazargan and his friends are wreaking their revenge."

13. Mehdi Bazargan, a former student at the École Centrale in France, was another of Mosaddeq's old supporters. After the fall of Mosaddeq he established the Freedom Movement of Iran, a party supported by highly skilled professionals with religious inclinations. He spent five years in prison under the Shah before heading the first government of the Islamic Republic and later falling out with the ayatollahs.

The Shah, half skeptical, half convinced, decided to change the subject. "What about here, inside the country? What's happening here? How did you find the political situation on your return?"

"The subject I wanted to raise with you, Majesty, is the arrest of Forouhar and Sanjabi three days ago. The arrest has been badly received both inside and outside the country."

"For once, when an arrest is legally justified, you say we're being criticized! It's very simple. In his press conference after his meeting with Khomeini, Mr. Sanjabi openly called the regime into question, and such an attack is expressly forbidden by the law.[14] He was therefore arrested. There's absolutely nothing irregular about it."

"Majesty, everyone at home and abroad knows that you've been trying to negotiate with the National Front,[15] that is to say, with Sanjabi and his friends, for the last two months."

"But what am I to do? Their decision goes against the constitution; they're saying that the monarchy no longer has any legitimacy."

"You know very well that the constitution has not been respected in the past. You cannot suddenly take refuge in a text which has been flouted many times over."

The Shah adopted his most persuasive voice and said, "I've always respected the constitution. I've always consulted it."

"Majesty, the people who speak about respecting the constitution are not referring to a purely formal respect or to mere words. For example, is the independence of the judiciary respected? Are all the special tribunals for ideological offenses constitutional?"

"The tribunals tried people who had threatened the security of the state—people who had engaged in espionage or committed acts of terrorism."

"Majesty, are you trying to say that for twenty-five years not a single person has been sentenced for political reasons? Were all the prisoners like Bazargan and his friends, or Ayatollah Taleghani and other mullahs, who had no links with any foreign powers, spies and terrorists? You yourself know that that was not the case. The regime

14. Sanjabi had signed a joint declaration with Khomeini in Paris questioning the legitimacy of the imperial regime because of its disregard for the constitution.

15. Partisans of Mosaddeq who, after his failure in 1953, formed a movement to keep alive his principles of independence from foreign powers, respect of democratic principles, and so on.

put any label it wanted on people it condemned for their beliefs. So, quite frankly, you're not in a position to appeal to the constitution. In the present political climate, in the middle of a very serious crisis, you cannot turn to a purely formal framework. Sanjabi taught at the faculty of law for many years, and he never called the constitutionality of the regime into question. Today, in an atmosphere of unprecedented political turbulence, he has allowed himself to do so. His action is therefore purely political. You too, Majesty, have no alternative but to act politically. The time for hollow formalities and legal niceties is over. You must resume your dialogue with them because, as you yourself are well aware, they are the only ones you can speak to; keeping them in prison is not going to solve any problems."

Wishing to demonstrate his magnanimity, the Shah replied, "They're being very well treated, you know. I gave orders that they should not be put in prison. They're in a place especially reserved for foreign visitors."

"That's neither here nor there, Sire. Dariush Forouhar is an old friend of mine. He has already spent more than twelve years in prison in the course of your reign, and under the harshest conditions. These days he has a bed and a carpet in his room, but he continues to sleep on the floor."

The Shah did not contradict me, but in an effort to surprise me he said, "We have also said that we will negotiate with them in an effort to find a solution."

"There was another matter I wanted to discuss with you, Sire: Hoveida's arrest."[16]

The Shah jumped upon hearing Hoveida's name, but he quickly composed himself.

I knew very well that the Shah had been living a Shakespearean drama since the moment, a few days earlier, when the military government had announced Hoveida's arrest, along with that of a

16. Amir-Abbas Hoveida was the Shah's prime minister from 1965 to 1977. He was a man with a lively mind, well versed in the problems of the modern world and fluent in several languages, including French. His weak point and the cause of his eventual downfall was his total submission to the policies of the Shah. The record of his thirteen years in power included important achievements but was marked by almost a kind of free-for-all in the misuse of power, political repression, and economic profligacy. Unlike the people in the Shah's entourage, he did not seek to enrich himself.

number of other ministers decreed to have been "accessories to corruption." The Shah knew, in fact, that during the previous year, 1977, when Hoveida was court minister, he had done everything in his power to combat the financial abuses of the imperial family and its entourage, an effort which must have earned him considerable ill will.

That was why the Shah felt uncomfortable whenever the conversation turned to Hoveida. When in July 1977 he named Jamshid Amouzegar as the new prime minister—a post Hoveida had held for thirteen years—the Shah kept Hoveida on by appointing him court minister. In that capacity Hoveida began taking determined steps to fight the all-pervading corruption of the establishment. He drew up, in particular, a directive establishing a kind of code of financial and economic conduct for the Pahlavi dynasty. The main element of the code was that the members of the royal family could not have interests in companies linked to the state. It took nearly a year to prepare the directive because the Shah was anxious not to upset his relatives and constantly asked for alterations. In the end the directive did not come to light until Hoveida had left the court—much too late, in other words, to have any effect.

Mohammad Reza Shah also knew that Hoveida had been totally loyal to him and that he could not really be accused of involvement in either misappropriation or repression now that people were calling for a settling of accounts. It was, in other words, obvious that the Shah was simply using Hoveida as a scapegoat to appease the masses. Yet at the same time he was aware that in government circles the arrest would be seen as a sign of the Shah's ingratitude toward those who had served him loyally.

For all these reasons Hoveida's name had become taboo at the palace since his arrest. This made the emperor all the more curious and anxious to hear what was being said about the affair in different quarters. He uncrossed his legs, adopted an air of superiority, as if he wished to practice and perfect his rhetorical technique on me so that he could be all the more convincing with future inquisitors, and said: "Due to the prevailing climate of insecurity, we thought it best to provide him with protection. I was asked repeatedly in recent weeks to authorize his arrest,[17] but I did not concede until I heard that

17. The Shah was referring here to either Sharif-Emami, the prime minister, or to General Oveissi, the military governor of Tehran, compared with whom Hoveida was, in terms of corruption, a saint.

General Khademi[18] had been assassinated by unknown assailants. [Later it was said that Khademi had killed himself as he was being arrested by the police.] I was told that Hoveida ran the same risk as Khademi. I telephoned him to warn him, and I let him know that military officers would be coming to fetch him to take him somewhere where he would be safe."

Had the Shah wanted to save an innocent or to bring an offender to justice? The ambiguity in his thinking in practice served as a justification for throwing Hoveida to the wolves, although he clearly never imagined that one day his faithful servant would be executed, as happened on April 7, 1979. This is why the affair tormented him until his own death.

"Majesty, you talk about Hoveida's safety. But since my return from Paris in the past forty-eight hours I've heard rumors that the military have prepared to plot to assassinate him and to make it appear as if he killed himself in prison. If that were to happen you would, like it or not, bear the responsibility for his death and its very grave consequences. You must prevent that at all cost."

The Shah looked horrified. "Why should they have such a plot?"

"Because the military have never liked Hoveida and believe that by doing away with him they will calm the people and spare you a trial which could prove embarrassing. They also think they can exploit the widespread rumor that the former prime minister belonged to the Baha'i sect."

The Shah's voice suddenly acquired new strength as he leaped to defend his former court minister and his own honor: "No. That's pure calumny. Hoveida is not a Baha'i. The people are talking nonsense."[19]

"At any rate, Majesty, you have to make sure that Hoveida's arrest is not exploited to settle personal accounts. If you want the people to believe in a policy of transparency and openness you must ensure that there is a trial. But it must be conducted with dignity and in the framework of the law. The reason I'm stressing this point, Sire, is

18. Khademi was chairman and managing director of Iran Air. While he was no doubt a capable company manager, he was implicated in numerous cases of bribery. He was at the same time a devoted follower of the Baha'i faith, condemned by Islam, to which he is believed to have made considerable financial contributions.

19. The Baha'is are a sect. For a Shi'i ruler there could be nothing worse than the accusation of having kept a Baha'i prime minister for thirteen years.

because I know that the military government is in the process of collecting Hoveida's expense claims for receptions and foreign visits. That's all nonsense and will convince no one. What matters is an investigation into the way in which the country has been run so that the people can see, for the first time, that their leaders are taking their constitutional responsibilities seriously and are prepared to explain the way they have behaved in important affairs of state. I have discussed the question with Ali Amini.[20] He believes that the trial should be political, not penal. Everyone knows Hoveida was not a thief. He just closed his eyes while everyone else stole, often with the connivance of the royal family. In order for such a trial to take place, Your Majesty must accept that, in accordance with the constitution, 'the prime minister and other ministers cannot justify their actions and behavior solely on the basis of the king's written or verbal commands.' I believe that, as I already said in our last meeting, we are now at a crossroads, Sire. The situation demands the greatest possible care and attention on your part in order that past mistakes may be undone and a new equilibrium established in the country."

It was at this point in the conversation that the Shah, looking totally dazed, made the following remarkable observation: "To tell you the truth, I don't know whether we're being attacked today for the good we've done or the bad."

"For both, Sire. I remember seeing Hoveida at his house a little over a month ago, just before my trip abroad. He'd just resigned from his post of court minister. I asked him if he intended to leave the country or stay in Iran. He said, 'I'd like to stay here and defend what we've achieved. That is also His Majesty's wish.' If that were true, he must be given a chance to plead his case before a legally competent tribunal. Undoubtedly, there are things which are not known. It may be possible to show that constitutional legality had to be sacrificed for the sake of economic efficiency or for other reasons. Who knows?"

The Shah made a gesture indicating resignation, and said, "Do you imagine that in the current climate of hysteria the people could be

20. Ali Amini was a former prime minister. He came to power in 1961, following pressure from the Kennedy administration for political reform, but was removed by the Shah after fourteen months. With the onset of the revolutionary crisis the Shah had overcome his suspicion of this independent statesman and turned to him for advice on several occasions.

made to listen? I myself have said to Hoveida: "Why shouldn't we reveal what we've done? Alongside the errors they accuse us of, we can also boast of great achievements."

"Majesty, that is what you must strive and hope for. The day of reckoning is now here. The people want to get to the root of things. It's not enough to say to them, 'We'll decide what's best for you. Leave everything to us.' Even at the price of slower development, we must pause, lay out records for inspection, and adopt a policy of openness and transparency."

"The problem is that, on the basis of the law as it currently stands, the government believes it is impossible to try high-ranking officials. Members of the government have told me that they're in the process of preparing a draft bill and drawing up new procedures that will authorize such trials. They'll probably submit them to Parliament soon."

"Majesty, I'd like to raise another thorny but urgent issue, though I suspect you'll find it irritating. It is a problem that is on the minds of all your most capable advisers, but they're too polite and timid to broach it with you.[21] Just this morning, before coming to the palace, I went to see Ali-Gholi Ardalan [the new minister of court].[22] When I told him that I planned to discuss the question of your assets with you, he embraced me and said, 'That's the best thing you could do for His Majesty!' When I was in Paris I heard of an Iranian publication, printed abroad, by the name of *Chap* (*The Left*) which contains a list of more than two hundred companies affiliated with the Pahlavi Foundation. In preparation for our conversation today I spent the whole of yesterday with economists, including a former minister in whom I have full confidence, checking the veracity of the list.

21. By "capable advisers" I meant Amini and Abdollah Entezam, a former minister of foreign affairs. Both had been seeing the Shah over the past twenty days. Both told me that in view of their long-standing but acrimonious relations with the sovereign, they were hesitant about raising this issue. It was easier for me to discuss the issue since there were no long-standing disputes between the Shah and me.

22. Ali Gholi Ardalan, who had just succeeded Hoveida as minister of court, was a relatively old career diplomat. He had been more or less out of favor because the Shah felt he had proved ineffective in silencing the American press on the subject of the royal family's activities when he was ambassador to Washington at the end of the 1950s. He was, as a result, totally untainted by the Pahlavis' financial affairs.

Unfortunately the information contained in the publication turns out to be relatively accurate."

I took the publication out of my briefcase and offered it to him, but he made no move to take it. Instead he asked me with obvious irritation, "When you talk about assets, you mean my assets as well as those of my family?"

"Yes, both, Majesty."

"I bequeathed all my holdings to the Pahlavi Foundation. As you know, the foundation is engaged in charitable and cultural activities. I don't understand what the criticism is about."

"Sire, you may have had such aims in mind when you established the foundation, but it has since gradually turned into a private commercial organization. That's clear for everyone to see today."

The charitable activities of the Pahlavi Foundation in practice represented a minute part of its activities. In fact it had three aims: first, to find sources of finance for commercial companies belonging to the Shah; second, to maintain the court's interest in the country's economy by investing in various fields; and third, to provide financial support for people considered loyal to the monarchy, or more precisely to the person of the Shah.

The foundation was established in 1958 with funds from the crown estates Mohammed Reza had inherited. The estates consisted of 830 villages covering a total area of 2.5 million hectares mostly seized in arbitrary fashion by the Shah's father. They included some of Iran's best agricultural land, part of which was situated in the fertile region near the Caspian Sea. After he succeeded to the throne, Mohammed Reza tried to redress the resentment felt against the Pahlavis on account of these acquisitions by selling them at fairly low prices to the peasants who worked the land—thus stimulating the beginnings of agrarian reform.

The foundation had a board of directors with ten members: five ex officio (the prime minister, court minister, president of the Senate, leader of the House, and the president of the Supreme Court) and five selected by the Shah himself. It engaged in a range of charitable and cultural activities: it gave scholarships to students belonging to families of police, military, and Savak personnel who were victims of confrontations with guerrillas; it also established an organization for the publication and translation of important texts which accumulated some five hundred books on its list—for the most part translations of Western classical literary, philosophical, and historical works. But its main activities were strictly commercial and highly profitable.

By the 1970s the foundation's assets came in the first instance from the Omran Bank, which had a capital of more than £600 million in 1978. The bank was itself a shareholder in a number of other Iranian banks and insurance companies. For example, it owned 80 percent of the Melli Insurance Company which reserved a large part of the public-service sector business for itself, including sole insurance rights for Iran Air, representing a net revenue of £3 million per year. The foundation was also a shareholder in companies producing sugar, cement, and cars as well as in large construction companies. It owned a big chain of hotels and casinos, claiming a near monopoly in the field. In 1973 it acquired the fifty-story Depinna building on Fifth Avenue in Manhattan, which was to be rented to Iranian state companies or organizations with offices in New York.

Most of these activities were carried out in the name of dummy companies (Iranian or foreign), which not only meant that the public was unaware that the Pahlavi Foundation was behind them but that even some government officials could not keep track of them. This lack of transparency did not help the royal family. Quite the reverse, the uncertainty gave rise to all kinds of rumors which magnified the foundation's commercial enterprises.

For my own part, I had been convinced for a number of years that these dubious operations were threatening the existence of the monarchy in Iran. Along with several friends who shared my qualms (notably Hoveida, who had to be discreet), I carried out an investigation to gather concrete information about the activities of the foundation. In the course of meetings I had with the queen, I used to present her with glaring bits of evidence which I hoped would indirectly convince the Shah that he would be running a great risk if he allowed these practices to continue. The queen would say to me on each occasion: "His Majesty is confident that all the fuss amounts to nothing more than baseless rumors. Where's the proof!" She would always take notes and sometimes filled page after page in her large notebook, but it was clear that she was unable to persuade the Shah that he should halt his family's sharp practices.

With all this in mind, I said to the Shah, "The foundation's affairs have always worried the supporters of the monarchy more than its opponents."

Surprised, the Shah asked why this should be the case.

"Because your supporters have always believed that if business became the prime concern of the royal family, it would corrupt it from within and render the crown indefensible; whereas for your opponents, who are determined to see you go anyway, the more rotten your realm, the easier their task."

The Shah remained unshaken in his determination to persuade me: "As you know, the foundation engaged in activities which the private sector would never have had the courage to touch. In the hotel business, for example, which attracted no investment at all, the foundation persevered with its efforts to provide the country with an infrastructure worthy of its name, even though it operated at a loss. It was also the foundation that took steps to encourage investment in the cement and sugar industries in areas where they had not existed before."

"Majesty, you must know that, even if these arguments were valid thirty or forty years ago, they are patently not so today, for, with the increase in oil revenue, the state itself is perfectly capable of carrying out these tasks. In view of the need for the monarchy to arouse the respect and trust of the Iranian people, it is difficult to understand why Your Majesty has become involved in such affairs. Why do you personally have to act as a model for economic investment? You occupy a very high position which carries a great moral force; that force can only be weakened by behavior of this kind. The clearest confirmation of the problem is that of today's businessmen, who owe their position to you but now consider you a rival. . . . It is they who speak at receptions and dinner tables about the affairs of the Pahlavi family with, it must be said, more than a little exaggeration. And that is where foreigners, be they businessmen or diplomats or journalists, gain their first impressions on arrival in Tehran. You can well imagine the disastrous consequences, both inside the country and abroad, of all these rumors?"

Clearly tired of all the things he had heard on the subject of his personal fortune, the Shah asked with deep resignation, "What must I do to put an end to all this?"

"Donate everything you own in one irrevocable act. And I mean everything, Majesty. To convince the people of your good faith, you must give up your possessions, both in Iran and abroad. You would thereby prove your firm determination to remain in Iran."

"All right, fine. But what form is this donation to take?"

"You could transfer it all to the Ministry of Education so that the interest can accrue to the well-being and education of the country's children. And in order to avoid falling into the same cycle of errors as the Pahlavi Foundation, you must place everything under government control, with a supervisory committee appointed by Parliament. You yourself should have no overriding rights; the status of the fund should be the same as the crown jewels, which were placed under sole responsibility of the Central Bank and thus kept out of your family's reach."

"So much for my own assets. What about the rest of my family's wealth?"

"You could order its nationalization."

He was horrified at the idea. "You're suggesting that I nationalize my family's holdings by force? Which law would you have me appeal to? Don't you think they'd protest against such an arbitrary act, as would any citizen, before national or international tribunals?"

"In the first place, Majesty, it is not a question of just any ordinary individual. In the second place, they wouldn't dare to protest."

"But tell me what methods am I to use in practice?"

"They could grant you the power of attorney, which is perfectly correct and legal, giving you the authority to dispose of their property as you deem fit. Or, if they reject this idea, you could order a government investigation into their business affairs, with the subsequent submission of a draft bill to Parliament aimed at nationalizing not all their belongings but those which are shown to have been acquired illegally. All this could be done within the framework of the law. Such a step would put you in a position of moral strength in the country. It would be an example to the well-to-do concerned and would allow you to undertake any social reforms you wished."

"Wouldn't my family claim that I'm depriving them of the right to own property, a right enjoyed by all Iranian citizens?"

"Majesty, they did not amass their fortunes through legal means. Their assets are the product of influence peddling. I'll give you an example. Two days ago newspapers announced the proceedings against the board of directors of a property company called Mahestan. Princess Ashraf is a major shareholder."

"But my sister has told me that she's already sold all her shares."

"How did she come by those shares in the first place, Sire? Allow me to fill you in on the background to the affair. Some years ago the Ministry of Agriculture presented a decree to the cabinet to allow the donation to the Pahlavi Foundation, free of charge, of several million square meters of land in northwest Tehran, for the purpose of constructing apartments for low-income families. Princess Ashraf set up a property company, the capital of which came by and large from the partial sale of this land, bought at a favorable rate from the foundation. The same company signed agreements with an Italian company for the construction of three thousand luxury houses. It then sold the houses at exorbitant prices on the basis of plans alone and never fulfilled its obligation actually to build the houses. Today, as a result of the purchasers' complaints, the company is being prosecuted. You can therefore see how the princess made several million in profit, benefiting from land acquired by illegitimate means, not to mention the sale of nonexistent properties. . . . That, Majesty, is the kind of business the royal family has been engaged in, and this is the kind of dishonor that it brings on the monarchy and the entire regime. . . ."

I sensed that, although embarrassed and silent, the Shah was not altogether displeased to be hearing these facts, with which he had rarely been confronted in so direct a manner. I was consequently encouraged to pursue my revelation about the business dealings of his twin sister and other family members. I continued:

"I'm certain they presented the company's plans to you with great enthusiasm, giving the impression that a new housing development would rapidly spring to life in suburban Tehran, at the foot of the Alborz mountains, and that it would leave nothing to be desired. Both its architecture and its planning would be comparable to that used in the latest housing developments in the West. I can also well believe that in their determination to impress you the Italian architects, presented to you by Princess Ashraf, showed you a model of this new town which took your breath away."

As if emerging from a dream, the Shah replied, "Yes, that's true. I saw interesting models but, if my memory serves me correctly, the visitors stressed they did not have sufficient funds. They expressed the hope that I might give instructions to the banks for them to obtain credit."

"Yes, you're not mistaken, but that's another story. Using maneuvers like the one you describe, they not only succeeded in illicitly obtaining land that was extremely expensive on the open market and selling unbuilt houses; they also secured credit at very favorable rates from various banks. Similar procedures were used by influential people besides the royal family. Your relatives, notably Prince Gholam Reza, also drew other advantages from the housing crisis. The municipal authorities issue building permits only within a strictly defined framework and on the basis of precise practices. And yet the prince was given permission to build exactly where he could gain maximum advantage, by special favor from the mayor of Tehran. This is the reason for the unpopularity of the unfortunate Nikpay [the former mayor of Tehran who was arrested on corruption charges at the same time as Hoveida and other ministers]. Whenever it suited him, the mayor would apply municipal regulations forbidding construction in urban areas without prior permission, razing the dwellings of the poor. But he cheerfully granted exemptions to companies associated with the prince and princesses for the construction of new urban developments."

The Shah looked pensive. I persisted: "This virtual monopoly, exercised by a few, aggravated the housing crisis and contributed to an endless spiral of rising prices. Left unchecked, the problem has become a source of anxiety for the new class of technicians and specialists who play a fundamental role in the country's economy but who are forced to spend more than 50 percent of their earnings on suitable housing. . . . That is certainly one of the causes of the discontent of the capital's residents, and revolutionaries have not failed to exploit it. But what's even worse, Majesty, is that the crisis could have been foreseen. I remember that, a little over five years ago, in 1973, Hoveida came to Paris where I was working with UNESCO. He invited me out to lunch, along with the director-general Rene Maheu, for whom he had great respect because he had been one of his students in philosophy at London's French Lycée in 1938. We and our wives had a meal together at the Hotel Bristol. In the course of a full two hours, Hoveida painted a glowing picture of Iran and its achievements in all areas. He stressed that all our socioeconomic problems had been dealt with except for the problem of housing. When René Maheu said that all that was required was a coherent policy to be adopted and maintained for several years, Hoveida replied, 'Yes, but big interests impede the implementation of a coherent policy.' You see, Sire, Hoveida could not bring himself to say any more. Today we can see what difficulties the pursuit of sordid interests can generate—difficulties which become grist for the mill of the revolutionaries. A former minister of economy, Dr. Alikhani, once said to me, 'If you were to stand on one of the hills of northern Tehran and look down on all the tower blocks built in recent years, you can assume that the royal family has had a share in every one of them; they would otherwise have never been built.'"

The sovereign looked disturbed. "Is that true?"

"Yes, Majesty, by and large."

In order to extricate himself from a tight corner and convince himself that the things he had been hearing about his relatives were unfounded, he said, "Recently we established a commission of inquiry to deal with any private complaints against the imperial family. I asked about the commission's work only this morning and was told there had been very few complaints."

"The current atmosphere is highly charged, Sire. The people no longer know what they think. They can't really believe that you're prepared to call your relatives to heel. I should also say, Your Majesty, that for the most part your family's interference in financial affairs has harmed the state and not private individuals. Allow me to give you a few examples. In 1977 the queen, in her capacity as president, called a meeting of the High Council for Scientific Research in a hotel in the Dizin Mountains. In the course of two days, members of the council discussed the different aspects of a science and research policy for the country. When I, along with a number of others, raised the issue of a transfer of technology, the queen, who agreed with our point of view and understood our concerns, hinted that we were unfortunately straying into forbidden territory and that because of the 'conflict of interests' we would under no circumstances be allowed to have a say on contracts of this kind."

"And yet I've always insisted that when it comes to a transfer of technology, Iranian personnel should be used at all levels. But in the area of advanced technology we were often short of Iranian expertise and we wanted to make rapid progress on the installation of new factories."

"Majesty, I sent a report to the Shahbanou when I took charge of the Institute for Research and Planning on Science and Education. I invited James Harrison, former assistant director-general of UNESCO for science and technology and former Canadian deputy energy minister, to examine the problem. He was in Tehran for two months, and he made a study of the contracts for six important projects undertaken by the Iranian government and foreign companies—in petrochemicals, nuclear energy, aluminum, and so forth. His final report stressed that in all the contracts the Iranian element was weak. 'If you don't seriously negotiate the conditions of these transfers,' he warned, 'you will never possess your own technology.' Mr. Harrison agreed that haphazard industrialization, without a distinct policy on science and technology, would make us more and more dependent on foreigners, and that we would never arrive at a point where we could rely on our own abilities. Isn't the problem that the climate which reigns during these contract negotiations is permeated with personal interests? Our real problems are always driven into second place. The financial acrobatics are such that even our commercial interests are neglected. Another example: at the end of that meeting of the scientific council I went for a walk in the mountains with Akbar Etemad, the director of the Center for Atomic Energy, and Reza Ghotbi, the director of television, who as you know is the queen's cousin. When I asked Etemad, 'Why don't Iranian industrial concerns include clauses safeguarding national interests on contracts concluded with foreign companies?' he replied that the financial stakes were too high and that the interests of the people in high places limited the negotiators' room for maneuver. He cited the example of nuclear power stations and related how he and others had resisted constant pressure from Princess Ashraf who pushed them to accept the offer of a German construction group whose bid exceeded that of other companies by £100 million, even though a few days earlier the prime minister, Amouzegar, had summoned Etemad to his office and told him that the princess's wishes had to be complied with in every particular.[23] Another example: a few years ago, the government completed a contract with a Canadian company to install and equip a paper pulp factory near the Caspian Sea. The contract was of the order of about $80 million. Sometime after it was signed, the Canadian company made Prince Abdol-Reza a party to the deal. The prince then went to your all-powerful finance minister, who managed to obtain from the government an additional payment of $20 million, in return for which the Canadian company paid about $12 million to the prince. As you can see, Sire, it always comes down to the same thing. There are countless examples of this kind of interference. How, in these circumstances, can national interests be protected? In effect, it's not up to individuals to make claims against this prince or that, because it's the interests of the nation as a whole that have been infringed."

The Shah tried to play down the significance of the corruption in his family. "These kinds of irregularities and practices are not confined to our country. There are many cases of it elsewhere, including Europe and America. One is forever hearing stories about influential people—senators, parliamentary deputies, or ministers—being involved in financial scandals. It's impossible to implement huge projects without a few minor infractions."

"In the first place, Majesty, the examples I mentioned were not minor. In the second, in the countries you mentioned there is a division of power. There are political parties, a parliament, a judiciary, the media, local governments, competition between companies, and so on. Here power is centralized. Everything emanates from you, and you must consequently be extremely vigilant. This is the price you have to pay for your power. As the proverb puts it, 'Being great costs a lot.'"

"I agree with you. We must safeguard the interests of the nation and not allow them to be compromised. And, as you yourself said, we must be very careful because we're under the glare of spotlights. That's why I would like you to discuss all of this with the queen. She

23. In order to illustrate the influence the princess exercised over the Shah and the monarch's own wariness of his twin sister, I should mention that a year after this conversation, when I found myself in Evin Prison, I ran into a Savak officer who told me an interesting story. He had once been summoned by the director of Savak to be told that the Shah wanted to know everything there was to know about the daily lunches the princess had with Amouzegar.

has shown a great interest in these matters recently, and she's keen to find solutions. Go and see her as soon as you can."

"With great pleasure, Sire, but I must confess to you that I've been discussing these problems with the queen for many years. She shared my concern but did not think she was in a position to act. Let's hope that she feels stronger now!"

"She has in fact been playing a very active role in everything recently, and I'm very pleased about that."

"One other thing, Majesty. Are you still determined to establish a coalition government?"

"Absolutely. Since I spoke on radio about ten days ago, I've had it in mind to set up a coalition cabinet, bringing together all the different elements of political life."

"I think that Sadighi[24] would, despite the twenty-five years he has spent out of favor, be prepared to take the plunge. Even in the face of the tremendous difficulties, he's bound to be enchanted."

Amazed to hear the name of one of Mosaddeq's best known ministers, who had never been prepared to surrender his principles, the Shah exclaimed, "What are you saying? Where did you get this information?"

"I went to see him last night. I sensed that he would be prepared to run the risk, unlike other nationalist politicians, with the proviso, I suspect, that you accept and abide by his conditions."

"I'm prepared to hear what he has to say. Tell the queen about this too. She'll be very pleased to hear it. Tell Amini and Entezam as well."

"With pleasure. I've really tried Your Majesty's patience today. With your permission I'll withdraw."

I rose. He walked toward me and accompanied me a few steps. Before reaching the door he shook my hand and said, "See you very soon!"

I left his office and went to the chamberlain's room. It was 12:30. I telephoned the queen's secretary and told him that I would like to

24. Gholam-Hossein Sadighi, a well-known academic, historian, and sociologist, was serving as interior minister under Mosaddeq when the latter was deposed in the 1953 coup. He spent more than two years in prison and afterward retired from political life to devote himself to scholarship. He "sponsored" the start of my academic career in 1957, and we always remained close. He died in 1991.

arrange a meeting with her. A few minutes later he rang back to say that she could see me right away. I went down the stairs, took the path cutting through the middle of the garden, and walked toward the queen's office.

Between Wife and Sister

And so I arrived at the Shahbanou's[1] small office, situated on the first floor of Niavaran Palace, adjacent to the royal family's private quarters.

Over the past ten years I had visited the queen many times in this room, where I could speak to her alone and entirely at ease. I had a family connection with her on my mother's side; but although this is a factor that engenders trust and plays an important part in the relationships between people in Eastern cultures, we never made an issue of it. Farah showed a great interest in nature conservation and the country's cultural heritage as well as in the welfare of children and the future of youth. In our meetings I spoke freely about all matters of importance for the country, be it the abuse of power, repression, or the machinations of the Shah's entourage and family.

On that particular day I hardly waited for us to be seated before taking out the famous list of companies affiliated with the Pahlavi Foundation. I placed it on the table in front of her and said, "I've just been to see His Majesty. I spoke with him at length about the affairs of the dynasty. He asked me to discuss possible courses of action with you. It may be necessary to establish a commission to deal with this terrible business."

1. Shahbanou, the "king's wife," is often translated as "empress" although in fact it means "queen."

The queen seized the list anxiously and her eyes grew wider as she skimmed through it. Her first reaction was to reach for a cigarette and then to breathe a deep sigh of relief: "I'm very glad to see none of my own family is on it."

She looked directly at me and asked, "What did His Majesty say when you showed him this list?"

"To be honest, His Majesty seemed to have no wish to read it. When I insisted, expecting him to make a decision on the question, he suggested that I come to see you. I was left with the impression that he hoped you would set a commission to look into the matter and make recommendations."

The Shahbanou crushed out her half-smoked cigarette and said wearily, "What good would a commission do? We're going around in circles. There's no doubt that a decision needs to be taken, but it has nothing to do with you, me, or any commission of inquiry. Whether he likes it or not, it's entirely up to His Majesty."

"As you know, the royal family's financial affairs are its weakest point—a cancer which must be cured immediately."

"I would go even further and say it should have been cured a long time ago. Unfortunately, nothing was done. I agree with you entirely when you say this business has caused great harm."

It was the first time the Shahbanou had spoken to me so frankly on this awkward subject. In the past, although she had heard me out with interest, she had usually refrained from commenting. Only once a few years earlier, when I painted a grim picture of the family's situation, had she allowed herself to remark, "Why should we, for the sake of gratifying the greed of a small group of fourteen or fifteen people, be expected to endanger the lives of our children? I'm asking you why?"

"You should put exactly this question to His Majesty the King," I had replied.

This was the only time she had spoken to me without reservation. She did not dare reveal her true feelings on the subject because she knew full well that it would be impossible to talk about the royal family's affairs without referring to the all-powerful Princess Ashraf, whom she feared to offend. Farah was acutely aware that Ashraf had played a role in the divorces between the Shah and his two previous wives, Fawzieh (the sister of Egypt's King Farouk) and Soraya.

Despite all the pomp and ceremony with which the Shahbanou had been surrounded in recent years, and despite her investiture in 1975 as future regent, she played no significant role in Iran's political life until 1977, the year before the fall of the monarchy. Nevertheless, although she remained in the background for a long time, Farah will be remembered for her positive contribution to the life of the nation, especially when compared with a husband obsessed with modernity and unconcerned with the environment or the country's cultural heritage. At times the views of the Shah and Farah were so far at odds that government officials no longer knew which way to turn. Pirouz, the governor of Fars Province, which has Shiraz as its capital, once confided in me, "I really don't know how to reconcile the royal couple's contradictory instructions. Each time the Shah visits Shiraz he tells us to construct taller and taller tower blocks in reinforced concrete; whereas the queen wants us to plant more greenery and make more use of local materials such as bricks, and she's forever saying, 'Not so high! Not so high!'"

The establishment of children's libraries in various cities and the development of extracurricular educational materials were two areas in which the queen's efforts proved particularly effective. But she also succeeded in repatriating large quantities of Iranian antiques, and she launched a kind of "cultural movement" in Tehran's high society which favored Iranian art. It was to the queen that we owed the creation of a number of beautiful museums, for glassware, ceramics, carpets, and paintings as well as modern art. A former student at a well-known Parisian school of architecture, she entrusted the design of the museum of modern art to Hassan Fathy, the famous Egyptian architect, who succeeded in giving the building a contemporary look while also using traditional designs.

As a director of the foundation which the Shahbanou established to supervise the work of a few dozen institutions set up on her initiative, I was in constant contact with her and can testify that she worked vigorously to avert the negative consequences of the Shah's haphazard modernization. Forming a kind of rampart against the excesses of a husband whose ignorance of Iran's culture almost bordered on contempt, she became a refuge and patron to a small group of artists and intellectuals who wanted to protect our identity from the ill effects of an increasingly oppressive and intrusive cosmopolitanism.

Thanks to the queen, despite the limited representation of this group among the directors of her foundation, we were occasionally able to question, in her presence and in the presence of the prime minister, the regime's policies in various fields.

I remember a particular occasion when we[2] managed to raise the problem of censorship in front of the queen and the prime minister. Our comments had immediate repercussions in the relevant organizations and Pahlbod, the minister of culture who was formally in charge of censorship—although in practice Savak held sway—was specifically informed of our complaints. (Pahlbod was the Shah's brother-in-law, having married another of his sisters, Princess Shams.) In meetings of the board of directors, we even took advantage of the Shahbanou's protection to criticize state policies and actions, although many things were also left unsaid where the Shah was concerned—a fact of which everyone was aware. This cast something of a shadow over all our discussions. Nevertheless, the Shahbanou succeeded, with tact and delicacy, in bringing the detractors of her husband's policies right into the palace, where they could meet in a room not far away from the man who was ruling the country with a rod of iron. . . .

A year before the ostentatious Persepolis celebrations the Shahbanou said to me, in the course of one of our private conversations, that she did not at all see the point of such elaborate events. I learned later that she had opposed the celebrations with such vehemence that the court minister, Alam, who enjoyed the Shah's confidence, had submitted his resignation to the sovereign in protest over the Shahbanou's endless criticism. In the event, Alam's resignation was not accepted and the festivities went ahead as planned. The queen nonetheless had an important moderating role in relation to her husband and was prepared to listen to the advice of informed people as well as to uphold her own deeply held traditional and religious values.

Princess Ashraf had an altogether different influence on her twin brother and had been privy to his secrets since the beginning of his reign. She owned property in Paris, the Côte d'Azur, and New York, and spent most of her time abroad. And with her passion for gambling and for glamorous possessions, she was a great spender. Once, when I

2. The historian A. H. Zarrinkoub and myself.

was eating lunch alone with Hoveida, Ashraf telephoned him from Juan-les-Pins. The prime minister spoke with her briefly, and when he replaced the receiver he seemed quite peeved. I guessed right away that the conversation was about money.

"Big loss at the casino?" I ventured.

Hoveida exploded, "Madam is demanding a large sum of money. And before this evening at that! She probably lost at the casino in Cannes and was forced to wake up at 11:30, French time, to call me. That's far too early for her since she goes to bed at the most ungodly hours, and it's probably why she was in such a foul mood. . . ."

Hoveida raised his eyes to the ceiling as if he had taken more than he could stand, but then made a signal indicating he was in a position to say no more.

"Why don't you resign?" I asked.

He put his index finger to his lips, and I had the impression he wished to alert me to the possible presence of hidden microphones. Then, in a loud clear voice, he said, "When one is serving His Majesty, one does not resign. . . ."

Since she combined audacity with seductiveness, Princess Ashraf had an enormous ability to enchant men and she always got what she wanted out of them. She was fearless and prepared to take on the most daunting statesmen, even a man of Stalin's caliber. In 1946, when the Soviet Union had failed in its attempt to seize Iranian Azerbaijan and the Shah was trembling at the thought of meeting the Kremlin leader, it was she who went to Moscow where she charmed Stalin to such an extent that he offered her an exquisite sable coat.

In 1947 she went to Washington to meet President Truman, and in 1972 to Peking where with Mao Tse-tung she laid the foundations for the new relations that were soon to be established between Iran and China. For many years she also headed Iran's delegation to the UN General Assembly in New York. She was always ready to take up the cudgels in defense of her brother when she was in a tight corner. She did not hesitate, for example—as she reveals in her own memoirs[3]—to meet representatives of the British and American intelligence services in the Bois de Boulogne in 1953 in order to hatch a plot to overthrow the prime minister, Mosaddeq, with the complicity of the

3. *Jamais Resignee* (Paris, 1983).

American General Norman Schwarzkopf.[4] Furthermore, she was given the task of secretly returning to Iran in order to persuade her still wavering brother to take a clear stance on the execution of the plan.

Princess Ashraf had a reputation for rewarding people in her inner circle, and she gave them important posts in the administration of her affairs. She believed that in their struggle for emancipation women should behave like men, in politics as well as on a more personal level. This approach, which directly contradicted the country's values and mores, never ceased to shock the public. So, although Princess Ashraf may have been a precious asset for her brother on the international level, she was little more than a liability on the domestic stage.

There is no doubt, however, that because she was his twin sister she had a particularly good understanding of the Shah. Her strong personality allowed her to act with determination where he was apt to hesitate, and she was prepared to take risks that the Shah himself would never have contemplated. Throughout the years 1941 to 1953, and particularly from 1941 to 1946, at the start of his reign, when Iran was occupied by allied armies, the Shah suffered countless humiliations, not just at the hands of the British and the Soviets but also from politicians who had come to the forefront again after twenty years of dictatorship under his father. During this period, when the regime

4. General Norman Schwarzkopf, father of the future commander of the coalition forces in the 1991 Gulf War, made his name as the chief of police in New Jersey by his determined efforts against the mafia. From 1943 to 1948 he offered his services to the Iranian officers charged with the task of reforming the national gendarmerie. He returned to Tehran on August 1, 1953, immediately after Princess Ashraf's clandestine trip to Tehran, and met the Shah secretly to confirm the plan his sister had divulged to him. The first attempt at a coup was made on the night of August 15, 1953, but Mosaddeq's supporters managed to thwart it a few hours later. According to the prearranged plan, the Shah was supposed to be at the Caspian with Soraya, but he left the country for Rome on his private plane as soon as he learned of the collapse of his attempt to regain undisputed power. On August 19 the plotters began spreading stories about a different version of events, involving the participation of a religious leader, Ayatollah Behbehani. This was followed by a series of pro-Shah demonstrations, thanks to which Mosaddeq's opponents succeeded in overthrowing him and in replacing him with General Zahedi. The day after the coup, General Zahedi invited the Shah to return to Tehran, beginning another chapter in a reign that was to become increasingly absolute.

was really hanging by a thread, the princess regularly took it upon herself to confront influential politicians or journalists who opposed the sovereign. And she often got her way because, like Catherine II and Pauline, Napoleon's sister, she would stop at nothing in her attempts to win over her opponents, or at the very least to neutralize them.

The Shah was well aware that in a Muslim country a woman could not easily take the place of a monarch—a fact that worked to her advantage since the Shah confided more freely in her than he ever did in his brothers, knowing she was unlikely to usurp the throne. Ashraf was, in effect, the Shah's alter ego, for she had all the psychological traits he would have liked to possess. On those occasions when the Shah felt compelled by events to seek compromise solutions he would rather have avoided—in his dealings with prime ministers, for example—she preferred to opt for intrigues aimed at undermining the minister's position instead.

While the Shah may have been grateful for his sister's help when he found himself in difficulty, he tended to turn away from her as soon as he felt more secure. Psychologically dominated by her and conscious of the power she had gradually gained over him in the course of their seven years of complicity, the Shah felt a certain unease. Their relationship was eternally ambivalent, and whenever the emperor wanted to rebuke her in any way he would delegate the task to someone else.

Houshang Ram, the head of the Shah's private bank, who was later detained with me at Evin Prison, told me that the sovereign had asked him on a number of occasions to tell his sister that she should stop interfering in the country's financial affairs. Ram said to me, "How in the world was I supposed to tell her that, when her august and powerful brother didn't dare do it himself?" That was why the Shah preferred her to stay away from affairs of state and to spend most of her time outside the country, especially during the last two years of his reign. Even then, she always managed to get her way if she set her mind on something. After the revolution, when the Shah was terminally ill, the princess showed that she was intensely attached to her brother.

The relationship between the Shah and Shahbanou had evolved in an altogether different way. Farah was very young when in 1958 she met the king who, eighteen years her senior, was already a man of experience and politically quite powerful. She did not possess Ashraf's political sophistication, nor did she have the same degree of influence on the Shah. For many years she remained in his shadow, without any governmental voice, but with a freshness and enthusiasm sadly lacking in a dynasty which because of its past had become suspicious of human beings and blasé about life itself. Eventually, however, Farah's media success and the public perception of her as a real fairy-tale princess—a young lady studying architecture in Paris who was transformed overnight into the empress of a great and ancient civilization—enhanced her standing in the Shah's eyes, obsessed as he was by his public image in the West. As a result he decided to give her an opportunity to oversee a wide range of sociocultural activities.

Unlike other members of the Pahlavi clan, particularly her husband, the Shahbanou was entirely at ease with ordinary people. In the course of her official visits to the provinces she often managed to escape the straitjacket of protocol. I witnessed this myself during one of her visits to Gilan Province, by the Caspian Sea. A few weeks earlier the provincial governor, whom I knew well, had told me that the way ministers and the queen's secretariat organized her trips did not allow her to discover anything about the people's real problems. He begged me to inform her of certain irregularities in the region which resulted from the abuse of influence by the Shah's entourage. He was particularly incensed about an outrageous procedure that allowed large tracts of forest to be granted to generals, among them General Nasiri, the head of Savak, who had succeeded in obtaining five hundred hectares. When I mentioned the problem to the queen, she asked me how she could unobtrusively arrange to have the facts brought to her attention. I replied, "The governor suggests that you let the organizers of your trip know in passing that you'd like to meet representatives of the local communities. He believes that, more likely than not, the local people, with their openness and frankness, will raise the problem of the 'schemes.'"

"All right," she said, "but on the condition that you come along with us." I accepted her invitation, and we in fact succeeded, with the help of high officials, in allowing the "ordinary" people to expose the land scandal. As usual the Shahbanou took copious notes. Soon after our return to Tehran she confided in me that she had raised the issue with the Shah. But, as might be expected, the story ended there. The organizers of the trip were in for another surprise when the queen decided one evening to pay an unscheduled visit to the prison in the city of Rasht. She managed to get her way, but she was forced to wait a good fifteen minutes at the prison gate while the guard set about obtaining authorization from his superiors to let her in.

The queen, in short, was not just interested in arts and artists but was also sensitive to the hardships suffered by her compatriots and the injustices to which they fell victim. And if she was convinced that what she was doing was right, she had no qualms about disregarding matters of state. For example, in 1973, when I was working in Paris, she received me on one of my trips to Tehran. I told her that Vida Hajebi, who had been one of her school friends and was now a militant in a guerrilla movement, had been tortured in a Tehran jail. I suggested that she ask Savak to let two of Hajebi's friends, Zinat Towfiq and Homa Nategh, visit her to find out about the conditions under which she was being held. The queen immediately called Sabeti, Savak's strongman, and obtained the necessary visiting rights—a privilege absolutely unheard of for prisoners held in solitary confinement and, like Hajebi, considered particularly tenacious and unyielding.

One year earlier, in 1972, the Shahbanou had asked me to help a left-wing writer-poet to join the academic staff of the new university in Hamadan, where he was put in charge of a museum of popular art and culture. In view of the fact that the poet did not possess—despite his many talents—a degree of any kind, or even a high school diploma, the queen's request seemed to me completely impossible, and I suggested another way of helping him. Since I knew that she had given him substantial financial assistance, which had most notably allowed him to go to Europe to "dry out," I said to her:

"The personal interest you've shown in this poet is most praiseworthy, but this kind of assistance should be generalized, and the state—in this case, the Ministry of Culture—should be made to help all poets and artists who face difficulties. I should also tell you that, however well meant, your solicitous efforts will not undo the disastrous effects of the royal family's behavior on public opinion. If you want to be remembered as a queen of historical importance in Iran, you must use your influence on His Majesty to make him understand that he must take decisive action to halt the Pahlavi dynasty's endless quest for money."

It was undoubtedly because she was not in a position to change the Pahlavis that the queen persisted, by way of compensation, in her attempts to help the revolutionary poets. She was in addition always prepared to respond favorably to requests put to her for the defense and promotion of community interests. For example, when preparations were under way for the World of Islam festival held in London in June 1976, I put it to the queen that it might be better if, instead of an official delegation—which in any case would be composed of the usual people—a group of real Iranian artists and artisans could be sent to London. Many had never traveled outside Iran, and this was a unique opportunity for them to meet and see the work of creative artists from other countries as well as experience international appreciation of their own work. In reply to a question from the Shahbanou, I said that in my opinion the delegation should consist of about 150 people. She asked me if I would take charge of the task of selecting the artists from throughout the country. I agreed, and late in the evening on that same day I received a phone call from Hoveida. He told me the government would be putting a Boeing 707 at our disposal and would pay the expenses of up to two hundred participants during their one-week stay in London. With the assistance of provincial radio/television centers and through the relevant professional associations, we set about selecting master artisans from each craft and, with the help of the National Congress of Iranology, appointing representatives from the field of history.

Her outlook on life and her persistent interest in matters such as this meant that the queen had very little in common with other members of the Pahlavi family who, for their part, felt only mistrust toward her. It is therefore not surprising that after the fall of the dynasty, members of the ancien régime, most notably those who live abroad, in the words of Talleyrand on the emigrés of the French Revolution, lost no time in holding her responsible for the collapse. They blame Farah for her systematic opposition to any attempt to crush the revolution in the autumn and winter of 1978, and some even claim that it was she who made the Shah leave the country.

In reality, even during the final years of the Shah's reign, the queen's activities never had a significant impact on the course of events because she did not have the means to curtail repression or to limit corruption. A single example will suffice to demonstrate that her efforts often amounted to little more than a straw blowing in the wind.

In Evin Prison, at the beginning of 1980, the architect Mohsen Foroughi, a great connoisseur of Iranian antiques, told me a story of how, ten years earlier, he had received a phone call from Parviz Raji, Hoveida's private secretary, informing him that the prime minister wished to see him at the earliest opportunity. In the meeting the head of government said to him, "Mr. Foroughi, I have here a round-trip ticket to Tokyo in your name, and a room has also been reserved for you there. This is what I would like you to do for me: a member of the royal family has taken some antiques out of the country illegally and is proposing to sell them in Japan in about three weeks' time. He's already published a catalog there and according to our information is displaying the antiques in the cellar of a bank. Your task is to go and see the pieces on display, to evaluate them, and to give me a report."

On his return from Tokyo, Foroughi told Hoveida that in his estimation the collection was worth about £600,000. Hoveida informed him that the prince was asking for £1.2 million. Foroughi ended his story with the following two points: one, that Hoveida had decided, on the basis of the Shahbanou's discreet advice, to buy the collection and bring it back to Iran, and two, that the prince had by that time controlled the illegal traffic of Iranian antiques for twenty years. The Shahbanou could ameliorate the effects of such activities, but she could do nothing to put a stop to them and therefore could not change the Iranian people's view of the dynasty.

The Shah began to draw Farah into politics after Jimmy Carter moved into the White House in January 1977. Aware of the president's disapproval of his regime and his human rights record, the Shah tried to exploit his wife's popularity in the United States to improve his public image there. He was especially keen to encourage Farah to make a number of trips to the States because he knew that President Carter and his wife Rosalyn were fond of her. But whenever the queen abandoned her role as guardian of the arts and patron of charities in aid of the underprivileged in order to help her husband politically, she would immediately fall prey to a handful of power-hungry politicians who wished to use her to further their own aims. In 1978 the Shah had Hoveida arrested in the hope of mollifying the revolutionaries. A week later, in the course of a conversation with the queen, I begged her to intervene to improve the conditions under which he was being held.[5] Much to my surprise—for everyone knew that Hoveida had always been a valuable support to the queen—she appeared extremely reserved.

I sensed that she had fallen under the influence of a number of politicians who had decided to make Hoveida the scapegoat for the regime. The clearest evidence was that two years earlier she had appointed a man as her principal private secretary who was known to have only one objective: to supplant Hoveida by any possible means. So the Shahbanou herself, who wanted to be the queen of the poor and of all the people, was in the end caught in the web of political intrigues for which she had no taste.

As for the accusation that Farah was responsible for the Shah's departure from Iran, my own impressions suggest the exact opposite. In a conversation I had with her in November 1978, I remember Farah saying, "More and more, people are advising us to leave. As to myself, I've always said that I would rather stay here, even with the children. If they're going to kill us, let them kill us all together in our own country. I would prefer that to spending the rest of my life wandering the world, from airport to airport, suitcase in hand." Indeed, she was at one point planning to remain in Iran with the children even if the Shah left the country, so as "not to give the impression that the entire family was on the run."

A final point: the queen's opposition to the iron-fist policy arose from her hope that a political solution acceptable to the country could be found without bloodshed, and her conviction that as long as the Shah was surrounded by a family and "servants" steeped in corruption and despised by the people, the regime would not be able to survive other than by force and with the support of the army. But as time moved on, signs of insubordination and rebellion were multiply-

5. Fereshteh Razavi, a doctor and university lecturer and cousin of Hoveida who was allowed to visit him, had telephoned me to say that Hoveida was being kept in a room with the curtains drawn and was not allowed to go out for air.

ing in the ranks of that very army, and the Shah's own entourage, sensing the danger, began to leave the country. At one of our meetings the queen told me with some bitterness of a political joke circulating in Tehran at the time which she had recounted to the Shah. It went like this: After one of the large-scale demonstrations, the Shah, like General de Gaulle in May 1968, asked, "Where, then, are my supporters?" The reply to de Gaulle had been, "On the Champs Elysées, General!" According to the joke, the Shah was given the same reply, with the same gravity, "On the Champs Elysées, Majesty!"

In these desperate circumstances the queen made every effort to encourage the Shah to take tentative steps toward National Front members, old supporters of Mosaddeq whom he viewed with mistrust but who had maintained a reputation as honorable patriots. The fact that her efforts, like those of other people of good will, did not bear fruit can only be attributed to the blindness of a regime that drove the country to the point of no return. By the time the Shah was prepared to allow his wife a political role, events were fueled by two factors entirely outside his control: the scale of the crisis within the country and the reduction of White House support for his government. Furthermore, because she herself had been excluded from politics before 1978, the queen did not know enough about the country's political problems or about the people who might have been able to address them to act effectively.

In her years in exile Farah has been unable, perhaps because of fear of isolation, to maintain her independence and her individuality. The Pahlavi family's disloyalty and cupidity have not escaped her, and she knows how much their blindness and irresponsibility contributed to the fall of the regime. Nevertheless, in her public statements on the subject she cannot surmount her bitterness over the loss enough to name the true causes of the revolution, and she always rallies, in a curious fashion, to the position of the rest of the clan which indiscriminately lays the blame on an international conspiracy.

A final irony of sorts: in the preservation of Iran's cultural heritage, which has the support of Iranians from all walks of life and to which the Shahbanou used to be passionately devoted, Princess Ashraf was able to make the greatest contribution in the end. Thanks to her personal fortune she was able to establish a foundation in the United States dedicated to Iranian culture, while Farah, for her part, wanders helplessly and hopelessly "from airport to airport, suitcase in hand."

Flowers on the Carpet
(Third Conversation with the Shah)

Wednesday, November 23, 1978, 10:30 a.m.

I entered the Shah's office in the Niavaran Palace. He was standing a few meters away from the door. He greeted me with a smile, offered me the seat facing his, and asked, "What's your assessment of developments since we last met? Anything new?"

"The strikes, Your Majesty—they're spreading throughout the country."

"Can you explain why these strikes are taking place? There are workers and laborers among the strikers who are relatively well paid. Their aims can't be either economic or professional. One must therefore ask whether something else lies behind it all."

"To be sure, there is a political will behind the movement, but if you examine the situation carefully you will see that this kind of action develops and spreads much more easily where conditions are conducive to it."

"You're trying to suggest that there are other motivating factors besides demands for more money and better working conditions. What are they?"

"The strikes in the bank, for example, are related to the way banks are run, Majesty. Let me explain what I mean. In the handful of private or state banks in which the honesty of the managers is not in doubt, there is no industrial action of any kind. But in other cases—that is to say, unfortunately, in the majority of our banks—frequent strikes occur, and their frequency is proportional to the extent of irregularities in management."

"What do you mean by management irregularities? Does the Central Bank not control all our banks? Don't its regulations hold everywhere?"

"It's a bit more complicated than that, Majesty. What is often being called into question is the origin and composition of the banks' capital, quite apart from any infringement of regulations. If you take a close look, you find that many of the banks which have been springing up like mushrooms in recent years have been set up by people who've been involved in industry, insurance, land and sea transport, construction, and so on—all at the same time. They've been granting themselves huge accommodating loans to finance their own businesses. To put it in a nutshell, Sire, they're crooked from top to bottom. They've been behaving in any old way they please and, to make matters worse, they've put all their friends and relatives in the top posts. That kind of nepotism obviously does not go down well with employees, who know exactly what their bosses have been up to. In the old days the employees didn't dare speak out because of the government's repressive policies. Now they're prepared to confront their managers. They know their superiors are not being frank with them, for the simple reason that all the major shareholders have decided to leave the country in order to enjoy peacefully all the money they've sent abroad."

"What you're saying relates to private banks and companies. But what's happening in public organizations?"

"In state organizations the problems are of a different nature. There are, for example, complaints about inequitable large differences between salaries; in some semipublic organizations the salary gap is of the order of twenty to one. This is unacceptable at a time when revolutionary and religious fervor is giving rise to concerns about equality and justice."

"Are the gaps between salaries less in industrial countries?"

"Not in the private sector, but in the public or semipublic sector, yes, they are less."

"But what about semipublic organizations like the telecommunications company or Iran Air where, I think I would not be wrong in saying, the average salary is quite high? What do they have to strike about?"

"The case of the telecommunications company is a significant one, because that's where tensions are at their highest. That's why I've made a point of studying it closely. The interruption of work there can have particularly serious consequences because it can cut off the country from the rest of the world. The company, which has a semipublic charter but which runs on state capital, approved—on the Pentagon's advice—a consultancy contract with the American company Bell International. As a result, Iran's telecommunications company has been using Bell's services for the past three years. More than 1,250 experts have been sent to Iran to date, and we pay the American company $200,000 a year for each expert. Iranian specialists working for the company maintain that, for one thing, the number of American experts by far exceeds Iran's technical requirements; second, not all the Americans have skills they're supposed to have; and third, they are occupying posts which ought to be given to Iranians. The Americans are, in effect, running our telecommunications. . . . Not only do our compatriots refuse to accept the huge differences between their salaries and those of the Americans, they also have political grievances. They believe the state has surrendered to foreigners its responsibility in an area that is integral to its sovereignty."

The Shah seemed to be searching his memory: "A few years ago a number of army officers informed me that we needed a master plan for our communications system—for military as well as for civilian use. We would then be able to meet all our requirements: telephone, telegraph, telex, and so on. We therefore suggested the civil authorities coordinate with the army."

"The people don't understand why civilian telecommunications have to be integrated with a military system in order to be modernized, Majesty. They don't understand either why things have to be run by American military experts. The whole business gives rise to such confusion that even a former minister I consulted admitted that he couldn't understand the system."

Pleased to be able to provide me with an explanation of one of his pet advanced technology projects, the Shah began to expand his theories with slow pedantic relish. "In the first place, you shouldn't be surprised that even high-ranking officials have been unable to follow everything we've been doing in the last few years to gain access to the latest technology. In the second, you should bear in mind that equipping a country with an ultramodern telecommunications system wouldn't make any sense unless we took into account our needs over the next twenty or thirty years. We therefore had to have a system which incorporated both our civil and our military needs—that is to say, a system capable of handling aerial defense using satellite technology. In view of the fact that the Americans are more advanced in this field than anyone else, we went to one of their big companies, which works for the Pentagon. Bell is a subsidiary of another big American company, American Telephone and Telegraph, which serves the U.S. Air Force. That's why they were selected to equip us with a military telecommunications system—because the U.S. Air Force acts as an adviser to our air force. You can now understand why we created a single system for military and civilian use and why the Americans were involved."

"All that may be true from a technical point of view, Majesty, but you must surely be aware that people don't see things only from a technical angle."

"Can the people you're talking about, the so-called patriots, not see that, thanks to a cooperation that has allowed us to benefit from American technology, we'll soon be joining an international telecommunications network that will place us alongside the most industrialized countries?"

"Unfortunately, your opponents are deaf in that ear, Majesty. Their lack of understanding, to say nothing of their political misgivings about the regime, prevents them from appreciating the benefits of the technology that the regime is bringing to the country."

"Don't they wish to see Iran advance and develop? How can we be a great nation without possessing the latest technology? Can they not see how Japan is surpassing the entire world, including America? Can they not see Korea industrializing at a staggering rate?"

"Majesty, you've put your finger on the most important and significant aspect of the current crisis: the huge gap between a people who are mistrustful of the regime for historical and sociological reasons and a regime that wants to achieve the maximum technical progress at any cost; the further the regime goes down its own path, the less the people follow it. They cannot see what this progress has to do with anything they care about."

"But how can one set about explaining all these complicated issues to the people? Would they really be interested?"

"Sire, for many years you and the prime minister and several officials held weekly meetings with your economic advisers. You would sometimes spend five or six hours discussing the most complicated documents. At one time, when they were published, I used to read the accounts of these meetings, and I'm convinced that if the people had access to them today they'd hardly understand a word, because the language used is almost indecipherable. They would conclude that each project must have concerned only a small number of people and been motivated by those people's personal interests. But let's move on to the example of another large telecommunications project: the installation of one million telephone receivers. At the time the government recommended a French company by the name of SOFRECOM, which was represented in Iran by Parviz Bushehri, Princess Ashraf's brother-in-law. It seems that Bushehri presented the price for each receiver, tentatively put at $413 by SOFRECOM, at more than double that amount, so that in the end preference was given to an American company, General Telephone and Electronics, with whom he had made other special personal arrangements. That's one clear case of sharp practice being denounced by today's striking telecommunications personnel. The interests of a handful of people, affiliated with foreign companies, ensures the virtual control of Iran by foreigners, to the most blatant detriment of the country."

"What's to be done if what you're saying is true?"

"You must, quite simply, annul the relevant contracts."

"Wouldn't the companies then lodge complaints against us in foreign tribunals?"

"I doubt it, since the contracts I've been referring to—like the one with Bell Helicopter[1]—were agreed during Nixon's term of office. Now that President Carter is talking about human rights, why not take advantage of his policies to condemn these one-sided contracts

1. At this time the manufacture of helicopters was about to begin in Isfahan.

and ask that they be revised on some kind of ethically acceptable basis?"

The Shah suddenly remarked, "Don't you think that the countries which keep harping on human rights are only using their campaign as a shield to hide their real objectives—of which exploitative contracts are only one example—and that they in fact want to establish their hegemony throughout the world? Do you really think they mean what they say? Is it not just a tactic to bring those countries into line which have not submitted to their policies and which have tried to maintain their independence? I have my doubts about their sincerity."

"That's just the point, Majesty. We should not provide them with opportunities to criticize our human rights record. That's precisely one of the issues I was hoping to discuss with you today."

"Tell me what's on your mind!"

"In two weeks' time, on December 10, it will be international Human Rights Day. It would be a good opportunity to release some of the political prisoners who have not been involved in acts of violence. Since, moreover, widely differing and at times excessive figures for the number of prisoners are bandied about, I've suggested to the minister of justice and to the associations concerned with human rights and political prisoners that they get together to clarify the exact number of prisoners in each category. In view of the fact that Savak and the military's justice department [dealing with political prisoners] have not been in a position to reveal the number of people imprisoned for political reasons, there's been too much room for speculation. I succeeded in persuading the minister of justice—whom I know very well because I studied with him—of the need for such clarification. But he has no authority over Savak or the military tribunal because they are under Your Majesty's direct command. If you find the idea acceptable, I think a meeting of this kind would go a long way toward removing misunderstandings and be a comfort to the prisoners' families and to public opinion."

The Shah, with the vexed air of an autocrat who is suddenly stripped of his power, retorted, "According to Savak reports, all the associations you were referring to are in the hands of the opposition, and it is consequently impossible to talk to them. Are you sure that they'll accept an invitation to sit at the same table with the minister without creating a disturbance?"

"I'm positive, Majesty. I've spoken to the president of the Association for the Defense of Political Prisoners, Matin-Daftari,[2] who told me he was prepared to see the minister and to bring his own list of prisoners. I can assure you that he'll keep his word, as will the heads of the other human rights organizations."

The Shah then asked the palace switchboard to put him through to General Behzadi, the president of the military tribunal, and told him, "Come to my office tomorrow with a list of political prisoners and the names of prisoners I can pardon. You can go and see the minister of justice afterward."

As the Shah was talking to the general, I whispered, "Ask for a complete list, Sire."

The Shah put down the receiver, looked at me with a smile, as if to emphasize the magnanimity of his gesture, and said, "What else?"

I was not about to miss such an opportunity. "Thank you for following my suggestion, Majesty. But I would like to stress, if I may, that the number of political prisoners was standing at about three to four thousand last year; if the officials responsible had made that clear at the time, Amnesty International and *Le Monde* wouldn't have announced there were 100,000 prisoners in Iran. . . ."

I sensed that the Shah had sunk deep into thought. Was he realizing that he had made mistakes in his political leadership? Did he think his advisers had led him astray? Did he at least acknowledge that the outside world was against him? After a few moments' silence I changed the subject.

"Another matter for concern, Your Majesty, is the situation of the National Oil Company and the question of the availability of fuel for the country."

"I've heard it said time and time again that there's nothing to worry about. Even if our domestic production doesn't meet our needs, we can always import refined products from the Persian Gulf countries, by plane if need be."

I was very surprised by his suggestion. How could such massive

2. Hedayatollah Matin-Daftari, Mosaddeq's grandson on his mother's side, had just been elected vice-president of the bar. He played an important role in the opposition to the Shah.

quantities of oil products possibly be transported by plane? When I put the question to specialists they replied that it could in fact be done, but only on a small scale, to a specific area, and over a relatively short period—and then only if the logistical requirements (the necessary number of planes, storage tanks at the airports, trucks with fuel reservoirs, and so forth) were available for an effective airlift. In their opinion the Shah's misguided conviction showed that despite his familiarity with the oil industry and military affairs, his knowledge remained seriously flawed. The bits of information he had learned about specific matters that interested him did not add up to a comprehensive picture or a firm scientific foundation.

"Sire, according to my cousin, Keivan Naraghi, who is in charge of the distribution of petroleum products, the strikes at refineries and related installations will mean disaster by mid-winter," I ventured.

"Why haven't I been informed then? I'm in constant contact with the people responsible."[3]

"They're afraid of giving you bad news. They tell you every evening that something of the order of three to four million barrels of crude are being loaded at Kharg terminal each day, which is very nice, of course, as far as it goes. More to the point, however, is that the production capacity at our refineries, for domestic consumption, is currently running at no more than one million barrels per day, and it's dropping steadily."

The military government was biding its time on the matter of domestic oil needs, assuming that a fuel shortage would discredit the strikers in the public's eyes and allow the army to step in to distribute petrol and kerosene and thus become the savior of the nation. But my cousin had convinced me that the army was deluding itself. It had forgotten that the National Oil Company was legally obliged to keep at least two months' supply of a variety of combustible substances in reserve for the immediate use of the army. Not surprisingly, National Oil Company employees sympathetic to the strikers and the revolu-

3. By "the people responsible" the Shah meant the assistants of the oil company's chairman and managing director, General Ansari, who briefed his chief of protocol each evening on the amount of crude oil loaded each day but made no mention of the serious problems of the oil industry in general. The Shah had also entrusted Ansari with the management of his personal fortune and Iran's public assets abroad. Using illness as an excuse, Ansari had been living in Europe for the past months—a cause of great discontent in the oil industry.

tionaries had allowed the army's forgotten reserve to be used for the public's everyday needs. In this way not only had an immediate fuel shortage been averted but also the Iranian army, which had harbored the ambition of becoming the third most powerful army in the world, could very easily be marginalized and neutralized by the civilian population. Despite the massive amount of credit at its disposal, the gigantic military machine would find itself paralyzed when it tried to come to the nation's rescue.

For their own part, the revolutionaries and the strike committees were working on the assumption that fuel resources were virtually inexhaustible. Since the National Oil Company had successfully distributed the precious manna to the country's most remote villages for fifty years, they did not imagine that a long-term suspension of production could deplete supplies. The contradictory ideas held by the Shah, the army, and the revolutionaries were thus all equally off the mark.

After hearing me out, the Shah asked:

"What, in your opinion, do we have to do to guarantee the supply of fuel?"

"You must separate the issue of domestic supplies from that of exports. You must then come to an understanding with the opposition by impressing upon them the gravity of the situation and by reminding them, for example, that throughout the years of fighting in Lebanon, none of the armed groups 'touched the electricity' in Beirut. Incidentally, I took Keivan to see Entezam, whom you're seeing tomorrow.[4] He agreed with our analysis, and he made it known that he felt Your Majesty ought to be warned against listening to the army on civilian affairs, because they haven't a clue."

The Shah seemed very confused. "Are there people, in the middle of all this, who are prepared to accept their responsibilities? Will the striking workers listen to the advice of such people? How can they draw a distinction—in the massive operations which include extrac-

4. Entezam was chairman and managing director of the National Oil Company until 1963 and had been out of favor since then. In December 1978 the Shah was forced to turn to him for help, and the first thing he did was to meet Bazargan and Rafsanjani to arrange a partial resumption of production at the oil refineries. These negotiations were difficult because the strike had been in progress for several months, and left-wing extremists accused the deputies of complicity with the regime.

tion, refining, and distribution—between oil which is going to be exported and oil destined for domestic consumption?"

"There are members of the national and religious opposition to whom one can speak. I've already had a word with my friend, Motahhari, who has the ear of Khomeini. It's also possible to talk to nationalist leaders like Forouhar and Bazargan; I'm going to put them in touch with my cousin Keivan. As for the striking oil workers, Majesty, they're among the most conscientious and responsible people in the country, and they know very well how to distinguish between exports and domestic supplies. They've even drawn up a program to ensure the provision of fuel on a priority basis to hospitals, bakers, and power stations, and have calculated a minimum threshold of domestic use, taking into account the requirements of state-owned and private industries—and, finally, the army. In brief, Majesty, they're ready to work to ensure that the public does not suffer in the winter cold and that minimum needs are met while at the same time not abandoning their protest action."

"I understand what you're saying, but would all this not mean that we had effectively submitted to the people who are opposing the regime, thereby granting them official recognition?"

"They exist, in any case, whether you choose to recognize them or not. As a matter of fact, the authorities should have come to terms with these people a long time ago and given them a chance to cooperate. I don't know if you've already been briefed about these things, Majesty, but I should tell you that they possess great verve and solidarity. In Isfahan's bazaar, for example, where people have been on strike for the past six months, the merchants have set up a relief committee to reschedule debtors' loans with the consent of the creditors. Islamic revolutionaries in southern Tehran have established a system of interest-free loans to help all the people who are experiencing difficulties."

"Where's the money coming from?"

"During the past few years hundreds of mosques have been built in Tehran, more than 100,000 students have registered for courses at Islamic centers, and hundreds of books have been published without the state spending a penny, Majesty. It has all been a product of Muslim solidarity. As for the bazaaris, who came into their own share of the oil money, no one could accuse them of being ungenerous."

"Why is it, then, that for all these years our technocrats and planners have failed to take this element into account in their program for social welfare?"

"Because, Sire, their conception of the state is based on an external model which not only disregards the specific cultural and religious characteristics of the country but is also extremely paternalistic, assuming that individuals must look to the powers that be for the fulfillment of every need."

"But can't you acknowledge what the state has done for them? Just look at the living standards of Iranians today and those of twenty or thirty years ago."

"One thing doesn't preclude the other, Majesty. We could very well have had social policies which relied on government action but which also took into account the Iranian people's own capabilities. Why could these two factors not have been combined? We may have made slower progress then, but at least that progress would have been better accepted and assimilated in the country."

We both fell silent. Once again the Shah turned his gaze to the flowers on the carpet. Was he resigning himself to a total rejection of his conception of development, which meant nothing to the majority of the people, or was he simply reluctant to accept my arguments? I was never to know.

The silence was broken with the arrival of a manservant with a tray in hand, which he lowered before the Shah. The sovereign took the medication and the glass of water offered to him and asked the servant to bring me some tea. As soon as the man had left the room, the Shah turned to me and said unexpectedly, "Do you have to take medicine too? I don't know why I've been so unlucky since childhood. All my life I've been made to take tablets for malaria, for stomach-aches, and for I don't know what. It never ends. Medicine, medicine, always medicine!"

"Majesty, thank heaven I've rarely had to take it myself. I haven't had a fever for the past thirty years."

"How lucky you are! I hope you appreciate it, because I've always had to take medicine."

He kept repeating the word "medicine" with a note of anguish that contrasted sharply to his usual reserve. At the time I assumed that he was trying to solicit my sympathy. But a year later, when I learned he was suffering from cancer, I realized it had been more than that; he had wanted to tell me something in a rare moment of frankness which he would ordinarily not have done.

Going back to our previous discussion, he said, in a friendly and lighthearted voice, tinged with curiosity, "I see that you still have some papers to show me. Go on, then, what's it about?"

"I have here a list of about sixty people considered to be particularly notorious in the influence-peddling game which has been so detrimental to our national heritage. The list has been drawn up by a number of honest high-ranking officials who wish to see these racketeers prevented from leaving the country and steps taken toward a rigorous investigation of their wealth in order to stop them from transferring their millions abroad."

"Haven't many ex-ministers and high-ranking officials been detained since the military government came to power?"

"The people who've been arrested are not, for the most part, the guilty ones, Sire. What they can be reproached with more than anything else is they kept quiet so they could remain in power, and ignored the theft of our national wealth by the people whose names are on this list. You are undoubtedly aware, in any case, that these people, whose fortune can be counted in the millions of dollars, have already placed most of their money in foreign banks, especially in numbered accounts in Switzerland. They've behaved in exactly the same way as colonial exploiters of former years. What public opinion is expecting from you now is decisive action which does not only target ministers."

The Shah had been reluctant in an earlier interview to look at the list of companies affiliated with the Pahlavi Foundation. Now he asked once again that I present it to the Shahbanou.

"Very well, Majesty. I'll obey your instructions. I will not miss an opportunity to see the queen. But what is needed now is for the government to submit a bill to Parliament establishing clear guidelines on how to deal with the offenders."

Asking the palace operator to put him through to the prime minister, General Azhari, the Shah instructed the head of government to speed up the preparation of the bill. Azhari replied that the minister of justice was extremely busy working on the bill and that it would be submitted to Parliament in the very near future.

"One last question, Your Majesty, on the subject of the national coalition you wish to create: I know that Amini and Entezam are going to visit Sadighi and Forouhar, the two nationalist leaders who are currently in prison, with the aim of soliciting their views about a possible government headed by Sadighi. What's your opinion?"

"I think it's a good idea. When do you want to go?"

"The sooner the better; tomorrow morning, if at all possible."

The Shah immediately telephoned General Moghadam, the Savak director, and told him to send a car the next morning to take me to the house in which Sanjabi and Forouhar were being held. He also said I was to be allowed to speak "freely" with them. He turned to me with a smile and said, "You'll see how well they're being treated."

"May I take them a few books?"

"Take whatever you like. Take them antimonarchical tracts if you want; there's no shortage of them these days. . . ."

"That won't be necessary, Majesty. They're already quite familiar with the activities of opposition groups. I'll withdraw now if I may."

I stood up. He walked a few paces with me, then he shook my hand. I bowed and left his office.

Don't Fire on the Crowd!

(Fourth Conversation with the Shah)

Tuesday, December 5, 1978, 4:30 p.m.

I stepped into the Shah's office in the Niavaran Palace once again. He greeted me warmly and offered me the chair opposite his. Then, hardly waiting for us to be seated, he said, "So, what do you think of the political situation now?"

"It's very bad, Majesty; especially since the start of the month of Moharram.[1] It's the fourth day today. Ayatollah Khomeini started the month with a call to the people to defy the state. For the first time he's asking people not to pay their taxes and instructing state employees not to follow their superiors' orders. The tension is mounting, and clashes between the people and the army are increasingly frequent. There are deaths every day, in the provinces as well as in Tehran."

"I've ordered the army not to use their weapons whatever the cost. They've been told to use tear gas instead and to shoot in the air to

1. Moharram is the first month of the Muslim lunar calendar. For the Shi'a it is a month of mourning, marking the martyrdom of Hussein, their third Imam, who was assassinated; he died on the tenth day of the month. Due to its powerful historical and religious connotations, it is the most important time of the year for Shi'i Iranians.

disperse demonstrators. It's because they're attacked more and more violently each day that they're forced to defend themselves."

Then the Shah leaned toward me and, as if he had suddenly understood the gravity of the situation, said dejectedly, "How are we to stop demonstrators who are not afraid to die? I've even heard that they're drawn by the bullets."

"That's precisely why we won't succeed in calming them down by calling in the army. Their new psychological tactic of crying 'Allah-o-Akbar' (God is Great) from the rooftops every evening is proving extremely effective."

"The army says they even use cassette recorders to amplify their voices."

"That only demonstrates once again that the unfortunate soldiers are trying to deceive themselves. I'll tell you quite frankly that my family and I have been going up to our own rooftop every evening, and I can assure you that during the fifteen minutes of chanting the entire city resounds in unison. You'd think Tehran had been transformed into a roaring ocean. It's simply breathtaking. Another thing that I see from my office window between 8:30 and 9 o'clock every morning is how the students of the three nearby secondary schools start chanting slogans whenever they see soldiers."

"I suppose the most frequent one is 'Death to the Shah'?"

Suddenly oppressed by helplessness before his fellow citizens and hopelessness over his own fate, the Shah exclaimed, "You're a sociologist. You try to understand why people behave the way they do. Can you explain to me why they shout 'Death to the Shah'? What have I done to them?"

"It's because we have a very hierarchical system, Sire, and everything redounds to the tip of the pyramid. The people who used to say constantly that the sovereign must reign, he must not govern, sensed that we were moving toward a crisis of authority. Today that crisis is here."

"Do you think the great powers, represented in Iran by various pressure groups, would ever have allowed us to achieve what we have in the absence of such a concentration of power? The calls for the Shah to reign and not to govern were merely the slogan of all those abroad who wished to see him turned into a puppet. The British, for example, had no wish to see real power established in our country."

"And yet they helped your father to become the strongman of a new regime."[2]

"You know as well as I that no sooner had he tried to embark on real reforms, especially industrialization, they brought him down."

"But then the Americans helped you in that respect. . . ."

"The Americans are a different breed. But they allowed themselves to be swayed by the British who fear our prosperity and our power. It would suit London to see a weak king, manipulated by their agents."

"You must also heed the arguments of politicians who are true patriots but who believe the Shah must keep aloof, Majesty. Then not only would the constitution be respected but the monarchy itself would be saved."

The Shah then added, in a grave and authoritarian tone, "That is a theory which originated outside the country. It has nothing to do with our national interests."

"If I may, I would like to suggest, Majesty, that it is on the contrary a wholly oriental idea."

"How can you say that?"

"Majesty, you are quite familiar with the game of chess. You'll concede that in chess the ultimate aim is to protect the king, and that the players' tactic is to sacrifice pieces when it is necessary to keep the king safe. But for all these pieces the range of activity is much greater than that of the king itself, which can only move one square at a time. So you see that in the Orient, too, the king is seen as someone who must be kept out of all enemies' reach."

"If I understand you correctly, you're saying that in the game of chess all the pieces must play the role assigned to them? After September 1941 the state was rendered powerless by the British and the Russian occupation; foreigners meddled in everything and our politicians sided with them.[3] It was imperative to assert the power of the state and to put an end to all the external interference."

"It's true that in the years since you took power our politicians have

2. In 1921 the British backed a coup d'état led by the Shah's father, then General Reza Khan, against the Qajar dynasty. The event culminated five years later in the fall of the dynasty and the accession to the throne of the Pahlavis.

3. The Shah was referring to the arrival in 1941 of British and Russian troops, the departure of his father to exile in South Africa, and his own accession to the throne—three events which coincided with political and social disorder in the country.

not sought—at least not openly—to establish special relations with foreign embassies, and that's something new. I remember how two years ago you forced out a government minister who had gone to the United States to renew his green card. Your critics say, however, that you've allowed the Americans to invade our lives and that you've relied on them to such an extent that you've practically become a member of the Republican party."[4]

"The problem is that the Democrats have no grasp of international geopolitics. They hold rigid views on many issues, whereas the Republicans are more subtle and take into account the political and strategic realities of different countries."

"The opposition believes we should keep our distance from foreigners, and they accuse you of not having done so."

The Shah obviously had no wish to discuss this matter any further and decided to change the subject. "I read your views in a French magazine about ways of overcoming the present crisis. You said there had to be a certain degree of 'de-Shah-ization.'[5] What did you mean by that?"

"I was thinking, for one thing, of an institutional de-Shah-ization, a situation in which not all economic, political, and military decisions have to emanate from you, Majesty. In other words, a division of responsibilities. In addition, on a purely symbolic level enlightened proponents of the monarchy believe that not every street and square, every dam and school, should necessarily bear Your Majesty's name. I remember discussing this matter with the Shahbanou three years ago. She agreed with this view and said—and I'm using her exact words—'Why do they have to name a dam after our daughter when it should be given the name of its location? With the present system I find that I no longer know where anything is in Iran.' I know that some people have been hoping for years that you yourself would order the removal of all your statues, which are in any case frequently in the worst possible taste. The army doesn't suggest it to you, but

4. Since the 1960 U.S. elections when Kennedy defeated Nixon, the Shah had supported the Republicans fairly openly and had made contributions to their funds. His liking for the Republicans dated back to the 1953 coup against Mosaddeq when he was supported by the Eisenhower administration.

5. Kenize Mourad of the *Nouvel Observateur* had asked me whether the regime stood any chance of survival.

they are forced to guard countless monuments day and night to prevent them from being damaged by demonstrators."

At this point the Shah interrupted our conversation to call his aide-de-camp on the intercom to give him the following instruction: "Tomorrow, when the prime minister comes to see me, remind me to tell him that demonstrators who harm statues should no longer be pursued."

"A very wise decision, Majesty. Given the sheer number of large and small towns involved, protecting monuments is an extremely onerous task. I can testify that the men who guard the statues are a provocation in themselves, inviting demonstrators to react. I passed a few such soldiers yesterday, and I couldn't help but feel sorry for them. I asked myself, 'What could they do if they were attacked? There would be no alternative but to use their automatic weapons or to allow themselves to be disarmed; for although they've been trained to fight external enemies, they've had no preparation for dealing with civilians in the middle of towns. They have received no technical or political training of that kind."

"That's why we've ordered special equipment from West Germany and Japan which will allow us to deal with such confrontations without any loss of life. We should have established special units, along the lines of France's CRS riot police, to deal with urban demonstrations."

"It's not just a question of having the right kinds of weapons and shields, Sire. It's more a matter of providing civic training for the army. Let me give you an example. A few days ago at Imam Reza's shrine in Mashad there was an incident which had the effect of a bomb exploding throughout the country—soldiers opened fire inside the holy building."[6]

"According to the information I have received, what in fact happened is that the pilgrims made up their minds that a noncommissioned officer belonged to Savak and cried, 'Get him! Kill him!' Frightened that his friend was about to be lynched, the soldier standing next to him pulled out his pistol and shouted a warning to the crowd. A stray bullet hit the ceiling of the main hall. That is all there was to it. The rest is simply a case of the opposition trying to

6. The shrine of Imam Reza at Mashad is the most sacred and revered in Iran. Reza is the only Shi'i Imam actually buried on Iranian soil.

put their own interpretation on the event and presenting it as a desecration of a holy place. . . ."

"As you can see, Majesty, the opposition has achieved its aim. The symbolic impact of the event has been such that they felt compelled to call a general strike the following day, in the bazaar, schools, universities, government offices, and so on, and to organize a demonstration in Mashad which turned out to be unprecedented in scale. It would be useful to learn a few lessons from this experience. In the first place, the NCOs who work for Savak dressed as civilians have failed to understand that times have changed. In the old days when they mingled with crowds of pilgrims they were undoubtedly locals who recognized them but were afraid to denounce them. Now that fear has gone and an attack on the regime is considered admissible and normal. In the second place, Savak and the army have become so unpopular that the slightest provocation inflames the crowds. Finally, the demonstrators have drawn attention to the sanctity of the shrine and the fact that it is forbidden to enter it armed. Even your father, at the height of his power, made a point of removing his revolver whenever he stepped into the Mashad shrine. Today the shrine's sanctity seems, if anything, even greater to the people, whereas the secular character of your regime has persuaded the agents of the state, including those working for Savak, that symbols have lost their power and that they no longer need fear public reaction."

"But I'm a believer myself, and I have great respect for religious values. I am, moreover, extremely devoted to the memory of Imam Reza. I've made a pilgrimage to his shrine every year since the start of my reign. I don't understand why the religious leaders regard me with hostility. . . ."

"Your belief doesn't alter anything, Majesty. As you know, there's an Islamic maxim which says: 'Don't concern yourself with what they believe; look instead at the way they behave.' The regime's behavior has belied the religious faith you proclaim. Your opponents are exploiting this contradiction today to discredit you. They're carrying out an extremely effective operation to undermine the state, of which the security forces and the army are totally unaware; the only thing they've been taught to understand is force."

"What is to be done then?"

"Withdraw the security forces from towns as much as possible. As long as they can do nothing but stand by and listen to the demonstrators shout their antiregime slogans, your soldiers will be of more use to you inside their barracks. Bear in mind also, Majesty, that there have always been rivalries among the police, Savak, and the army. Perhaps you even encouraged that rivalry in more stable times to prevent any one of them from gaining the upper hand? You may have been able to control and harness the rivalry then, but that's no longer the case. At a time of profound social upheaval, the conflict has become yet another aggravating factor. If you study the situation carefully you'll find that this unhealthy rivalry between the services is the cause of many of the confrontations with the public and that it leads to deaths and injuries every day. In Tehran, for example, the antagonism between the military government and Savak is severe. Thanks to his experience, General Moghadam [the director of Savak] has a better grasp of the situation than General Oveissi [the military governor] who knows nothing but force."

"I received General Oveissi yesterday.[7] He said that because he's responsible for maintaining order in the capital, he must be given the sole right to make the necessary decisions."

"Sire, General Oveissi is most definitely not the man for the job. He doesn't understand that although his brutal methods may have stopped demonstrators in the past, they also sowed the seeds of today's problems. At any rate, he's preparing to crush the demonstration called by Ayatollah Taleghani for the ninth day of Moharram. If you don't stop him, thousands will die and the day will prove even more dreadful than 'Black Friday' for which he already bears the blame."[8]

"I've been told that the demonstrators intended to march on the palace."

"That's just the kind of nonsense we've come to expect from General Oveissi and the gentlemen of the army. As you know, Majesty, there is a distance of twenty kilometers between their starting point and Niavaran. . . . It would probably take the thousands

7. In his capacity as commander of the imperial guard, General Oveissi violently crushed the first uprising led by Khomeini in June 1963.

8. Friday, September 8, 1978, was the date of the first armed clash between soldiers and protesters taking part in a large demonstration organized by religious leaders at the end of the fasting month of Ramadan. The clash left hundreds dead.

of demonstrators an entire day to cover the distance on foot. The general's suggestion is patently absurd. In any case, the authorities can simply ask the demonstrators to identify their route. In the light of the conversation I had with members of the organizing committee, it ought to be possible to reach agreement on every aspect and even to ensure that there won't be any chanting of hostile slogans."

The Shah broke in to say with perplexity, "If we withdraw all our military forces from the city and if we authorize the demonstration there will be an enormous crowd. Don't you think the opposition will exploit the situation and turn the demonstration into a kind of referendum on the regime?"

"Certainly! But by authorizing the demonstration the regime will prove at the same time that it has enough life left in it to show tolerance and prevent bloodshed."

"But why should we tolerate it if we don't stand to gain from it?"

"Quite simply, because there is no alternative, Majesty. There is no doubt whatsoever that a confrontation between the army and the demonstrators will lead to a horrific bloodbath. Are you prepared to add another massacre to the regime's record? Whatever happens now, Majesty, historians will have to acknowledge that at this point in your reign you chose tolerance over violence. As long as the crisis takes its inevitable course, isn't there more satisfaction to be drawn from this option? At least you'll have avoided tragedy, against the military government's advice. Amini and Entezam are of the same opinion as I on this. Professor Sadighi, whom you'll be meeting the day after tomorrow, is also entirely against violence. He'll tell you exactly what I've been saying today. And I know that the queen, too, shares this view."

Although I had partially concealed my thoughts, I sensed that the Shah understood very clearly the implication of my remarks: "Even at the price of abandoning power, don't let your hands be covered with blood."

He crossed his legs, was silent for a few moments, and then looking directly at me, he said deliberately, "Very well, I'll speak to the gentlemen tomorrow."

The army, which over the past months had occupied Iran's major cities and on which the Shah was relying without much conviction, had originally been the creation of Reza Khan. He had begun to establish it in 1921, that is to say, before his accession to the throne, which ended the rule of the Qajar dynasty in 1925.

The organization of a modern defense force had been a long-standing aim of reformist politicians in the late nineteenth and early twentieth centuries. Reza Shah's underlying objective, however, had been not so much the protection of the country's borders but the establishment of internal security. At the time the people were suffering from exactions of feudal lords and armed tribes dispersed throughout the country. So the idea of a proper national army, even one geared to internal security, was welcomed by the people. In the event, it served at once to assert the authority of the central government and to strengthen the new dynasty.

In 1925, as part of his effort to create a modern army, Reza Khan, by then prime minister, submitted a bill to Parliament instituting compulsory conscription. Given the fact that the new law applied to all men without exception, for the first time the concept of citizenship itself gained real currency in the country. Before this, military recruitment had relied on a traditional system known as the *bonicheh*[9] which was administered by tribal chiefs or religious leaders. The conscription law provoked the wrath of the religious establishment in particular since, on the one hand, as Shi'i clerics they did not fully accept the authority of the state, and, on the other, the law applied equally to mullahs as it did to everyone else. Thus the law gave rise to the first demonstration by Shi'i clerics against Reza Khan's reforms and notably to the first gathering of clerics in Qom, where, according to a contemporary witness, a young student by the name of Ruhollah Khomeini was among the most vociferous protesters. Together with Ayatollah Haeri, the senior religious figure at Qom, Reza was forced to formulate a compromise solution whereby mullahs were to be exempt from military service.

After he became Shah, Reza Khan maintained close control over military affairs. All the commanders of provincial units were appointed by him, and he chose them from the ranks of his friends from the days when he had himself been a soldier. He thus held an iron grip on the maintenance of order, ensuring that he was in constant

9. Under the *bonicheh* system, mayors would conscript men for military service according to the needs of the army and with the consent of the local population.

contact with tribal chiefs, religious authorities, and the heads of local and civic associations. In other words, through the army he gained control over all the elements which could possibly have undermined the authority of a state, which during his reign was to become increasingly domineering.

The surprise attack on Iran launched on August 25, 1941, by allied Anglo-Russian forces on the pretext of combating a German "fifth column" in the country, and the subsequent occupation of Iran which allowed the transport of American military equipment to the Soviet Union, met with little more than desultory resistance from an army which had never been intended for the defense of the country's borders. Reza Khan, the absolute ruler, was forced to abdicate and to depart for exile in South Africa, leaving the throne to his son, Mohammad Reza, then twenty-one years old and a graduate of the École de Rosay in Switzerland. Unlike his father, Mohammad Reza was shy, modest, and initially a democrat who spoke in a tremulous voice about the sanctity of the constitution.

He was also to develop a very different relationship with the army. Whereas Reza Khan had come to power through his control of military resources and had constantly relied on the army to reinforce his own power, his son ascended to the throne at a time when the army was in total disarray and had to look to the monarch for its eventual reconstitution. Moreover, at first Mohammad Reza Shah, knowing full well that his father had unseated a constitutional monarch with a military coup d'état, did not entirely trust the army.

Five years after the start of Mohammad Reza's reign the Iranian army enjoyed a brief spell of popularity when the Red Army withdrew from Iranian Azerbaijan. Stalin had failed in his attempt to annex the province on the pretext of creating a democratic republic (entirely contrived by the KGB). The Shah was well aware that the Red Army's evacuation of his country—a unique occurrence under Stalin—had more to do with the astuteness of the statesman Qavam Saltaneh[10] and the ultimatum issued by the Americans than with any

10. In 1945, on the day he was appointed prime minister, Qavam Saltaneh left for Moscow to negotiate the evacuation of Azerbaijan. In return, and by way of compensation, he promised the Soviet Union an oil concession in the north of Iran (which was later canceled by Parliament). Iranian troops then occupied Azerbaijan, and the pseudodemocratic republic was dissolved. It should be added

action taken by the army. Nevertheless, one way or the other, the restitution of Azerbaijan to the country was a boon to him and to the army's prestige. Seven years later, in 1953, the Shah faced a political crisis precipitated by Mosaddeq's attempt to turn him into a constitutional monarch. This led to an Anglo-American coup in which the army played a part. Later the Shah was to strengthen the army as an instrument of international policy, but unlike his father he never really counted on it as a force dedicated to maintaining internal security.

Up to 1966 the Iranian military machine was a reasonably modest affair. It was based on the American model and largely financed by Washington. Then, however, rising oil revenues made the Shah more ambitious. In February 1967 he went to Moscow and bought Soviet arms for the first time, amounting to a total of about $110 million. His improved relations with the USSR in turn drove the Americans to sell him even more weapons, and in 1969 Nixon, encouraged by Kissinger, gave the authorization, without the Pentagon's approval, for Iran to purchase any military hardware it wished from the United States, with the exception of nuclear arms.

So the Iranian army suddenly entered a new phase. The military budget grew rapidly during the 1970s, from less than $1 billion at the beginning of the decade to $10 billion in 1978, on the eve of the revolution. These huge sums of money allowed Iran to place orders with the United States which not only helped the big American firms, such as Northrop and Lockheed, to grow even more prosperous, but even played a part in allowing a firm like Grumman to build its Tomcat planes. Furthermore, the sophisticated new hardware created the need for highly skilled personnel who were not to be found in either the Iranian army or Iranian industry. So the Shah, not surprisingly, turned to foreign experts, and who better than the Americans who were already familiar with the equipment? By the middle of 1978 there were 45,000 Americans in Iran, of whom 80 percent worked for the army.

All this was an inevitable consequence of the Shah's eagerness to turn his army into the third most powerful in the world. But the

---

that the previous prime minister had already complained to the UN Security Council about the Soviet Union. The Americans later claimed credit for this protest which was the first issue to be referred to the Council after the establishment of the UN.

resulting dependence on the United States did not tally at all with the image of a nation striving to become a regional superpower. It was also very difficult to know whether this enormous army fell under the authority of the state or of the Shah alone. According to the constitution, the minister of war was responsible, before the cabinet and Parliament, for all matters relating to the army. In reality the Shah maintained direct contact with the chief of staff as well as with the different armed forces commanders. Of course, high-level training for junior officers in military tactics and the handling of advanced weaponry was provided by American instructors, either in Iran or in the United States. But when it came to the issue of national strategy, a subject reserved for higher ranks, training was severely hampered by the fact that it was impossible to cover the relevant ground without reference to the country's economic, social, and political problems. The army preferred to remain indifferent to these: for while junior ranks were totally terrorized by the files which the Intelligence Department kept on them, high-ranking officers feared the Shah's mistrust of them. It was not at all unusual for such a superior officer to suddenly find himself forced into early retirement.

The army, consisting of 400,000 men, including 20,000 officers and 150,000 NCOs and technicians, turned into a professional military machine possessing increasingly sophisticated weapons and existing as a self-contained entity. As far as the Shah was concerned, its commanders, as well as the American experts, led a separate existence, completely detached from everyday problems of Iranian society; the ranks, on the other hand, shared all the vicissitudes of normal Iranian life. Internal security, the main function of the army under Reza Shah, was left to Savak, with the police and gendarmerie acting as its instruments. Military tribunals were used for the trials of political offenders only so that the trials could proceed as quickly as possible. By the time the revolutionary crisis broke, the army was totally apolitical. And yet it was to the army that the authorities turned to confront the revolutionary state of the country.

The Shah asked me to tell him about my conversation with the National Front leaders, Sanjabi and Forouhar, who were being held in an undisclosed place. He wanted to know their views about the possibility of a government headed by Sadighi.

"I went to see them and spoke to them at length."

He said magnanimously, "First things first: are they being well treated?"

"Very well, Majesty. They are living in a beautiful villa at the foot of the mountains. Their guards led me to a drawing room complete with grand piano and exquisite carpets. I was even offered creamed coffee, served on a silver platter by a manservant in tails and white gloves."

"I suppose they share everyone's view that I should leave."

"More or less, Majesty."

"What do they really think of Khomeini?"

"I have the impression that Sanjabi doesn't take Ayatollah Khomeini's supposedly philosophical and legal approach very seriously. He believes that Khomeini's writings will not really have much impact. For him the whole business is political and the alliance established in Paris between the Ayatollah and secular leaders is purely tactical. He said to me with great confidence, 'Once we're afloat, we'll take the helm.' "

"How does he feel about the Sadighi government?"

"Sanjabi told me that neither he nor his companion would be prepared to take part in such a government, but they wouldn't oppose it either."

"I've been told that he's willing to see me, even while he's being detained."

"It doesn't seem worthy that you should meet a politician while he's under a cloud and while there are doubts about his attitude toward yourself, Majesty. First release him, then talk to him, Sire."[11]

The Shah agreed.

"I wanted to discuss another matter with you, Majesty, something which has been causing quite a stir. I'm referring to a list, published by the strikers at the Central Bank, containing the names of people who are said to have sent currency abroad."[12]

11. I later learned from Forouhar that the idea of seeing the Shah while still in detention had come from Sanjabi himself. He felt this would allow him time to talk to the king while being able to say to Khomeini that he had been taken to the meeting as a prisoner.

12. This act of psychological warfare, carried out by the extreme left opposition, struck like a bombshell. The 120 names consisted of military and civilian officials who were said to have taken funds amounting to 1.5 billion out of the country with Central Bank complicity. After the revolution it was acknowledged that the list was false.

Clearly indignant, the Shah said in a loud voice, "Pure lies! Pure propaganda! I received reports from the Central Bank this very morning informing me that the list was totally false."

"I'm also convinced that it's unfounded, Majesty, but public opinion is so set against the regime that it is determined to believe that the list—hitherto taboo—is true."

"These revolutionaries who accuse the regime of corruption and dishonesty, themselves distort everything and sully the names of people who never sent money abroad. The list includes, for example, the names of businessmen who sent currency to other countries, using their own accounts, in order to purchase imports. Is that misappropriation of funds?"

"The best solution, at any rate, is to ask the Central Bank itself to publish, with the procurator general's permission, the names of individuals or companies who really did send capital abroad in 1977."

The Shah called the director of the Central Bank and told him to consult the justice minister with the aim of eventually drawing up such a list.

It was around six o'clock then, and night had already fallen. All of a sudden, every single light in Tehran went out. Behind the Shah, who had his back to the window, it was as if a curfew had been declared at that instant and the entire city blacked out. Thanks to its own powerful emergency generators, the palace lights promptly came back on, and it was as if nothing had happened.

For some time now the country had been in the grip of a near-general strike, and the paralysis was spreading steadily. In the provinces electrical workers had refused to go back to work in the big power stations which supplied Tehran. In the capital itself electricity could be switched off at any time simply on the instructions of the strike leaders, and the cuts had been affecting different parts of the city at different times.

Until this December day the power cuts had been only sporadic, but on that evening the city was plunged into total darkness for the first time. An entire city, with a population of five million, suddenly vanished into the jet-black night.

In the seconds between the power cut and the restoration of light by the emergency generators, the huge glowing chandelier in the middle of the ceiling had gone out, along with all the other lights in the room. Despite the almost instantaneous restoration of normality, the Shah looked as if he had been caught in a trap, set for him each evening by the electricity workers, at the moment he had been least expecting it.

At that precise instant I saw the beat of a nervous pulse in his taut face, and I knew he was in a state of extreme tension. As if to shake himself free, the Shah said with agitation, "So here we go again! . . ." Unwittingly he revealed that he saw the cuts as an unavoidable reality. Abandoning his usual composure, he rose to his feet and moved toward the windows from which he had formerly contemplated the capital of his kingdom, extending to the horizon in the vast plain. But with not a single light left shining, the Shah could only peer out absently, looking for a city that was simply not there. . . .

I felt it only polite to rise as well. I strode toward him, but I stopped at some distance, as was expected. All at once, emerging from his torpor, the Shah approached me. He came right up to me in a way that was extremely unusual, because he made it a point to keep a certain distance from his visitors. In a voice at once shaken and resigned and looking directly into my eyes, he uttered a brief sentence, laden with meaning, which lent itself to a multitude of interpretations: "The whole city has sunk into obscurity! . . ."

It was as if he were speaking of the fall of another person, as if he were watching an unfolding drama that no longer had anything to do with him, as if Tehran had suddenly dissolved before him. . . . Embarrassed that I had involuntarily become a witness to the fall of an immense power, I looked away and lowered my head. We were silent for a long time, like people who had just seen someone fade away on his deathbed. To end the uncomfortable silence, I said, "I think I've tired you enough for one day, Sire. I'll withdraw now if I may."

"No, no," he protested, as if suddenly awakening from a dream, "you don't tire me. Please come and see me whenever there are things you wish to tell me."

He walked a few paces with me. I bowed and shook the hand he extended toward me. I left his office, went down the stairs, and crossed the garden. I stepped into my car, and in oppressive darkness we began the descent to the city. My driver—although a firm supporter of Khomeini—seemed disturbed at the thought that the

Shah might be without electricity. As if to reassure himself, he said, "They have their own generators at the palace, don't they?"

Then he asked me a few questions about the Shah's mood and state of mind. I told him a bit about the conversation I had just had, and he suddenly exclaimed, "They hadn't been telling him the truth. Isn't that right, sir?"

Like millions of other Iranians, this good man preferred to nurture the illusion that the Shah had been misled, rather than to believe he may have been guilty.

Even Judges

(Fifth Conversation with the Shah)

Wednesday, December 13, 1978, 10:30 a.m.

I was received by the Shah at the Niavaran Palace. On entering his office I bowed as a sign of respect. Smiling, he took a few steps toward me, shook my hand, and indicated that I should take the seat facing his. Then, skipping all preliminaries, he asked, "How do things stand now? You must have news about Sadighi. Does he still feel up to the task?"

"Yes, Majesty. I went to see him before coming to the palace, and we made a general assessment of the situation together. Although he's fully aware of the scale of existing problems, he seemed optimistic about the prospects of a government of national reconciliation, which he's prepared to form if Your Majesty accepts certain conditions that he considers to be absolutely essential."

"What do you mean by conditions?"

"Sadighi is hoping that Your Majesty will carry out a number of measures yourself before his appointment is officially announced."

"I'm quite prepared to discuss his conditions and to take any steps he deems to be imperative. But first tell me, what are his conditions?"

"Since I believe you are to receive Sadighi tomorrow, I would prefer to let him explain them to you himself. Sadighi's an extremely meticulous man who carefully weighs his words. But he did authorize me, in case Your Majesty asked questions today, to give you a general overview. He hopes, on the one hand, that Savak will be dissolved, the state of emergency lifted, and prisoners released. On the other hand, he wants you to adopt severe and decisive measures to deal with the royal family's business interests. He also wants preliminary investigations into the cases of new prisoners—mostly former ministers and officials in charge of economic policy—completed as rapidly as possible, because once the state of emergency is lifted the government will have no legal right to detain them. Sadighi has no preconceived view on the guilt or innocence of the detainees; he feels nonetheless that since the military government's declaration of a state of emergency in Tehran and in other big cities, the military authorities have been able to arrest whomever they please. As for the arrest of ministers and businessmen—carried out to appease public opinion—Sadighi is worried that in many cases it may have been purely arbitrary. That's why he's hoping that the cases of the accused will now be handed over to the Ministry of Justice and that a proper dossier will be established for each containing watertight evidence. Otherwise he'll feel obliged to release them. He would therefore like Your Majesty to instruct the relevant services to gather proper evidence, seriously and with objectivity, to support the charges."

"Wouldn't it be better if he were to announce these decisions himself so that he can benefit from the resulting goodwill when he establishes his government?"

"Sadighi believes there are decisions which depend specifically on Your Majesty, most notably with regard to measures to restore the royal family's holdings to the state."

"We've already set up a committee to deal with individual complaints against members of my family, with the aim of making good any losses incurred."

"Majesty, I've explained to you before that in the case of members of the royal family it is not so much a question of settling disputes with individual litigants but of undoing acts which have harmed the economy of the state."

"On this matter too I'm in a position to announce that I have already specified, in a detailed circular, that they are henceforth forbidden to interfere in the state's economic and financial affairs. The court minister has just sent the circular to all the members of my family as well as to the relevant government organizations."

"Majesty, with your permission, I must say, with the deepest regret, that the simple act of delaying the public revelation of this circular has removed any possible advantage it might have yielded. Everyone knows that all the members of the royal family have now left the country. Perhaps you will allow me to tell you about what I tried to do personally in this connection some months ago—unfortunately in vain."

While obviously puzzled by my remarks, the Shah did not seem altogether displeased to find that there were people who had been taking an interest, from a distance, in matters which concerned him directly. He prompted me and said, "Indeed? Tell me what you did, then!"

"In the spring of 1978 I learned that a circular had in fact been written but that because of pressure from your family—and notably from Princess Ashraf—you were unable to decide whether or not to make it public. As you know, at the beginning of summer Flora Lewis, the *New York Times* correspondent, came to Tehran to interview you. Before your meeting with her she visited me to get an idea of how things stood in the country. I mentioned the existence of the circular to her in the hope that she would raise the matter in the interview. I saw her again after she met you. She told me that she had made a point of asking you about it and that you had unfortunately confirmed your intention not to make it public. You did, however, give her permission to report it abroad at a later date. While obviously respecting your decision, Flora Lewis tried to send a brief dispatch on the subject on July 3, but the censors did not allow it.[1] Again, knowing that you intended to hold a press conference in August, I suggested to my friend Mahmoud Enayat, who is a moderate and scrupulously honest journalist, that he use the occasion to ask you about the circular. To the best of my knowledge he put the question to you with the greatest possible sensitivity and correctness, but your only response, delivered in a stiff tone, as if you'd been offended, was, 'Yes, we've taken certain measures!' And so, another

1. The dispatch was published in the *New York Times* on July 3, 1978, under the title "Shah of Iran Forbids Royal Family to Make Profits on Business Deals."

opportunity—an exceptional one at that—was lost for dealing openly with the question and for giving the public some information which would certainly have been a comfort to your supporters."

In a voice tinged with regret, as well as with irritation over the "embarrassing affair," the Shah replied, "Perhaps. But what is to be done at this moment? Are you of your usual opinion—if I understand you correctly—that it is once again too late?"

"Majesty, you must act without any ambiguity! You must take radical measures without delay!"

"Well, then! You should know that we are, at this moment, in the process of finalizing the details of a procedure that will allow me to obtain power of attorney from the members of my family and subsequently to take any necessary action."

"How exactly do you propose to obtain power of attorney from them?"

"I'm going to send messages to the different members of my family abroad, asking them to send me the authority to dispose of their holdings as I see fit."

"I very much fear, Majesty, that it may again be too late. Public opinion is so highly charged that it wants to see decisions which will have immediate effects; it will not be satisfied with mere preliminaries. You should, moreover, bear in mind that people do not consider the members of the royal family to have acquired their fortunes lawfully. They are seen as usurpers of the national patrimony. In any case, it's extremely unlikely that Princess Ashraf will ever grant you such a power of attorney, because she, like your brothers and sisters, maintains that the bulk of the fortune bequeathed to you by your father was—thanks to you—converted to the Pahlavi Foundation's initial capital. The members of your family claim they had to pursue economic and financial activities in recent years because of the rising cost of living. They further argue that it was all the more difficult for them to maintain their princely life-styles because they were not receiving a penny from the Pahlavi Foundation. That's why their fortunes are inextricably intertwined with yours. It would therefore be best to make a prompt decision embracing your assets as well as theirs—although even this may fail to appease the public, which is convinced that your family has already transferred most of its capital abroad."

Looking helpless and dejected, the Shah replied, "We'll see what we can do. But let's go back to Sadighi's conditions."

"One of the most pressing issues is to close as quickly as possible the files of people who've been arrested on charges of corruption but whose cases cannot be tried due to a lack of evidence."

"I've spoken several times to the prime minister and the minister of justice about this. I have the impression that the magistrates become obstructive the minute they're asked to deal with cases in which they know we have an interest. Isn't it interesting that those same judges who organize strikes and shout revolutionary slogans do absolutely nothing when we put the cases of the expropriators of public property before them? In fact, they give every impression of being at one with the global plan to disrupt and paralyze the country."

"Majesty, you should pay close attention to the judges' grievances all the same and try to understand their behavior."

"One thing is for certain, whenever they're faced with one of the offenders I was referring to, they do everything in their power to absolve and acquit them. Why?"

"It's very simple. The judges maintain that for many years the government has only referred the cases of miserable second-rate culprits to the judiciary, whereas the big shots have been let off scot-free. That's why they resort to acquittals. They know very well that they're not dispensing justice, but they claim the regime is forcing them into it."

"And yet quite a few people have been arrested who are not exactly wretched paupers!"

"The circumstances are different now. In any case, the judges suspect that these arrests are motivated by political factors and have nothing to do with justice. This attitude, taken by magistrates over cases referred to it by the government, may only be coming into the open today, but it has always existed beneath the surface, at a more discreet level. The judiciary cannot forgive the regime's interference with their prerogatives. For example, they've never accepted the establishment of an Imperial Inspectorate, which to them represents a blatant violation of fundamental laws stipulating that investigation is the right of the judiciary."

"But everyone recognizes the integrity and competence of the judiciary."

"To be sure, Majesty. But the Inspectorate—totally hallowed territory—is completely out of the hands of the judiciary, and it has always been headed by an army general enjoying your confidence. Moreover, virtually none of the important cases it has investigated have ever been made public."

"Fine. Let's suppose the judges are feeling frustrated. What about attorneys, who've been a privileged class on the professional level?"

"Attorneys, while admittedly better off than judges, feel equally frustrated, although in a different way. In the first place, a judicial system that doesn't function correctly discourages legal counselors just as much as judges, because they're both prevented from carrying out their duties properly. Under the current system an attorney's professional success depends less on his skills than on his talent for cultivating people in high places. In any case, the eminent attorneys hardly ever plead a case in court."

The Shah looked bemused. "What do you mean? What do they do, then? How do they win their clients' cases?"

"In hallways and corridors, Majesty, using all kinds of tricks and ploys. They're not so much lawyers as brokers. To play this part well they must have connections. And by favoring bigwigs the regime has done nothing but reinforce this tendency. It's this kind of misconduct that has alienated lawyers."

"In what ways has the regime reinforced the tendency?"

"The association of lawyers, established forty years ago, was until about the 1960s the last independent organization in Iran. The regime deprived it of its independence by arbitrarily selecting and imposing its own presidents of the bar. The younger members of the profession never accepted this, and as soon as they sensed a degree of opening in 1977 they systematically backed attorneys opposed to the regime."

"This same lawyers' association has not desisted for one moment over the last year from activities in support of demands for human rights, demands which have driven it into the arms of foreigners who are plotting against the regime."[2]

2. When he spoke of foreigners the Shah referred to the Americans. Minachi, who was minister of information in the Bazargan government after the revolution, told me of a visit he and his colleagues made to the State Department in the summer of 1978. The delegation was received warmly, and State Department

"For the reason I just mentioned, Majesty. As you know very well, lawyers and professors the world over take an active interest in human rights simply by virtue of their profession. But the minister of justice has never permitted them to inspect our prisons. . . ."

"Have we not invited Amnesty International and the Red Cross to visit Iranian prisoners regularly during the past two years?"

"Certainly, Majesty. Iranian lawyers and jurists feel, however, that if you had allowed them to pay such visits in the past, you could have avoided recourse to foreign missions of inquiry."

Shaking himself free of the deep thoughts my suggestions had set in train, the Shah exclaimed, "Let's go back to Sadighi and his conditions!"

"They include, notably, the dissolution of Savak, as I mentioned."

"I'm not against it in principle, but don't you think that in view of our present difficulties such a decision would provoke deep resentment in the ranks of Savak personnel, and that they would throw in their lot with the opposition? With all the information and resources at their disposal, wouldn't they organize plots against us?"

"When Sadighi speaks of the dissolution of Savak, he doesn't mean that all its personnel should be dismissed. What he has in mind is a redistribution of responsibilities, according to which the protection of citizens' rights would be kept distinct from operational activities which would be transferred to the police and gendarmerie, as demanded by the constitution. Intelligence and counterintelligence activities would be made the responsibility of another organization which would have no executive power."

"If it's carried out properly and carefully, I would have no objections."

"You must remember that Sadighi is a perfect legalist. Of course, his motto, 'Everyone in his own proper place,' won't be easy to fulfil in practice, even for you, Majesty."

"Why won't it be easy for me?"

"Because for the past twenty-five years no one has contradicted the will of the king with the demands of the law. The implementation of

---

officials asked to be informed discreetly of human rights violations in Iran so that they could pressure the Shah through the U.S. ambassador. It was agreed that from the following day an attaché responsible for such matters would be available at the American embassy to receive verbal or written complaints from the human rights organizations.

Sadighi's principle would therefore imply a measure of sacrifice on the part of Your Majesty."

"Even if I agree to abide strictly by the constitution, it shouldn't be forgotten that the constitution also gives me certain rights."

"Without a doubt, Majesty! Rest assured that Sadighi will be just as diligent in protecting your rights as he is in protecting those of the people." I smiled and added, "Given the fact that the rights of the people have been substantially eroded in recent years, it shouldn't be too surprising that the pendulum is swinging in the other direction now. . . ."

"Very well. What else?"

"Sadighi wants to see the credibility of the legislature restored."

"What does he think about a possible dissolution of Parliament?"

"As a disciple of Mosaddeq, he prefers a bad Parliament to no Parliament. As I'm sure you're aware, Majesty, with the current system of elections, the Parliament enjoys no credibility with the people, even though some deputies have recently dared to criticize the government if not the regime itself."

"It's almost as if some of the deputies have all of a sudden started seeing Robespierre in their dreams every night. Deputies who had never said a word before are suddenly launching into the most inflammatory tirades. . . ."

"Bearing in mind that these deputies owe their seats in Parliament to the powers that be and have not been legally elected, is it so surprising, Majesty, to find that they suddenly start singing a different tune the moment they suspect those powers are under threat? Not only do they often turn into cynical demagogues, they also tend to go to even greater extremes than popular speakers. It's as if they have some kind of score to settle with the powers to whom they owe their fictitious mandates. . . ."

"I don't follow you. Why do they have a score to settle? Why are they throwing everything overboard all of a sudden? And why such a rage and fury in their speeches?"

"Sire, a totally fake deputy is a man who feels deeply humiliated because he knows that he's held in contempt by the general public as well as his own constituency. As soon as he senses that the wind is starting to blow in a different direction and that the authorities may be tottering, he doesn't want to lose a minute in changing his colors.

When one hears some of the speeches by deputies whose names were conjured out of the ballot box by Savak, one can't help but notice that their language is a good deal more revolutionary than that of people who've just emerged after many years in Savak prisons. . . . The deputies seem to think they can win some credibility by outbidding everyone else."

"Do you think free elections would produce good results in the current turbulent climate?"

"I have no doubt, at any rate, that anyone elected today would behave in a more responsible and dignified manner than yesterday's so-called deputies."

"I'm interested to know Sadighi's plans for the army and its command."

The Shah was asking me this question because he had a strong suspicion that Sadighi, in the mold of all prime ministers who—like Mosaddeq—wanted to uphold the constitution, would not be prepared to see the monarch maintain his role as head of the army.

"For Sadighi the command of the armed forces is the responsibility of government, Majesty."

"Does that mean the king has no role to play?"

I knew that Sadighi did not want to throw the Shah out into the cold, not only because of the many other strict conditions he intended to impose on the sovereign but also because he felt the Shah could exercise a positive influence on the formation of a government.

"For the time being, Majesty, Sadighi intends to consult you on the subject of selecting the armed forces' minister, on the understanding, of course, that consultation does not necessarily mean complying with Your Majesty's decisions. He believes furthermore that the question of the army's budget is the government's concern only, as are all other aspects of the budget; it must, in other words, come under control of the court revenue."

"What is Sadighi's opinion of our position in CENTO[3] and our relations with our allies?"

"He believes that Iran should distance itself from CENTO and abandon its policy of unconditionally following America."

3. CENTO, or the Central Treaty Organization, was a military defense pact signed by Pakistan, Turkey, and Iran in 1958 and was backed by the United Kingdom and the United States.

"What kind of foreign policy does he have in mind for the country?"

"He favors nonalignment. He'd like to halt our oil deliveries to South Africa and Israel because these links trigger negative reactions from African and Arab states."

"What's the National Front's attitude to Sadighi?"

"It should firstly be said, Majesty, that Sadighi is no longer a member of the National Front. Nevertheless, when I went to see Sanjabi and Forouhar in detention they told me they would not oppose Sadighi's nomination because they see him as the best candidate in the present circumstances."

"Why was it, then, that when Sadighi came here to see me the National Front put out a statement saying that Sadighi had been brought to the palace by force?"

"Because Sanjabi is trying to benefit from Ayatollah Khomeini's backing as well as Your Majesty's."

"I would like to ask you a question now about 'your' liberals and 'your' intellectuals. I've been told that they took part in the demonstrations on Ashura [the tenth day of Moharram, marking the anniversary of Imam Hussein's death] and that they marched under the banner of the 'Islamic Republic.' Do they believe in that slogan? It appears that many of the demonstrators, men and women, were from the well-to-do classes of northern Tehran and that they mingled with the religious and revolutionary marchers. How do you explain this?"

"Your question is a very significant one, Majesty, because it relates to a fundamental problem which the country's authorities have never addressed. The regime's analysts have failed to understand that this rebellion is not motivated by economic factors. Their blindness may, paradoxical though it may seem, be attributed to the fact that most of them are Marxist. Over the past thirty years the regime's political and ideological posts have been filled by repentant members of the Tudeh party [Iran's communist party]. They're people who have held on to their Stalinist rhetoric and, to get on the right side of Savak, have simply put you in the place of Stalin. They are also well versed in using Savak's flattering language. Since the top Savak officials aren't very well educated and don't possess much political awareness, they've accepted these people as analysts useful to the regime. As you know, former Tudeh members believe that religion is the opiate of the masses and that it's always a reactionary element."

"Yes, I understand what you're saying, but I have to add that our Anglo-American advisers haven't been much help either. How would you explain the fusion of so many disparate groups at this particular moment?"

"As I've said before, this opposition is not based in any way on economic factors. It came into being at the time of the coup d'état against Mosaddeq in 1953, which aroused only revulsion in the opposition and contempt among the general public. In reality, religion helped give shape to those feelings, and it brought about a kind of collective hypnosis, pulling everyone in the same direction."

The Shah interrupted me and said, calmly and deliberately, "And the collective objective is to remove me from power?"

"Sire, your removal is a pretext cloaking a multitude of emotions. If we take as an example the well-to-do class you were talking about, which is not satisfied with the state of the country, it's clear that in recent years it has found an outlet in that slogan."

The Shah seemed hurt and saddened by the ingratitude of this prosperous group and said, "It is dissatisfied? What about? About the good living standard it has achieved in so short a time? About the trips it can now take? About the strength of our currency? About the fact it can now send its children to schools as good as any in the West?"

I replied in a lighthearted tone, "Sire, it is perhaps precisely because the members of this class have achieved a high living standard so quickly and so effortlessly that they're dissatisfied. They're hoping, at any rate, that they'll now be able to play an active part in the running of the country."

"Let's take the case of an engineer who is making the equivalent of £6,000 a month [about $9,000], who has a villa on the Côte d'Azur and whose wife buys her clothes at Christian Dior. What can he possibly have in common with the small shop owner in the south of the city who has no other pastime but to go to the mosque and to pay a pilgrimage to Mashad once a year?"

"These two different types of people nevertheless share a common frustration, Sire: the regime has not allowed either of them to develop their personalities. Let me explain. You have led the country singlehandedly; you have been the one who has taken responsibility for every single decision, assuming perhaps that nothing else would be needed as long as the country made progress economically and technically and as long as the country was modernized at breakneck speed, relieving the population of all its worries."

"Hasn't it been the case that, since our defeat at the hands of the Russians in the nineteenth century,[4] when Iranians became aware of the army's technological backwardness—that is to say, of their country's backwardness—all Iranian patriots have sought access to Western technology? Today they also want their country to have railway tracks, paved roads, and a national electricity grid. Did nationalist and revolutionary patriots at the turn of the century not have a long-standing wish that Iran should have its own steel industry? Well then, has all of this not been achieved?"

"No doubt Iranians did harbor all these dreams. But now they feel as if they've had nothing to do with their realization because you alone have made all the decisions. When you go to a village on the first day of Moharram you can see local people organizing communal meals and ceremonies with men and women, rich and poor, mingling together and helping in the preparation. Everyone is invited to the ceremonies which go on for ten days. They serve as occasions on which everyone can work together and feel a sense of solidarity. Since the regime has kept aloof from such traditions and activities, the people have made the commemoration of Hussein's martyrdom their own and turned it into an opportunity for defying the regime. One other point has come to light in this connection: when the well-to-do middle classes rediscovered these religious rituals, which for many years had been driven out of public view by the regime, they were not only surprised to see how dynamic they were but also felt deep resentment against a regime that had deprived them of a valued tradition in the name of a superficial secularism."

"Do you know what their slogan was throughout the Ashura demonstration?"

4. The Shah was referring to the wars between Iran and Russia at the beginning of the nineteenth century which resulted in the loss of Iran's provinces in the Caucasus and northern Azerbaijan and the signing of the 1828 treaty recognizing Iran's defeat.

"Yes, Majesty: 'God, the Koran, and Khomeini.'"

"Is it possible that all these educated people, who have gone to university in Iran and abroad, really want to back Khomeini? Is it possible?"

"For them Khomeini is, more than anything else, a symbol. Aren't there countless examples in history of religious leaders who became symbols of nationalist movements?"

"If I'm not mistaken, one of the agreed conditions was that the armed forces would be withdrawn from the city for forty-eight hours and that it would be handed over for the duration to the demonstrators on the understanding that they would not chant violently anti-regime slogans. As you know, that understanding was not respected on the second day."

"Majesty, the agreement that we reached with the organizing committee concerned only the first day of the demonstrations. And that agreement was fulfilled to the letter, as reported by all the journalists with more than a little amazement. On the following day the committee was outmaneuvered by the extremists who admittedly organized an openly antireligious demonstration."

"In that case, the people who claim to be in charge aren't in charge of anything. On whose behalf are they speaking?"

"They're faced with a particularly difficult task, Majesty. They're outflanked on all sides. I'll give you an example. On the day after the second demonstration [on Ashura], my wife and I went out before sunrise to see the tail-end of the event. We walked for two hours along the route of the marchers. We saw so much graffiti and so many posters on walls and shop windows that the sight defies description. I said to my wife, 'It's as if an ocean had spat out its entrails onto the shore in the course of a stormy night.'"

The Shah asked, partly with sarcasm and partly in despair, "Perhaps you could tell me, in a few words, what you saw in these entrails?"

"An irrevocable denunciation of the authorities; a total lack of confidence in them; the frustration of an entire nation. . . . In a word, Majesty, a total rejection of the regime."

Like a man who knows exactly what is going on behind the scenes, the Shah replied with the following comment about the Ashura demonstration: "It appears that it was the Fedayin-e Islam[5] and the Islamic Marxists [the Mojahedin] as well as a number of Tudeh members who organized the Ashura demonstration."

"Majesty, Savak is determined to make you believe that whenever there is a demonstration anywhere, it's systematically the handiwork of the communists or the extreme left-wing parties. This only serves to show that they're seriously underestimating the depth of religious feeling and that they understand nothing about the movement it's galvanizing. I remember taking part in a procession more than fifteen years ago, Majesty. It was organized by the residents of south Tehran and it crossed the entire city. Lasting more than three hours, it brought thousands of people together. I can testify that the procession was very orderly and yet at the same time remarkably vital. There were cultural displays, music, and religious singing which could compare favorably with other large-scale celebrations I've seen elsewhere in the world. What I'm trying to say is that the traditionalists in the south of the city, who constitute the majority of Tehran's population, are very adept at integrating their social experiences and their religious traditions into their political life. Khomeini has, in any case, convinced them that they are themselves the creators of this alliance of politics and religion."[6]

In order to remind me of his magnanimity toward political prisoners, whose liberation he had ordered on the recommendation of his new "advisers" (including myself), the Shah exclaimed mockingly, "It

5. The Fedayin-e Islam (the devotees of Islam) came into existence in 1946 with the assassination of the well-known historian Ahmad Kasravi, whom they accused of having abandoned Islam. It continued to disturb Iranian political life until 1953 and was responsible for spectacular attacks on the court minister in 1950 and the prime minister in 1951. The movement was dismantled in 1956 after its leaders were executed, but it continued to haunt Iranians until the time of the revolution.

6. Traditionally, religious associations exist in all Iranian cities. Their principal activity is the arrangement of funeral ceremonies and religious celebrations in mosques and public places as well as in private houses. The associations mostly recruited young people, preparing them for playing a role in the demonstrations, and they served as a ready-made instrument for the Shi'i clergy as the revolution began to surface. Because Savak was totally obsessed with the communist threat and with the Tudeh party, its manifestation, it had no idea of the role being played by these associations. They were fundamental in mobilizing mass participation both during and after the revolution.

appears that the political prisoners we recently pardoned marched at the head of the demonstrators!"

"What did you expect, Majesty! After being unjustly imprisoned and at times subjected to violence, they're not likely to forget in a hurry how they've been treated. With time their bitter memories will fade, but what is essential is that this kind of detention should never recur."

"We've formally instructed the army and Savak to avoid any kind of violence."

"I must inform you, Your Majesty, with the greatest regret, that at this very moment the violence is continuing inside and outside prisons."

"Are you certain? Do you have evidence?"

"Yes, Sire. On the day before Ashura, when the military were arresting people they described as 'ringleaders,' they arrested Homa Nategh and her husband Nasser Pakdaman[7] as well as Haj Seyyed Javadi.[8] I telephoned the Shahbanou to beg her to intercede with you on their behalf, and I know that you spent half an hour on the telephone trying to contact the relevant military officials. Thanks to your prompt intervention, they were released and taken home the same evening. I'm very grateful to you, Majesty. I only allowed myself to disturb you so late in the day because I'm convinced that the violent methods being used by the military won't solve anything."

"You were going to tell me about instances of violence?"

"Yes, Majesty. Homa Nategh told me that during the few hours she was in detention in military barracks, along with other women clad in chadors, she saw the soldiers behaving indecently toward these women. As far as violence outside prisons is concerned, I can cite the eyewitness report of a journalist known for his integrity, Paul Balta of *Le Monde*. He was in Isfahan watching a procession of demonstrators when he saw soldiers swoop down on a young man of about eighteen who was quietly washing his car, brutally ordering him to shout 'Long live the Shah!' Since the teenager remained stunned and silent, they put a bullet straight into the back of his neck. That's just one typical example of the acts of brutality being carried out by the military in an

7. Academics associated with left-wing circles.
8. Haj Seyyed Javadi is a gifted writer who in 1976 addressed a two-hundred-page open letter to the Shah denouncing the regime's transgressions.

attempt to generate false promonarchist reactions, which are utterly futile and do nothing but tarnish Your Majesty's image."

"The army, on the other hand, claims that it's a question of spontaneous reactions to provocative antimonarchist demonstrations."

"Sire, we've seen countless examples of how the army—and I'm talking about the people at the top—is prepared to do anything to mislead Your Majesty. They're trying to make you believe that these are spontaneous actions, whereas we know for a fact that the military governor of Tehran has deliberately established a special committee—with the help of his henchman, who is, to say the least, of dubious moral character—which has the task of organizing faked demonstrations. The committee, which is said to be carrying out Your Majesty's express wishes, is extorting large sums of money from businessmen. Several people concerned about the future of the monarchy, who knew I would be coming to see you, begged me, as a matter of urgency, to inform you about all this."

Agitated and annoyed, the Shah threw back at me, "What you mean to say is that all these people are expecting the crowds to chant 'Down with the Shah!' and they're amazed when they hear the reverse."

"Majesty, if people want to shout 'Long live the Shah!' no one is going to stop them. Unfortunately the military is behaving with such ineptitude at the moment that the public attaches no credibility whatsoever to promonarchist demonstrations. Moreover, General Moghadam, the Savak director, himself believes that there must be a stop to these machinations because he knows the people behind the whole operation and he knows that with their dubious reputations they'll only harm Your Majesty."

The Shah tried to reply more calmly this time and said, "Very well. How do we put an end to all this?"

"By speaking to the prime minister, Sire; he's the most sensible member of the officer corps."

"Fine. I'll do that. I accept that the machinations you're talking about must stop, but I want you to know that I'm not about to ask him to halt all spontaneous demonstrations in support of the monarchy. . . ."

"For the love of heaven, it is absolutely imperative that the military does not launch political initiatives. Perhaps Your Majesty could be so good as to stress this crucial point?"

"Very well. Was there anything else you wanted to tell me?"

"The military is continuing to use live ammunition; people are being killed and badly injured every day."

"I instructed General Toufanian[9] over two months ago to obtain plastic bullets from abroad. He informed me that the Americans, to whom we regularly send our orders for military equipment, said they didn't have any; they suggested that we go to the British. But the British keep postponing things, and I'm forced to ask myself whether that's just an excuse. I really don't understand what's happening."

Without pausing for breath and in a voice tinged at once with sarcasm and disillusion, the Shah then made the following surprising comment: "Perhaps the British are delaying delivery of the kind of bullet we've been asking for because they prefer to have people killed in Iran every day, so that their BBC can have sensational material to use in its provocative programs."[10]

"I'm not qualified to say anything on this subject, Majesty."

"Whenever we've submitted protests to the British they've replied that the government doesn't have the right to intervene. We've stressed, for our part, that while respecting the BBC's right to freedom of expression, we considered that it was taking things too far. The information it was broadcasting about the situation in Iran was virtually tantamount to instructions to the opposition on how they should behave from one day to the next. Does that constitute objective news? Or would the term 'manipulation' be more appropriate? One way or the other, it's exactly as if the BBC has turned into the mouthpiece of and the link between the Iranian opposition."

"It's true, Majesty, that the BBC has a very large audience in Iran. During the time when it broadcasts its evening program, from 7:45 to 8:30, I've noticed the city looks completely different because so many people go home to listen."

"Do you listen too?"

9. The deputy war minister responsible for the purchase of military equipment.

10. The Shah was once again revealing the anger which the BBC's Persian-language transmissions aroused in him. The BBC gave detailed reports of opposition activities in Iran, and it had a large audience there. The Shah had twice sent his minister of foreign affairs to London to protest to the British government and had even tried to use American intermediaries to make the British halt the offending broadcasts. It was all to no effect.

"Certainly, Majesty. The program is very interesting. It provides news and comment about Iran that one doesn't hear anywhere else."

"Don't you think there is a political motive behind it all?"

"Although, due to my own prejudice, I hardly ever believe the British are innocent regardless of what they do, in the present circumstances I find it hard to see what their motive could be. If anyone is in a position to know, it is yourself, Majesty. Have you offended them by giving the Americans pride of place in Iran or by buying weapons from the Americans rather than the British? Or might it have something to do with the fact that you transferred our foreign currency assets, amounting to more than $14 billion at the time, from London to New York? The little information I have on these matters hardly allows me to form an opinion. In any case, setting aside any problems directly related to British diplomacy, I may be able to suggest an explanation. It has two dimensions: one British, the other Iranian."

"Go on then! I'm listening!"

"As far as the British dimension is concerned, is it not conceivable that a country like Great Britain, which is finding it hard to accept the loss of the world's most powerful empire, is pleased to see that it can play a role in the political life of an Eastern country simply through the transmission of radio programs? And all the more so since the United Kingdom is aware of the slipping away of a country that it once regarded as its own private reserve? As to the Iranian dimension: do you not think, Majesty, that the current infatuation with a foreign radio station would never have occurred if we had had our own radio and television program which dealt openly and squarely with national problems?"

"And yet we gave such a free rein to our radio and television that Savak was constantly agitated, denouncing them as a communist nesting ground. Haven't I always protected radio and television against Savak attacks?"

"If you'll forgive me, Majesty, I have to say that you clearly did not protect them enough. By way of evidence I need only cite the confidences of Reza Ghotbi,[11] of whose loyalty you're fully aware, on

11. An engineer who graduated from the national school of telecommunications in Paris and a cousin of the Shahbanou. Ghotbi was at once a skilled technician and a committed patriot. He was passionately devoted to the development of Iranian radio and television.

the subject of Savak intrigues and those of others in your entourage. Despite all the harsh criticism to which he was personally subjected and the constant pressure he was under, Ghotbi did not think twice about providing every possible opportunity for expression, at least on an artistic level, to those intellectuals who didn't toe the official line. If you had allowed radio, television, and the press the freedom without which they cannot seriously carry out their task, Iranians would no doubt have never felt the need to turn to foreign sources."

Hoping to bring the conversation to an end without waiting for the Shah's reply, I said, "Majesty, I'd like to request your permission to withdraw."

I stood up to take my leave and bowed as a sign of respect. He shook my hand and I left his office.

The Impossible Renunciation
(Sixth Conversation with the Shah)

Monday, December 25, 1978, 10:30 a.m.

I stepped into the Shah's office and bowed. He came toward me, indicated a chair, and, stopping for a moment in front of me, asked his usual question:

"Well, what's new?"

"Before going over the political situation, Majesty, I'd like to convey a message to you from a young engineer."

"What do you mean? Which young engineer?"

"I met him on the way to the palace, Majesty, while I was hitchhiking."

"Are you without a car then? Why don't you ask protocol to send you one?"

"The strikes are now also affecting our Institute's employees, Majesty. Although the strike committee has for practical reasons authorized my driver not to interrupt his work, I decided to do what everyone else is doing and hitchhiked instead. It worked out very well. The young engineer who gave me a lift was a nice man, and I had a very interesting conversation with him."

"What did he say to you?"

"When he realized, much to his amazement, that a university

professor was hitchhiking to Niavaran Palace to see the Shah, he was amused and said, 'I thought everyone who went to see His Majesty went in a Rolls Royce or a Cadillac. I'd never have believed that anyone might hitchhike.'"

Extremely curious, the Shah pressed me: "What did you say in reply?"

"I told him, Sire, that the people he was referring to were now all driving their cars in California or on the Côte d'Azur and that only the hitchhikers were left in Tehran to go to see His Majesty. . . ."

The Shah seemed pleased in a way that despite the severe crisis confronting the monarchy, there were still people left among his subjects who had not abandoned him and who were even prepared to hitchhike to see him. But it clearly broke his heart to find that he had placed his trust in an entourage that was falling over itself to abandon him in the face of adversity. He asked in a friendly voice, "So what did the young engineer tell you? What was his message?"

"He's an agronomist working in Khuzestan,[1] and he was wondering if you realized when you were presented with, say, a plan to construct a dam beneficial to agro-industry, that the project would do nothing to improve the daily lives of the peasants working the land."

"What was he getting at? Did he think we should totally renounce the building of dams? Didn't he think it necessary to create a national electricity grid worthy of the name?"

"What he no doubt meant to say, Majesty, was that proper development of the agricultural sector doesn't necessarily hinge on the building of huge dams. The clearest proof is that the Khuzestan Dam, where he's currently working and which was built about fifteen years ago, has not yielded any appreciable benefits in the absence of an adequate irrigation network. If water had been pumped along the course of the great Karoun River instead, the peasants would undoubtedly have benefited much more."

"If I understand him correctly, the engineer's criticism was mainly directed at the planners. He seems to be suggesting that a more sensible plan would have taken the interests of the peasants into account."

"What he was trying to say was that technocratic planning, when it

1. A southern province bordering on the Gulf and Iraq.

is conducted from high, cannot by its very nature take the interests of the local populations into account. We have seen countless projects in recent years which have more than anything else benefited foreigners and their Iranian associates, who are now in Europe and the United States."

In response the Shah made a surprising remark which revealed a degree of creeping disappointment with foreigners and, in particular, Americans: "I have to acknowledge with regret that foreigners did indeed impose some projects on us which may not have taken our interests into account."

"Hasn't it in fact been the case, Majesty, that you've been surrounded by people who did everything they could to convince you that if you placed your trust in the Americans you would no longer have any worries?"

"You're right. It was a bit like that."

"There was an article by Richard Helms[2] in *Time* magazine on December 18 which clearly illustrates the consequences of this excessive trust. If you read the article you might believe that Helms is rushing to your defense; but in reality he has done you great harm. He criticizes Jimmy Carter for his suggestion that 'he did not believe that His Majesty would emerge unscathed from the current crisis,' but adds that the United States should not allow you to fail since you have been upholding American interests. He states that during the Arab-Israeli conflict of 1973 you hastily sent an envoy to Egypt and Saudi Arabia to try to prevent the imposition of an oil embargo against the United States. He also reveals hitherto secret information, according to which you're said to have sent a squadron of F-5 combat planes to help the Americans during the Vietnam War. I'm sure you can imagine the disastrous effects of such an article in our current volatile political climate."

Clearly beside himself, the Shah raised his arms in the air and cried, "Suggestions of this kind are certainly not aimed at defending us; quite the reverse! It was exactly the same when the British foreign minister declared two months ago that I had to be supported because I had defended British interests in the region. These gentlemen are

2. A former CIA director and later ambassador to Tehran 1974–1977. Even before his appointment to the Tehran embassy he enjoyed a close relationship with the Shah.

determined to go out of their way to persuade my people that I was at the service of foreigners. Instead of really supporting me, they malign me. Their treachery is without limit."

"Everyone imagined that the British and the Americans were your friends, Majesty."

"Not at all. The British never sincerely supported me, and for about a year now the Americans haven't been supporting me either. It's exactly as if they'd agreed between themselves to do away with me."

"Why would they adopt such a policy, Majesty?"

"I have no idea. Maybe because they don't want to see a strong country in this region. I have the impression that they're worried about their interests in the long term."

"If you were aware of what they had in mind, why didn't you alert the people?"

He looked at me skeptically and replied, "Do you think one can turn to the public with secrets of this nature?"

"But you had nothing to gain keeping it to yourself, Majesty. At a time when you're being accused of having served foreign interests, you're telling me that these same foreigners have every intention of eliminating you. . . ."

"Their animosity toward me goes back a long way. Neither the British nor the American oil companies ever forgave me for reaching an oil deal with Mattei that was very different from previous agreements with oil companies. And you know what happened to Mattei.[3] Oil companies are extremely powerful in the United States. Whenever I put pressure on the oil consortium to raise the price of petrol, there were demonstrations both inside and outside the country. Only Nixon proved capable of controlling those companies. Since he left the political stage they've been influencing American administrations again. As for the Democrats and Jimmy Carter, you might as well forget it! They're like putty in the hands of oil men."

"The Iranian people would have been very interested to know all this."

3. In 1957 Iran signed an agreement with the Italian Enrico Mattei, president of ENI, the Italian national oil company. Mattei, who was well known for his refusal to submit to the dictates of the old oil companies, died in 1962 when his private plane crashed in Italy. Since a bomb had earlier been discovered on the aircraft, the circumstances of the accident remain mysterious.

"I've never subscribed to the Mosaddeq school of thought which advocates playing the martyr to gain the people's backing. I believe that the task of a leader faced with difficulties is not to rush onto the public stage, giving ammunition to enemies, but to solve the problems."

"If I understand you correctly, Majesty, you ended up in the same position as Mosaddeq."

"With the exception that we are able to do away with control of foreigners over our oil industry and that we created and strengthened OPEC, which has been the bugbear of the big oil companies for years.[4] We finally succeeded in wrenching out of their hands a large part of the profits, whereas by closing the Abadan refinery and supporting agitation Mosaddeq did nothing but strengthen their resolve and make them more united."

"I would like to move on to another subject if I may, Sire. Don't you think that what is currently being said in the United States about the CIA's erroneous analysis of the current situation in Iran is worth thinking about?"[5]

"It's all a big charade aimed at justifying the change in American policy. The new leaders want to put the blame for this crisis on the CIA, which at our request under the previous Republican administration refrained from having any contacts with our opponents. All the things they're saying today are untrue. In reality I simply said to Nixon and Kissinger: 'Since you deem yourselves to be an ally of our country and since there are many Americans in Iran, be so good as to stop infiltrating our administration and suborning our diplomats and officers and turning them into spies.' Since I attached particular importance to preventing the patriotism of our officials from being undermined with enticing propositions, I told them that our services, including Savak, would be prepared in return to put at their disposal any information which could prove useful to them on the activities of communists and Soviet agents in Iran. Everything is different now. It is common knowledge that the CIA has no qualms today about developing its information channels within Iran and its contacts with

4. The Organization of Petroleum Exporting Companies founded in 1960, of which Iran was and still is an active member.

5. On December 21, 1978, the *New York Times* reported that Carter had ordered an inquiry into the CIA's analysis.

the Iranian opposition abroad, against our wishes; in fact, a large part of that opposition is not only in the United States but is operating under the protection of the American government."

In reality the CIA had in the past reduced its contacts with the opponents of the Shah for two reasons: the first was that during the 1960s and 1970s the main aim of the American intelligence services was to gather information about Soviet activities in the region. The CIA, which was in constant contact with Savak, also had its own direct operations inside Iran thanks to a highly advanced eavesdropping system installed along the Iran-Soviet border, allowing the Americans to intercept Soviet defense communications and to survey missile and rocket-launching bases situated in the USSR's southern republics.

The second reason was that during the fast-moving period from the coming to power of Lyndon Johnson—following Kennedy's assassination in 1963—to Carter's arrival at the White House (1977), American leaders considered the Shah to be the only viable political option for Iran. They believed he had eliminated once and for all an opposition which had never amounted to much anyway. And the Shah was in regular contact with the CIA's head of operations inside Iran, in much the same way as he met the American ambassador to Tehran on a regular basis. There was hardly any other head of state in the world who felt the need to receive CIA officials regularly. It was, in effect, so important to the Shah to maintain personal control over the Iranian intelligence services that he could not bear to give the task of briefing the CIA to anyone else. Since the Shah had reached an agreement with the Americans according to which Savak provided them with information about Iran, the intelligence went around in a closed circuit comprising the CIA, Savak, and the Shah, a system which allowed errors to occur and recur without being detected.

The CIA completely failed to recognize the importance of the religious phenomenon and its revolutionary potential precisely because the Shah and Savak did not consider Shi'i Islam to be revolutionary. Obsessed as they were by the communist threat to the exclusion of everything else, they passed information and analysis to the CIA seen only from this one angle. Consequently the Shah had no right to be indignant about the confusion reigning in Washington on the subject of Iran, because his own blindness was partly to blame.

During the relatively long period of Republican administrations, from 1968 to 1976, the Shah became a kind of spoiled child of the United States who was allowed to behave in any way he pleased. It was really no surprise, then, that he felt completely disoriented by Jimmy Carter's puritanism when the Democrats came to power. He suddenly felt traumatized by the new American attitude and acted like a deceived lover. Even though he was not prepared to admit it, everything about him indicated that he wanted to say to the Americans, "I went along with you on every level. Why have you adopted this ambivalent attitude toward me now?" The only point on which we didn't see eye to eye was that thorny business of human rights, which Carter, the presidential candidate, turned into his battering ram.

There was no one in the Shah's entourage who could explain to him what was happening in Washington. He could not understand that the climate had changed with Carter's arrival and that the sumptuous receptions at the Iranian embassy were no longer an adequate instrument in themselves to influence a team which had just emerged from the Vietnam War and the Watergate scandal.

A few weeks after Jimmy Carter's election as President of the United States, I spoke with someone close to the Shah who seemed particularly adept at understanding his state of mind. When I asked him what attitude the Shah was going to adopt toward Carter and his policy on human rights, he said, "The Shah, who is sure Carter won't win a second term, believes he can gain time by appearing to liberalize the regime. But his undoing will be that until now he's been able successfully to juggle a number of ideas, including the notion of revolution [he was referring to the "White Revolution"], and to keep them all in the air. But he's making a serious mistake if he thinks he can now juggle with freedom in the same way. In the hands of a political ruler who has always held it in contempt, freedom can turn into a bomb which may blow up in his face at any moment."

It could be said that when the Carter administration came to power, the Shah decided on an inch-by-inch policy instead of adopting a general strategy of response to demands for liberalization of the regime. This put him in an especially vulnerable position: he was bewildered time and again when his every step inevitably ended in failure.

The Shah was so tormented by the American attitude that he did not wish to pursue the conversation further. He turned to another subject: "What's happening with Sadighi? We're waiting to hear about the outcome of his consultations."

"Sadighi will no doubt be coming to tell you about them in the next few days, Majesty. I see him every day, and I can testify that he's under a great deal of pressure."

"Pressure from whom?"

"His political friends."

"Yes, I heard that his National Front friends went to see him and that one of the front's leaders wept as he spoke to him. What was it all about?"

"It's true, Majesty, that when Dariush Forouhar was trying in vain to dissuade Sadighi from accepting your offer, he began to weep. His tears revealed the awkward position in which the National Front now finds itself."

"What awkward position?"

"On the one hand Forouhar and his friends have great respect for Sadighi's outstanding moral rectitude, and on the other they are afraid that the basis on which he's planning to form his government—that is, the 1906 constitution—has already outlived its time. They don't want to see Sadighi lose his credibility."

"Has the National Front not always harped about respect for the constitution? Well then, let it put its words into practice!"

"They believe that, after flouting the constitution for so many years, Your Majesty cannot be a constitutional monarch."

"Have they thought about the country's future? Do they have any guarantees that in the event of an alternative scenario their freedoms will necessarily be respected? What do they want to put in place of the constitution? Do they realize they will soon have nothing else to do but to follow the mullahs, with no role of their own to play? Do you have any idea what they want to do with this country?"

"The fact is, Majesty, that the protest movement is now of such a scale that they no longer dare to support the monarchy, constitutional or otherwise. As for Sadighi, I believe I can say that he'll probably refuse Your Majesty's offer for him to form a government."

Surprised and disappointed, the Shah wanted to know the reasons for his refusal.

"He stipulated conditions which have not been met, Majesty."

"Which conditions?"

"The one calling for the release of prisoners, for example. Even though the minister of justice met the representatives of various organizations and the people in charge of the military tribunal and prepared a list of prisoners who could be pardoned, nothing has been done."

"What's holding things up? I'm prepared to take immediate action. What can I do to help?"

"The quickest solution, Majesty, would be for you to ask the minister of justice to inform the army and Savak immediately about Your Majesty's decision. He would be happy to carry out this task."

"Would it be all right by phone?"

"Of course, Majesty. Having spoken to the minister yesterday, I have a feeling he'll be in the Senate just now."

Several minutes later the palace operator put the Shah through to the Senate. He repeated to Najafi, the minister of justice, exactly what the minister had asked me the evening before to have the Shah say to him.

Resuming our conversation, the Shah asked, "What else?"

"Yesterday evening Sadighi gave me a document which showed that the Pahlavi Foundation is still continuing its activities as a commercial organization."

The Shah immediately telephoned the court minister to obtain the latest information about the Pahlavi Foundation and, notably, about the instructions he had given for a halt to all the financial activities conducted in his name. He told the minister to bring the final decree for him to sign the following morning. He then turned to me and said, "Which of Sadighi's other conditions have not been met?"

"Two very central points, Majesty: the command of the army and the regency council."

"As far as I'm concerned, there's absolutely no doubt that the command of the army is one of my prerogatives."

"Sadighi, standing on legal precedent, maintains that, like other royal prerogatives, the king's supreme command over the army is symbolic. In his opinion the army is in practice the responsibility of the cabinet and not of Your Majesty."

"Sadighi is suggesting that I'm not the commander of the army!"

"If I may be permitted to clarify this delicate point, Majesty: the objective opinion of all legal experts is that the imperial prerogatives are strictly symbolic where they have to do with executive matters."

"Well, I believe that, as far as the army is concerned, the king's prerogatives are complete. We'll discuss this with Sadighi."

"A related problem, Majesty, is the question of who's responsible for ordering military equipment. Sadighi wants this also to be placed under government control."[6]

"Tell me about Sadighi's views on the regency council."

"In the course of two weeks of consultations, Sadighi has concluded that the regime must change in certain ways in order to survive. After careful consideration he's decided that Your Majesty should not leave the country but that you should distance yourself from day-to-day affairs for a while and delegate your prerogatives to a regency council."

"The appointment of a regency council and the delegation of royal prerogatives has only been foreseen in cases where the monarch is outside the country. What sense could it otherwise have?"

"Majesty, since it is stated in the constitution that 'in the event the Shah is abroad or absent, a regency council shall be appointed by him,' you could very easily, should you decide to stay away from day-to-day affairs temporarily, appoint a council and remain in the country."

"You'd like me to stay in the country after I've appointed a regency council?"

"Yes, Majesty."

Clearly annoyed, the Shah said sarcastically, "What you're saying, in effect, is that I should accept that I'm little more than a minor who must be assigned a guardian!"

6. The Shah attached particular importance to maintaining control over orders for military equipment. For more than twenty years he had taken personal charge of arms purchases from other countries and the weapons industry at home, and he had become very skillful at achieving the right mix in his international orders. He purchased fighter planes, submarines, and sophisticated aerial defense equipment from the United States, for example; armored vehicles and warships from the United Kingdom; missile-launching patrol boats from France; and anti-aerial missiles and transport vehicles from the Soviet Union. These purchases were made through various commission agents, including a number of former kings (including those of Albania, Bulgaria, and Greece) who enjoyed the Shah's confidence.

"You really haven't any choice, Majesty. It's precisely because you granted yourself powers which the constitution did not allow that you've become the focal point for all the criticism and condemnation directed at the regime today."

The Shah nervously shifted his position in the chair. "No, no, no! What you're suggesting is against the constitution, and I cannot accept it because it would give rise to the view that I'd abandoned my responsibilities."

"If you accept Sadighi's proposal I can assure you that no one will speak against it. Isn't it the case that often when a commercial company is experiencing difficulties the shareholders appoint a management committee to sort out the problems?"

"Let me tell you categorically, this solution is unacceptable to me."

"In that case, Majesty, Sadighi won't accept your offer to form a government either, because for him this condition is a *sine qua non*."

It may be appropriate to explain why Sadighi (unlike Bakhtiar who advised the Shah the following week to leave the country) wanted the Shah to remain in Iran and to withdraw with the Shahbanou to their villa by the Caspian Sea. Normally whenever the Shah intended to leave on official visits to other countries he appointed a regency council consisting of the presidents of the House and the Senate, the prime minister, the commander of the armed forces, the president of the Supreme Court, the court minister, and, on occasion, one of his brothers.

Sadighi wanted to see an enlargement of the council to include respected political and possibly religious figures, so that it would be clear to the country and the opposition that the situation had changed and so that the council could henceforth guarantee the legitimacy of power. Sadighi was, moreover, insisting that the Shah stay in the country because he was hoping this would keep the army out of the melee and prevent attempts at a coup d'état. Although the Shah had lost his credibility with the public, he still enjoyed a certain popularity in the army, and his continued presence in the country would serve to reassure it. Indeed, the liberals were worried that there might be an insurrection in the army with the consequent possibility of a civil war. Finally, Sadighi was particularly eager for the Shah to stay in his kingdom because in this way he hoped he would be in a position to restore the regime. But the Shah was both physically weakened by illness and lacked the moral strength to accept such a solution. And to make matters worse, the British and Americans were, through their ambassadors (who were seeing the Shah regularly at the time), urging him to leave.

Before withdrawing I said, "Sadighi would like to propose another condition, Majesty, namely, that you should tell your British and American friends to stop pledging their support for you every day. If he becomes prime minister he intends to ask Jimmy Carter to cease his regular declarations of support for the Iranian regime. Sadighi believes that declarations of this kind are humiliating for the Iranian people."

"We're not certain, anyway, to what extent these statements are merely hypocritical," the Shah replied pointedly.

The Shah had already confided to me on a number of occasions that the British and the Americans were not really supporting him. Farah had also suggested as much to me. Nonetheless, the Shah remained in direct contact with the Americans, notably Carter's adviser Zbigniew Brzezinski, through the intermediary of his ex-son-in-law, Ardeshir Zahedi, the ambassador to Washington. He used this channel to solicit American backing—it was clearly difficult for him to give up a thirty-year-old habit. Faced with the inconsistencies between American statements of support and American actions, however, the Shah felt completely lost. His condition was compounded by the conflicting advice he received from the people around him. They could be classified into three categories.

Some, like Princess Ashraf, maintained that the Americans had abandoned him and that the crisis could be resolved only by relying on the army and by means of a military coup d'état.

Others, like Ardeshir Zahedi, continued to count on the Americans because they deluded themselves that the United States would not, in the end, allow the Shah to fall, and they interpreted even the slightest gestures from Washington as a sign of continued support. There were, finally, new advisers, such as Sadighi, who were telling the Shah that he should renounce American support once and for all and turn entirely toward the Iranian people.

All these contradictory suggestions served to heighten the Shah's inner uncertainties and increasingly pushed him toward the decision to leave. On the day of our conversation the Shah bore a strange resemblance to a person trapped in a dark room who, groping along the walls, tries desperately to find some light.

For my own part, I had perhaps gone too far in suggesting that he should renounce to such a drastic extent the powers he had accumulated over the course of years. Before taking my leave of him I tried to give him some moral comfort by telling him the following story:

"Majesty, this morning as I was conveying to you the wishes of those who want you to give up your powers, I tried to imagine how you might be feeling. I recalled an incident from my youth. When I was a twenty-year-old student in Geneva, one of my friends, who was a seasoned mountain-climber, asked me to accompany him on an expedition. We spent the night with some friends in Chamonix, and at four o'clock in the morning we began our ascent. I wasn't accustomed to climbing, but as we mounted we were rewarded every fifteen to thirty minutes with breathtaking views. They made me light-headed with pleasure, and the physical exhaustion failed to register. After we had reached the glaciers we continued to climb for a good while. Around noon we were at an altitude of about 3,500 meters. At that point I turned around to see the sheer drop behind us, and my head spun at the thought of what lay before me on the way down. But we had hardly had time to swallow our sandwiches and cast an awed look at the magnificent panorama when my friend said, 'Well, it's time to head back down!' Your situation can be compared with that of a climber, Majesty, who, in the course of twenty-five years has made the step-by-step ascent up the steep mountainside to reach the summit at last—or, in this case, to gain absolute power—and who is suddenly asked to make the descent back to the valley in a very short time. On the way up the climber always feels confident about where he'll put his next step, but on the way down a rock may dislodge itself from under his foot at any moment. The steeper the descent, the more hazardous the journey. All this is entirely comprehensible, Majesty; I don't for a moment underestimate your fears and anxieties. But there is no other solution."

As I was speaking the Shah gazed at the floor, looking at the designs on the carpet, and I had the impression he had plunged into a mental abyss. Then, as if surfacing from a dream, he suddenly said, "Was there anything else you wanted to tell me?"

"Majesty, an old friend of mine, Thierry Desjardins from *Figaro*, is currently in Tehran. Although I know you haven't been granting interviews for several months, he would nevertheless be grateful if you would receive him, even if you made it clear that the meeting shouldn't take the form of an interview. He's an honest journalist, and I can assure you that he won't distort your remarks."

"Fine. Tell the director of protocol to arrange an appointment for him."

"Thank you, Majesty."

I rose to take my leave. He shook my hand and I left his office.

What Is Happening in Guadeloupe?
(Seventh Conversation with the Shah)

Monday, January 8, 1979, 10:30 a.m.

My audience with the Shah was to be at 10:30 a.m. Observing protocol, I arrived at the palace a half-hour early. At the top of the staircase, in the main corridor, I ran into Thierry Desjardins, who had just concluded his interview with the Shah. I asked him if it had gone well. He told me that although the Shah's analysis of the situation was quite lucid, he was still uncertain about the action he should take. Desjardins added that at the end of the meeting something quite unusual had happened, too personal for him to mention in his article.

The Shah had walked over to the window looking onto the city, through which one could hear the distant rumble of chanting demonstrators shouting something resembling, "Death to the Shah!" Looking directly at Thierry Desjardins, he had suddenly asked, "What would you do in my place?"

Hoping to relieve the strained atmosphere, the reporter replied, "I would take up journalism, Majesty."

The Shah, in a manner at once both familiar and grave, had patted him on the stomach, saying, "This is not the time for jokes, Monsieur Desjardins!"

At 10:30 it was my turn to enter the imperial office. The Shah came to greet me, shook my hand, and asked with amusement, "Well, did you hitchhike again?"

Walking toward the armchair in which he invited me to sit, I replied, "Yes, Sire, but this time it was not a question of running out of petrol or being caught in a strike; there were other reasons. . . ."

"What reasons?"

"Since the situation has become very serious, I thought it best not to tell my colleagues that I was coming to the palace. . . ."

Surprised and resigned at the same time, the Shah sighed. "Oh, I see. So that's how it is. . . ."

"I just saw General Jam leaving here.[1] Has he accepted Bakhtiar's offer?" I asked, to change the subject.

"I don't think he will agree to become defense minister. For one thing he has a handicapped son who needs constant attention, and for another he does not want to have blood on his hands. I know Zahedi and Seyyed Jalal Tehrani are going to see him, but I don't think they will convince him."

When I heard this I realized that deep down the Shah was hoping that General Jam would not return to office.[2] Jam had been appointed chief of the army's joint staff in 1970. He was an able officer entirely at ease with the latest military techniques, but his personal integrity had made him impatient with the Shah's interference in army affairs. The Shah had dismissed him some years back and sent him to Spain as Iranian ambassador. He clearly feared that if Jam were to return now as the army's savior and the guarantor of the country's security, it would be seen as a definite retreat. In addition, after more than twenty years of absolute power, the Shah was not prepared to accept that important decisions could be taken out of his hands. Deep down he did not want Bakhtiar to succeed either, because even though circumstances had forced him to turn to Bakhtiar, he had no confidence in a man who had supported Mosaddeq for thirty years.

I asked him, "Is it true that Your Majesty is planning to leave the country?"

1. General Jam was a former brother-in-law of the Shah (Princess Shams had been his first wife).

2. Jam stated later that during his conversation with the Shah he had asked, "If I become war minister, who will take care of the army?" To which the Shah had replied, "The same person as always!" (meaning the sovereign himself).

"It is Bakhtiar who is asking me to leave," he answered, as if to say, "If it were up to me, I would stay here and accept all the risks."

"Majesty, you yourself have chosen Bakhtiar. What right has he to tell you what to do?"

The Shah gave me the following, extremely surprising reply: "It is not just Bakhtiar. It is also the others who are telling me, 'If you don't leave the country and if Khomeini does not return, the crisis will not be resolved.'"

The Shah was constantly trying to make "others" shoulder the responsibility for his departure: Bakhtiar, the Americans, and God knows who else. As for myself, I sensed that between Sadighi, who was advising him to stay in Iran but to steer clear of politics for a while, and Bakhtiar, who was pressing him to leave, the Shah preferred the second solution. For him, staying in the country and accepting Sadighi's solution would require a real psychological metamorphosis; it would be a kind of penitence to expiate the sin of vanity committed over many years. So as not to endure such a trial, he preferred to abandon one of the most celebrated thrones in the world.[3] That is why I am convinced that the Shah had made his decision even before he asked Bakhtiar to form a government.

Additional evidence for this view comes from Michel Poniatowski who was sent to Iran toward the end of December 1978 by President Giscard d'Estaing to prepare a report about the political situation and the Shah's state of mind before the Guadeloupe summit—a meeting of the heads of state of the Federal Republic of Germany, the United States, France, and the United Kingdom, to be held on January 5 and 6, 1979. In the course of a long conversation I had with him much later in Paris, Poniatowski told me that when he met the Shah on December 27, 1978, his impression had been that the monarch was already well on his way to making the decision to leave Iran.

3. One day during my conversation with the queen, I said to her: "The function of the Shah, with all the connotations which the word has in our country, is unique in the world. As you know, in the Persian language, when we want to indicate that something is most handsome, the biggest, the most accomplished, we add the prefix 'Shah' to a word. In order to identify the best verse of poetry, the longest road in the country, the most delicious fruit, we use the prefix 'Shah.' Is it not the case that our greatest epic poem is called the Book of Kings, Ferdowsi's *Shah-Nameh*? But unfortunately the Shah's function has become unworkable—like a Rolls Royce which, despite all its capabilities, finds itself useless in a rocky terrain.

Poniatowski, of whose mission Helmut Schmidt and probably Jimmy Carter had been informed by the French president, also told me that the Shah was not pleased with the attitude of his Western allies. "Not only are the British not helping me," he confided to Poniatowski, "but the Americans too are adopting contradictory positions which change from one week to the next, depending on whether you're talking to their intelligence services, their military, or their diplomatic personnel.[4] The Western powers should know that if there is chaos in Iran, the Soviets will intervene. That is why I hope that a clear stance will emerge from Guadeloupe on a collective position vis-à-vis the Soviet Union."

At the same time Poniatowski told me that while the Shah was calling for the West's support and for a united position on the Iranian crisis, he did not himself have a clear strategy on the question of remaining in the country or leaving. He tried to give the impression he was still undecided, whereas in reality he was increasingly inclined toward departure. In the meantime his message to the four presidents was that his ultimate decision depended on whether the Western powers would support him; for without their backing he believed he would be irreparably harmed by his opponents.

When President Giscard d'Estaing's envoy had raised the idea of speaking—in his prison cell—to the former prime minister, Hoveida (whose lucid analyses he had always appreciated), the Shah had replied, "It's true that Hoveida can analyze political situations very well; but at the moment he enjoys no credibility with the public. In any case, it would be difficult to obtain permission to see him even if the meeting were to be very discreet."

There are other indications, besides these, which suggest that after

4. To understand the political atmosphere of the time I should refer the reader to the January 5 issue of *Le Monde* and the following dispatch by the paper's special correspondent at the Guadeloupe conference: "Another sensitive subject for Monsieur d'Estaing: Iran, about which Mr. Carter wants to speak at length. The actions and positions of Monsieur Giscard d'Estaing could plead guilty to the charge of having been right too early. Whereas the Shah's fate is now being seen as desperate, even in Washington, the President of the Republic could claim that he had been justified in maintaining a 'link' with the man who could soon have a considerable influence on the course of events, Ayatollah Khomeini. Is the United States not declaring itself ready, today, to maintain the best possible relations with the Bakhtiar government, and does it not acknowledge that it is trying to increase its contacts with the forces of the moderate opposition?"

Black Friday (September 8, 1978) the Shah's desire to go into exile grew steadily.[5] He was only looking for excuses to justify his departure.

Before going to meet the Shah on that day, I had stopped by the office of General Pakravan, who had been appointed deputy minister at the court some time before, to gauge his opinion of the situation. Having already warned me a month earlier that the Shah no longer had the heart or the will to deal with the country's affairs, the general now expressed the fear that his reserves of strength were gone and he wished to leave. He said, with great feeling, "His departure would be an abnegation of responsibility. He must not be allowed to leave!"

As for myself, I had good cause to believe that the Shah had already made up his mind. Every topic he raised that day showed that he felt the country had become ungovernable. On the subject of the court's and his family's financial affairs, for example, he told me in an irritated tone, "Of course the newspapers don't publish my decisions on this matter. Haven't the revolutionaries always declared themselves to be against my own and my family's intervention in any financial affairs involving state organizations? But now that a clear decision has been made on the subject, the newspapers are silent, because they have been terrorized by those same gentlemen."

"Your Majesty, people of goodwill are always glad to hear about your decisions, while thinking, all the same, that you should have made them long ago. . . ."

In order to convince me—or perhaps to convince himself—that there was nothing he could do, the Shah gave another example: "I will ask you to explain to me something which happened this morning. Half an hour ago I learned that the doctors and nurses at the cardiology hospital—which was funded by my mother with her own money and with private donations, and which consequently bears her name—have demanded that the name be changed to that of Ali Shariati. . . ."

Then, punching his chest angrily with his fist, the Shah gave vent to his indignation: "My mother's hospital! Built by my mother! How do you explain that?"

5. On December 7, 1978, when he received Sadighi for the first time in the presence of Ali Amini and Abdollah Entezam, the Shah informed them of his decision to "establish a regency council and go abroad for a time."

I responded calmly, "Sire, this is a rebellion arising from a sense of dispossession. The people feel that nothing belongs to them. That is their perception, even when your mother has had a state-of-the-art hospital built for them. It is true that they are the beneficiaries; but they are nevertheless frustrated to find the imprint of your family on everything. Now that they have the opportunity to make themselves heard, they want to name the hospital after one of their own. They want to prove to themselves and to others that they exist. It is a reclamation of identity. But when all is said and done, Majesty, the matter is not all that serious. Perhaps all that is needed is for your mother to say, 'I built this hospital for you. If you would like to give it a name of your own choosing, I am quite happy to let you do so.' The simple people also feel the need to be recognized, Sire. . . ."

Events at the hospital had deeply wounded the Shah, and while I tried to comfort him with my suggestion, I could not help but feel that the breach between him and the people had become unbridgeable. The dramatic behavior of the hospital's personnel, recruited and administered as they were from the court by the queen mother's secretary, could not be attributed to a political party or to an international conspiracy of some kind. It simply showed that the game was up, that the entire country was turning its back on the dynasty, and that all links had been irretrievably severed. Nevertheless, in order to put a brave face on things and to show some measure of optimism, the Shah went on to say in a neutral but not very convincing voice, "Let's see what Shapour Bakhtiar can do. I hope he can put our paralyzed economy back into action as soon as possible."

"That will be a difficult task, Majesty. Most of the men he has asked have refused to join his government."

"That's because the people can only have their eyes on the streets these days. Look at the parliamentarians. They are going out of their way to pour oil on fire!"

"They want to be reelected, Majesty!"

"They're dreaming. The mullahs will have nothing to do with them!"

"History will be the judge."

"You are quite right. History will have the last say. Is it not, in fact, our final court of appeal?"

On those words, I withdrew.

Visa for Egypt

(Eighth and Last Conversation with the Shah)

Sunday, January 14, 1979, 10:30 a.m.

My audience with the Shah had been arranged for 10:30 a.m. When I arrived at the palace I ran into a number of generals on their way out. Clearly disturbed by the news that the Shah was planning to take a trip abroad, a couple of them said to me, "When you see His Majesty you must persuade him not to leave."

As for myself, I simply felt that it was too late: whatever his decision, it could no longer make any difference to the destiny of a man who, because of his temperament and his health (about which we were yet to learn the worst), was no longer in a position to face the violent storm shaking our country.

I took a seat in the chamberlain's office, and as I heard the telephone conversations conducted around me, I realized how much pressure the Shah's entourage were putting on him to leave on one of the cargo planes taking his family's belongings to the United States. I understood also that a select few of the entourage had obtained His Majesty's permission to leave the country. Even so, the Shah himself was still doing his best not to give the impression that this was in fact the "great departure"; indeed, until the very eve of his flight, the date and destination were kept secret.

At exactly 10:30 the chamberlain announced me and I entered the Shah's office with a respectful bow. He welcomed me with a big smile, invited me to take a seat, and asked me the usual question, "What's new?"

"The most important news is the announcement that Your Majesty is leaving."

Hiding his emotions, he said in a neutral tone, "Yes, I'm thinking of leaving for a while to give Bakhtiar's government a free hand and to allow him to resolve the crisis."

"Has Your Majesty chosen his destination?"

"I've decided to go to the United States."

"Your Majesty, your decision to go abroad on holiday was first announced in Washington two days ago by Secretary of State Cyrus Vance, who described it as 'wise.' Nationalist circles would have preferred the announcement to have been made in Tehran. Besides, Majesty, aren't you afraid that with the anti-American sentiments currently raging in the country, your choice of the United States will further inflame the hostility being directed at you?"

The Shah preferred not to reply to my first observation, and judging by the way he crossed and uncrossed his legs, I understood that he had been hoping it would be the Americans who would announce the trip so that they would feel responsible for all that might follow.

As to my second remark, he replied, "Our visit is a private one, and we'll be staying with friends.[1] In any case, we've chosen the United States because our safety could not be guaranteed anywhere else."

"But, Majesty, any country which accepts you will have to guarantee your safety."

"Which country are you thinking of?"

"A Muslim country in the Middle East."

"In that case the revolutionary Muslims would not be silent, and we would create problems for our hosts. In America it is a different matter; the security system is structured in a way that will ensure our personal safety. At any rate, we have also received an invitation from a friendly Middle Eastern country.[2] We will decide what to do for the best."

1. A reference to Walter Annenberg, a former U.S. ambassador to London, who had invited the Shah to stay at his house near Palm Springs.

2. From the Egyptian president, Anwar Sadat.

When William Sullivan, the American ambassador in Tehran, informed the Shah that President Sadat had invited him to stop over in Egypt for a few days, the Shah was reluctant to accept, so great was his hurry to reach the United States. (Once in Egypt, the Shah must have noticed that the Americans were increasingly reluctant to renew their own invitation.)

Aslan Afshar, imperial chief of protocol, who stayed with the Shah during his last months in Tehran and later accompanied him to Egypt and Morocco, confided to me that the Shah had said on several occasions that he hoped to go to the United States so that he could "explain to the National Security Council and the Foreign Affairs Committee of Congress the dangers which threatened Iran and the region, because neither the American embassy in Tehran nor the Iranian embassy in Washington had been capable of conveying the reality of Iran to the Americans."

The Shah imagined that the Americans perceived this reality as something apart from him. He did not realize at the time that for more than twenty years he himself had been the main component of American foreign policy in the region. Marvin Zonis, an American political scientist who knows Iran very well, has recently published a book on the Shah and his relations with the U.S., in which he demonstrates that America was unable to see Iran other than through Mohammad Reza Shah.[3] Zonis argues that the deep involvement of the United States in Iranian life manifested itself during practically every phase of the Shah's reign and of the revolution which so categorically rejected that regime. The Americans were responsible for what happened in Iran because they were so intimately linked with the Pahlavis. Had they acted differently at various points in the Shah's reign, his fate would also have been different. The United States contributed, perhaps decisively, to the transformation of the Shah into a despot. It encouraged his dreams of grandeur by contriving his regime's economic and military strength, and it encouraged him psychologically by allowing him to use America and its presidents as if they were his personal property.

Now the Shah was desperate to get to the United States in any way possible, whether for security's sake, or for the sake of "explaining

3. Marvin Zonis, *Majestic Failure: The Fall of the Shah* (Chicago, 1991).

things to the Americans," or possibly on health grounds (as became the case a few months later in the course of his exile in the Bahamas and Mexico), or even, as the revolutionaries in Tehran maintained, in order to gain access to the money he had sent to America. His idealization of America and his profound attachment to that great power never diminished even during his years of exile. More than any other factor, it explains the personal and political tragedy that engulfed the American embassy in Tehran when he was admitted to the United States in 1975. After the revolution both the American administration in Washington and the Bazargan government in Tehran foresaw such an explosion and did everything possible to prevent it. It was the Shah's tenacity that made nonsense of their efforts.

During my conversation with him on January 14, 1979, I saw before me a man totally obsessed with—even possessed by—the United States. Although deep down inside he blamed America for his fall, when he abandoned his throne he still longed to go there.

To ease the tension, I said, "For sixty years now, whenever Iran has been faced with an uncertain future my father has consulted the poetry of Hafez.[4] He has done so again now, thinking of the current crisis and your Majesty's destiny."

The Shah was very intrigued and asked, "So what did Hafez say?"

I answered with an attempt at humor. "Given your lack of interest in poetry, Majesty, I think it might be better if I give the poem directly to the Shahbanou, but I can give you an idea what it said: In the face of adversity it is wise to keep one's distance, because once the turmoil and agitation of this world have died down, it is the good we have done which will finally remain of us."[5]

Looking pleased and relieved, the Shah nodded twice, saying, "That is good! It is comforting. . . ."

"Your Majesty, I will withdraw now. It only remains for me to wish you a safe journey."

4. It is an Iranian tradition to turn to the poetry of Hafez in order to throw some light on the future. A volume of the poet's complete work is opened at random, and the future is read from the poem selected.

5. The verse from Hafez which I read to the queen over the telephone that same evening was, "In golden letters 'tis written in a crystalline sky: Good deeds will live, all else will die." Clearly moved, the queen bade me farewell and thanked me for the frankness with which I had spoken to her of the country's affairs.

"Very well! See you soon . . . that is, I hope we will meet again."

"I hope so too."

I stood up to take my leave. Contrary to custom, the Shah accompanied me to the office door. When he took my hand I had the distinct impression that he held it longer than usual. He peered into my eyes in a way he had never done before, and his eyes were bright with emotion. I felt as if I could read in them a sense of recognition as well as regret and remorse. It was as if he wanted to say, "Why did you not come to me earlier, when I needed so badly to be told the truth?"

To which my answer, like that of many others, could only have been, "Because, Majesty, for a long time you preferred to listen to people who chose to hide the truth from you."

I was never again to see Mohammad Reza Pahlavi, the last Shah of Iran. Two days later he left with Farah on an "official visit" to Aswan, Upper Egypt. He returned to the Nile valley in 1980, after incredible tribulations on both sides of the Atlantic, to die and be buried.

PRISON

Youngsters as at Vincennes...

(First Detention, April 1979)

I was arrested for the first time in early April 1979. My detention at what used to be the Savak premises lasted only four days, because the late Ayatollah Motahhari[1] interceded with the revolutionary "committee"[2] on my behalf, asking that I not be kept long without reason. As a result my interrogation was brief, but thoroughgoing for all that. The people questioning me were young left-wingers with slight Islamic tendencies. They had great respect for the Islamic theorist Ali Shariati but also displayed some of the psychological characteristics that typify many Stalinists. Their questions reminded me of those my left-wing students used to ask when I was teaching sociology in Vincennes in the early 1970s. For them, everything that happened in the world was willed and planned by American imperialism and more directly by the CIA. The whole of Western Europe and all international organizations, including UNESCO, were under the command

1. Morteza Motahhari, a theologian receptive to Western schools of thought, taught at both Tehran University and the Qom seminary. A disciple of Khomeini, he advocated reformist ideas within the Shi'i religious system, and, enjoying the full confidence of Khomeini, he became the main theoretician of the Islamic revolution. He was assassinated in May 1979 by an anticlerical Islamic group.

2. After the revolution in February 1979 committees were established in workplaces and neighborhoods "to fight collaborators of the former regime and to safeguard the advancement of the revolution."

of the United States. Iran was similarly beholden to the Americans, and everything that went on in the country was orchestrated by Savak. Whenever my interrogators were unable to uncover any trace of the Savak, they simply constructed ever more elaborate theories of CIA intervention.

They asked me questions about the Institute for Social Studies and Research which, as I explained earlier, I founded at Tehran University in 1958. The Institute had been a sanctuary for a good number of independent researchers and had produced many studies on various aspects of Iranian society. None of these had any direct relevance to state policy, so those examining my case concluded that the Institute must have been protected by a hidden power, which again could only have been the CIA. At the same time, because Bani-Sadr had been one of the Institute's first research officers—something of which he was still proud—it was difficult for them to claim that it had actually been an arm of the CIA. In the early days of the revolution the future president, Bani-Sadr, was considered to be a close adviser of Khomeini, and my interrogators, their leftism notwithstanding, refrained from attacking him openly. At this time and throughout the first year of the revolution (1979) all extreme left-wing groups in Iran supported Khomeini and tolerated his entourage. Their immediate aim was to get rid of the Bazargan government and the institutions of the young Islamic Republic, with the exception of the revolutionary tribunals.

I was released after more than fifteen hours of interrogation during which my captors demonstrated a total ignorance of national and international affairs. But they gradually abandoned their initial arrogance and ended up by giving the impression that they regarded my answers to their political questions as interesting and instructive. Thanks to the oldest among them, I was given to understand that despite my position as a prominent intellectual, the examination of Savak archives had not revealed any complicity between myself and the Pahlavis.

Upon my release I was treated with great courtesy by the young committee member who took me home in his own car. As I was saying goodbye to him he asked very shyly if he could have copies of the books I had published during the last years' reign of Mohammad Reza Shah, which he heard about when he himself was in prison before the revolution. One of my sons brought the books, and the young man begged me to autograph them for him, using his pseudonym, Alavi. . . . Before leaving he gave me his telephone number, saying I was to call him without hesitation if I had any trouble. This same revolutionary, on the evening of my arrest, phoned my wife to let her know that I was being held as a "guest," that I was conducting a political seminar, and that he would be bringing me back home as soon as possible. . . .

The next day the main evening paper, *Ettela'at*, published my photograph on the front page next to that of the minister of justice in the former Hoveida government, accompanied by the headline, "The Pahlavis' Theoretician and the Former Justice Minister Have Been Arrested." I immediately phoned the committee man to ask what this was all about.

"We did everything humanly possible," he replied, "to keep the news of your arrest out of the papers. Indeed we took you out through a back door because we heard that a journalist who was desperate to see you was about to arrive at our offices. We wrapped things up quickly to avoid meeting him. In any case, you should phone the paper now and tell them you are at home, without mentioning the arrest."

He admitted to me during this conversation that he had not received an order for my arrest. I could understand less than ever why I had been cross-examined at all. I could also not account for the presence of a journalist at committee premises to which one could gain access only after being checked several times.

When I contacted him the editor-in-chief of *Ettela'at* confessed to me that he had no power whatsoever over the new revolutionary editor who had been installed at the paper.

"Unfortunately, I'm unable to rectify anything. The journalist who followed your case was able to obtain the twelve tapes of your interrogation, and he thinks they are very interesting since they can clarify certain points about a range of institutions and personalities. He is in the process of transcribing them for publication in a series of articles which he believes will cause a sensation."

I protested vehemently, stressing the fact that I had testified before a judicial organ of a revolutionary state, but that I had had no intention of making my statement public. It was no use. The editor-in-chief had been terrorized to the point where he feared he was to be relieved of his post.

Since I knew the Bazargan government's information minister (Mr. Minachi) well, I told him about the *Ettela'at* incident and pleaded for his intervention.

"Although the paper has been nationalized and therefore in principle is within my jurisdiction, I'm actually powerless," he said to me. "All I can do for you is to call Tehran's procurator general at the Ministry of Justice[3] and arrange for an injunction against the journalist."

I decided to let the matter drop. Nevertheless, I remained worried for several days until one evening, around midnight, I received a phone call from someone who did not wish to give his name. Almost in a whisper he said, "I work for the paper and I have great respect for you. A couple of friends and I have learned that, by some means or other, a tramp, passing himself off as a journalist, has obtained copies of tapes containing your statements to the committee, and that he intends to use them for a scoop, breaking all the rules of journalistic ethics. In view of the current anarchy, no one has either the authority or the ability to stop him. We've decided to steal the tapes and destroy them. That's what we've just done. Good night and sleep well."

He hung up.

In the course of my two other arrests I was to discover no trace of those fifteen hours of interrogation in my records. According to the judge at the Evin Prison's revolutionary tribunal, this was because at the end of the first year of the revolution the magistrates who questioned me had been ousted for being on the extreme left, and they had taken the tapes of my interrogations with them.

3. To be distinguished from revolutionary tribunals, over which the Bazargan government had no control.

Surprises in a Prison Hospital

(Second Detention, December 1979–April 1980)

Despite the ambiguities surrounding my first detention, I was reassured by the knowledge that the revolutionary authorities were now aware of the stance I had taken under the former regime. I should perhaps say, in my interrogators' defense, that my position was rather peculiar and if not actually inviting suspicion could at the very least give rise to a degree of confusion. The truth of the matter was that I had condemned the regime's "forced developmentalism" and relentless Westernization with as much if not greater passion than the Marxist or Islamic opposition. I had, moreover, not only criticized the American model of liberalism but had also firmly opposed the communist model. The result of all this was that Marxist intellectuals considered me a nuisance, and the Islamists, while exploiting my analyses for their own ends, were unhappy with my reformist approach and with the fact that I did not share their radicalism. That is why they found me difficult to place and why any or all these groups could use me as a scapegoat whenever things started getting "hot."

Given the revolutionaries' hypersensitivity toward intellectuals, I had written to Bazargan to let him know that I wished to publish my conversations with the Shah which I believed would serve to throw light on some of the more obscure aspects of the deposed regime. I also told him that I wanted to go to Paris for a few months to see my eldest son who was taking a business course at university there, but I made it clear that I had no intention of leaving Iran for good and that my wife and two youngest children would be remaining in Tehran. Bazargan had asked his close friend, Professor Yadollah Sahabi, who was a minister of state, to keep an eye on the situation as my passport went through the process of renewal. In the following weeks Sahabi telephoned me several times to reassure me that the necessary authorization had been granted and to tell me that he could not understand why the passport office had still not given me my papers. He attributed the delay to a department close to his, headed by an undersecretary of state[1] who was below him in rank but who apparently did not share his faith in me.

The affair went on like this until the beginning of November 1979 when a group of students occupied the American embassy in Tehran and took the diplomats hostage. Bazargan resigned soon after this event, and Bani-Sadr took charge of several ministries, including foreign affairs. Close to Khomeini and an influential member of the Revolutionary Council, Bani-Sadr was in a position to act as my character reference, and I was thus able to obtain my passport with the approval of the revolutionary tribunal. There was one last hurdle left to negotiate—an authorization from the prime minister's office. Here again Bani-Sadr intervened. With the final stamp on the document, someone from his office telephoned me to give me the necessary reference number and to let me know that I could leave on the Air France flight to Paris the following day. And so I arrived at the airport on December 30, 1979, and checked my suitcases which contained my notes about the Shah. I was having my passport examined at the control point when a young man suddenly appeared from nowhere and demanded to see it. The policeman at the control post was clearly not very happy about the unexpected intervention, for he turned to me and said, "Mr. Naraghi, I'm giving you back your passport, which is in order. The gentleman's business has nothing to do with me."

The "gentleman" said he only wished to detain me for an hour or two to "ask a few questions." But as he led me to the revolutionary

1. He was referring to Mostafa Chamran, who had lived in the United States and Lebanon for fifteen years and who, unlike Bazargan, was not familiar with either the country or its people.

tribunal's office at Mehrabad airport, I realized that I was in fact being arrested. I had a strong suspicion that the same person who had phoned me from the prime minister's office to tell me I could leave had also called the office of the revolutionary tribunal to inform them of my time of departure. All these people were clearly obeying orders from somewhere.

For my own part, I had just enough time to ask some passengers booked on the same flight to notify my son in Paris so that he could collect my bags at the Orly airport. I was actually feeling quite relieved because the manuscript of my conversations with the Shah—which was quite possibly the reason for my arrest—was in those bags. Soon afterward I got into a Volkswagen containing three young men in civilian clothes who drove me to Evin Prison, in the northern foothills of Tehran.

Although I was rather annoyed by all this, I comforted myself with the thought that a few hours' questioning by a judge anxious not to disturb my travel schedule unduly would not be too unbearable and would help complete the earlier statements I had made before the revolutionary committee. As a result I was feeling quite relaxed and hummed to myself throughout the journey, much to the amazement, if not the amusement, of my travel companions.

After about half an hour we arrived at Evin. The prison's imposing gate swung open. We passed through another barrier, and the car headed toward a building which, I was to learn later, was known as Number 9.

In the early days of the revolution, prison administrators and most examining magistrates were chosen from the ranks of the Shah's former prisoners. They used Savak methods in their interrogation and in the running of the prison. In the 1970s, whenever Savak arrested any guerrillas its aim was to make them "rat" on their friends to reveal the locations of arms caches and the details of planned assassinations and attacks. A variety of methods was used to extract the desired information, including physical torture. In order to demoralize the prisoners they were thrown into small, dark cells, where they were kept in solitary confinement and allowed to see no one other than their Savak interrogators. Then, as they began to "spill the beans," they were gradually transferred to the communal sections where the cells were more comfortable and where they were treated less harshly. The ex-prisoners in charge of Evin subjected their captives to much the same rituals, although they did not torture them.[2] There was one other notable difference: the former ministers, senators, and generals who now formed the prison population were on the whole predisposed to talk, for they had no wish to stay in prison a moment longer than necessary, nor, in view of the overthrow of the Shah, did they need to worry about their confessions being used against them.

When we arrived at building Number 9 the warder told the people accompanying me that "according to orders" I was to be taken to the medical section. I understood then that my arrest had led to some string-pulling in high places and that in all likelihood I was to be confined in the medical section to diminish the severity of my detention. I was even more certain of this when I found myself in a room with washing facilities, a convenience unheard of elsewhere in Evin. These luxuries also made me realize that, contrary to the revolutionary guard's promise at the airport and contrary to what I had first imagined, I would be in Evin Prison for rather more than a few hours and would not only miss that day's flight but those of the days to come.

The infirmary consisted of six rooms leading to a corridor where the patients or pseudopatients could pace up and down. Since supper was already over, the pasdar (revolutionary guard) on duty made me an omelette, and then I went to bed. People usually find it difficult to sleep in their first night in prison, because they suddenly find themselves in an unknown environment without any idea what the future may hold—a state of complete uncertainty, in other words. I experienced this predicament once again.

The next day a very obliging pasdar, who was acting as the medical attendant, brought me breakfast: bread, cheese, and tea. The door opened again a few moments later and two men entered my room. One was small and stocky with a big grey beard; the other was young. The man with the beard wore a slightly bitter smile and had a gentle look in his eye as he glanced at me, but he tried not to let the pasdar

2. From February 1979 to June 1981, the period in which the prisoners were for the most part former officials of the monarchy, torture or humiliating treatment was not used against prisoners at Evin—although of course a number of people were executed.

see. I suddenly recognized a former health minister whose death sentence had been commuted to life imprisonment on the condition that he act as a prison doctor. He quickly made me understand that I should not appear friendly toward him while the pasdars were present. The visit to my room was part of his regular round. After a few days—I spent twenty in the infirmary—I was able to speak to him freely on several occasions. During our first conversation he told me that since he had started working in Evin he had never seen any other prisoner brought directly to the hospital. He believed this indicated that they did not have much against me and that I therefore had no need to worry.

On my first full day in prison I was keen to convince myself that the man at the airport had been in earnest when he told me I would only be asked a few questions and that "the whole thing would not take more than two hours." As a result I was expecting to be called before the examining magistrate at any moment. Toward the end of the afternoon I acknowledged that I was being unrealistically optimistic and that to protect myself against anxiety and depression it would be better if I bowed before the facts and patiently endured the setbacks.

Normally a rapid interrogation followed an arrest when there were major charges against a detainee; in all other cases time was irrelevant. When a prisoner was held for a long time without interrogation—say, six months to a year—it meant that there was not enough to charge him with. The examining magistrates were biding their time, waiting for evidence to emerge from somewhere.

I also noticed that a delay of this length ultimately became a point in the prisoner's favor. So whenever prisoners complained about how long they were being held, I would console them by saying, "The longer you remain here, the easier will be your eventual release. One fine day, without ever having been cross-examined, you'll be told 'you're free.'" All the same, the twenty days I had to wait before I was called before the examining magistrate seemed like a very long time to me.

On the fourth day of my imprisonment I was summoned to the office of the hospital director where I found one of Bani-Sadr's assistants at the Ministry of Finance and Economic Affairs. I recognized him right away because his boss had pointed him in my direction as soon as he had been put in charge of diplomacy and economy. I had informed him, among other things, that a considerable number of contracts signed between the imperial government and European, American, and Japanese industrial firms, worth a total of several billion pounds, risked not being honored—something that was all the more alarming in view of the fact that since the rise in the price of oil in 1973 the Shah had made it a policy to pay in advance. The reason why Bani-Sadr had sent his assistant to see me on several occasions was that he felt I was in a position to give him reliable information. The revolutionary government faced many problems because the ministerial records to which they had access concealed more than they revealed, and the people who might have filled the gaps had either left the country before the revolution or been driven away indiscriminately afterward by the revolutionaries.

When I approached Bani-Sadr's assistant in a friendly manner in the presence of the pasdar, he adopted a very cold attitude which I found difficult to understand at first. In a very officious tone of voice he told me, "I've just been to see the revolutionary tribunal's procurator general. They say you were intending to go abroad without having your papers ready."

I found this behavior all the more baffling since he had been fully aware of my travel preparations. I took out my passport to prove to him that my arrest had been totally groundless. The pasdar left the office at this point and we were briefly alone. He took advantage of the opportunity and whispered hastily in my ear, "What became of your manuscript in the airport?"

I assured him that I had placed the manuscript in my luggage and that it had gone to Paris in the plane's baggage hold. . . . He breathed a deep sigh of relief. When the pasdar returned he resumed his terse tone and declared, "Very well, then. I'm going to report all this to Mr. Bani-Sadr! The magistrate will of course take the appropriate decisions regarding your case. Goodbye!"

I was not to learn for quite some time exactly what had happened. The former minister of foreign affairs in the Bazargan cabinet, Ebrahim Yazdi,[3] who was no longer a member of the government but who

3. A specialist in pharmaceuticals, Yazdi had lived in the United States for more than twenty years and had acquired American citizenship. Like his friend Chamran, he had lost touch with Iran.

had maintained his links with the Islamic revolutionaries, was afraid I might be intending to write in my book about things that the Shah may have said about him, or possibly to mention his close links with American circles. Having become Bani-Sadr's remorseless rival and suspecting that I may have tried to help Bani-Sadr to resolve the American hostage crisis,[4] it was he who had been behind my arrest.

The time I spent in the prison hospital proved very useful since it allowed me to understand how Evin worked. Almost every evening the prison director, Mohammed Kachoui (assassinated a year and a half later by the Mojahedin), would visit the doctor and the small number of prisoners who were ill. He was an Islamist who had fought the Shah and had spent several years in Evin before the revolution. He had been a bookbinder in the Tehran bazaar. He had received only a primary school education, but because of his profession and his activism he took an interest in books and authors and consequently in me. After his evening tour he would stand in the doorway of my room chatting with me. One day I insisted that he come in and sit down for a moment or two. He refused: "As you know, people here have twisted minds. If the pasdars, most of whom are very simple people, saw me sitting and talking with you, they wouldn't understand because they can't make any distinction between the prisoners."

Mohammed Kachoui was a very conscientious prison director, and he was always prepared to listen. During the four months I spent in Evin on that occasion and even after my release, he always responded positively to my interventions on behalf of other prisoners. For this reason officials of the former regime, who unlike the Mojahedin (an organization with an Islamic Marxist ideology) were not contesting political power in the Islamic Republic, held him in great esteem. I have very fond memories of him, and I remember in particular the role he played in the case of a religious panegyrist by the name of Javad Zabihi, whom I met during my detention.

At the time of the Shah, Zabihi used to sing religious eulogies, with his beautiful voice, at high-society occasions and on radio. Since the

4. At the time (December 1979) Bani-Sadr was minister of foreign affairs and was about to leave for the United States where the problem of the American hostages was to be discussed at a UN Security Council session. For my own part, I had simply advised Bani-Sadr that it was up to the government of the Islamic Republic to persuade the students to release the hostages without further delay to ensure that the Iranian state would not become implicated in the affair.

radical Islamists considered him a traitor and of weak moral fiber, it was more or less taken for granted that he would be arrested soon after the revolution. A few months later, when the tension had subsided, he was sentenced by the revolutionary tribunal to three years' imprisonment. He benefited later from amnesty which reduced his sentence to one year. When the moment of liberation arrived he went to the prison office armed with a letter from the procurator permitting him to leave; but without giving any explanation, the prison director refused to let him go. The panegyrist pleaded with me to intercede on his behalf. I did as he asked, but when I tried to speak to the prison director he looked directly into my eyes and said forcefully, "You should understand that by urging me to release him, you're pushing him to his death. Be so good as to explain to him that he's much safer here than outside. Tell him to have a little patience!" I was convinced that Kachoui was telling the truth, and I did what I could to persuade the prisoner that he would be taking a risk if he left. He agreed to wait. After my release two months later, in April 1980, I learned that Javad Zabihi had eventually managed to leave Evin and that within a few days a gunman had taken him from his house to the outskirts of the city and killed him.

Another interesting character from my stay in the Evin infirmary was the doctor I mentioned earlier. He too, like Mohammed Kachoui, made a habit of visiting us almost every evening after he had finished his medical round. On these occasions he would tell us about life in other parts of the prison. By dint of his dynamism and his ability as an organizer, he had succeeded in gaining the goodwill of the procurator general and other officials in a remarkably short time. On the whole, doctors came to be appreciated by the Islamists well before other Western-educated professionals. Thus from the moment they arrived at the prison they were given a privileged status even if their offenses were quite serious as far as the Islamic Republic was concerned, and very few were ever executed.

The Prison as Microcosm

Having spent a total of nearly three years in Evin (if this and my later terms are added together), I can say with some confidence that the prison society included all the different elements which made up the Islamic Republic. From the start it was a point toward which all the disputes and competing forces converged, and it became a sociological microcosm accurately reflecting the realities of the revolution. Because of the important role played by doctors and nurses in the prison, I came to learn—through the medical staff's confidences—that the highest Islamic judges, who struck fear in the hearts of all the prisoners and who were considered to be "impervious" to all outside influences and "inflexible" in the performance of their duties, behaved with the same degree of vulnerability as ordinary mortals when it came to their own health and that of their families. The fact that they were not robots gave us hope that we might be able to move them on occasion after all.

During the initial three weeks of my detention I spent much of my time with the two men I had as neighbors in the adjoining rooms. They taught me a great deal about the circles from which they came: one had been a colonel in the imperial guard, and in the course of our conversations he helped me to understand the attitude of elite officers toward the regime and the dynasty; the second, a young man whose family was totally dedicated to the cause of the Mojahedin, was the archetype of the militants fiercely opposed to Khomeini's regime.

The colonel had been a member of the Immortals, a military unit responsible for the security of the Shah and his family. Listening to him, I realized the extent to which officers of this division had been kept apart not only from the country's political and social realities but from all that concerned the Shah himself. It very quickly became clear to me that as a result of their training the Immortals felt boundless devotion to the person of the Shah, whom they saw as superhuman and as a myth. But they were largely uninterested in and even contemptuous of the rest of the imperial family (including the queen). This idolization of a man they considered to be infallible drove them systematically to put the blame for all the regime's shortcomings, including corruption, on others. Later they were also to blame others for the fall of the Shah.

Although I was used to hearing—in a variety of circles, and especially in high society, which sought through such gossip to justify its own actions—about the greed and unprincipled behavior of the royal family and its entourage, I was still amazed to hear the colonel's ideas. Because of the things he and other officers I later met in prison said to me, I concluded that the loyalty of servants such as these would certainly have disintegrated had there been long, drawn-out confrontations between the regime and its opponents. It must surely be the case that if people do not have the same attachment to a system and to the values on which it is based as they do to the top man himself, their devotion will last as long as the regime is not under serious threat; but no sooner does it begin to waver than they will no longer be in a position to provide adequate support.

My other neighbor, the young Mojahed, was raised in a family deeply hostile to the Shah and wholly devoted to the opposition cause. Sa'id was twenty-one years old. His sister, Mahboubeh Mottahedeh, and her husband, Alad Push, had been killed in an armed clash with Savak. Keen to exploit as martyrs those of their fellow strugglers who had fallen in the battle against the powers that be, the Mojahedin had turned Mahboubeh into a national heroine. Thus it came about that under the Bazargan government the women-only university in Tehran, which had been called Farah under the monarchy, was renamed Mahboubeh. One can easily imagine the aura with which Mahboubeh's personality had been surrounded after her death and the hold it had exercised on her younger brother, who wished both to avenge his sister and to establish greater justice among men.

Sa'id's character was complex: on occasions I would enter his room to find him seated before *The Sayings of Imam Ali* (the Prophet's son-in-law and the "father" of Shi'ism), deeply absorbed in his reading. He used to say, "It's magnificent! This text really takes me far away, very far away." At other times I would catch him in the middle of his karate exercises and he would say, "A militant should always be in good physical shape and ready to confront the enemy."

Who was this invisible enemy? I suppose he described as such anyone who did not share his ideals and those of his organization. I could see how the poor child was torn between religious spirituality, which for him constituted the ultimate end, and an attraction to violence, which had to be perpetrated as a means to that end.

Soldiers of Marx and Mohammed

To understand the politics of the Mojahedin and their position in the revolutionary struggle, one has to go back to 1953. After the campaign against Mosaddeq, the Shah succeeded in eliminating his opponents and banned all political parties. The National Front, composed of the former prime minister's collaborators, consequently distanced itself from the dynasty and—at least in principle if not very effectively—denounced as "illegal" all the subsequent governments put in place by the Shah. They were unable, however, to instigate any mass political action.

The first prime minister of the revolution, Mehdi Bazargan, contributed more than anyone else to the formation within the National Front of a more active current, which bore the name "The Freedom Movement." With the help of the militant antimonarchist Ayatollah Taleghani, he gave the movement an Islamic orientation, making it different in this way from the National Front itself. But the younger generation, which had placed its hopes in the secular National Front or the more Islamic Freedom Movement of Iran, was frustrated after a decade or so of just waiting, and decided to choose more radical methods instead. Another group, the People's Fedayin, deeply disillusioned by the Tudeh party and the USSR but attracted to Marxism-Leninism in the style of Fidel Castro, Che Guevara, and Ho Chi Minh, established a guerrilla movement in the 1960s with the aim of overthrowing the monarchy. At about the same time the Mojahedin-e Khalq, the People's Mojahedin, was also set up, its inspiration coming from Islam.[5]

The Algerian revolution and the Palestine Liberation Organization (in its activist phase) served as models for the Mojahedin. Contrary to the Marxist People's Fedayin, who committed themselves to an armed struggle almost from the outset, the Mojahedin took some time before deciding on the same route. The two were alike, however, in the extent to which they distanced themselves from the country's political traditions; neither was prepared to follow anyone with experience, and they chose leaders whose ages did not exceed thirty.

The Mojahedin's doctrine rested on two pillars: on the philosophical level they swore entirely by Islam; on the level of practice they claimed allegiance to Marxism. They believed that by setting aside the philosophy of dialectical materialism they could base their revolu-

5. "Mojahed" is an Arabic term meaning fighter in a holy war or *jihad*.

tionary actions on Marxism. To them Marxism was a tool of analysis that allowed them to explain social, political, and economic phenomena and to understand and define an "egalitarian Islamic society." As far as Islam was concerned, they fell back on the abstraction of the original faith, disregarding fourteen centuries of theological debate, which left them with a Shi'i fundamentalism grafted onto a purely Stalinist Marxism-Leninism. The doctrinal and eschatological element of this strange but potent blend of two ideologies was taken from Islam, but the Mojahedin also followed Marxism as one might follow a religion.

The Mojahedin's political and military organization was modeled on the PLO, and they sent a number of their militants for ideological and military training to camps set up by Yassir Arafat's Fatah in Lebanon. The Mojahedin lost about a hundred of its activists in the urban guerrilla war against the Pahlavis, in the course of which "targeted" assaults were carried out, for example, against Americans working with the army's communications division. Although immediately after the revolution the Mojahedin enjoyed prestige accorded to revolutionary parties, their organization had in fact been destroyed under the Shah. Their methods had failed, and only a few activists, such as Massoud Rajavi (their leader after the revolution), remained in prison at the time of the revolution.

So when the leaders of the Islamic Republic—from Khomeini to Bazargan—expressed any sympathy for the Mojahedin, it was solely as a tribute to their past; for they had been completely out of the picture in the years 1977 and 1978. In those decisive years the initiative had been in the hands of Bazargan and his liberal allies in the front line, and in the rear with Khomeini and his followers. They were the ones who, relying on an extensive network of more than 100,000 religious activists, gradually increased the pressure in the course of 1978 by organizing lengthy strikes in the bazaars of big cities. Nevertheless, although the Mojahedin played only a small part in overthrowing the Shah, they remained convinced that they had been the true initiators of the revolution, and in that capacity they were always ready to judge others severely. They had no qualms about labeling Bazargan's liberal and Khomeini's religious followers as "soft conservatives, virtual accomplices of American imperialism," who were putting at risk the gains of the revolution.

That was their attitude and their circumstances in December 1979 when I found myself in Evin Prison, in the room next to Sa'id's.

Despite his youth Sa'id had already spent several years in prison and had attempted a number of escapes. It was almost as if he had deliberately chosen death as his ultimate aim. Determined to pursue his activism one way or the other after the victory of the Islamic revolution, he had put himself at the disposal of the movement for which his sister had fallen, fully prepared to become involved in difficult and even dangerous missions.

So Sa'id found himself assigned to the task of robbing a jewelry store in a well-to-do area of Tehran. If he failed and was arrested, he was to say that he had intended to sell his jewels and distribute the money among the poor workers in the south of the city. Armed with an automatic pistol, he had ordered the jeweler to open his safe. But the jeweler's staff, who were in the adjoining room, rang the alarm, and the amateur burglar, gripped by panic, was unable to use his weapon. Sa'id had rushed out of the shop and tried to flee. The jeweler had picked up the pistol and fired at Sa'id, hitting him in the foot. Arrested and sent to Evin—armed robbery fell under the jurisdiction of the revolutionary tribunal—Sa'id had ended up in the prison infirmary.

The boy, who had wanted so much to become a hero like his sister, had a number of reasons to be dispirited. Not only had his attempt at playing Robin Hood failed in its own right, it had also failed to trigger a more extensive movement to reclaim "illegitimately acquired property." As if this were not enough, he also had to contend with the fact that the Mojahedin condemned his initiative for the sake of maintaining its public image of legality; this had particularly hurt him. What he had taken to be an act of heroism was viewed by the revolutionary authorities as mere vandalism, and to make matters worse he was being forced to carry all the blame for the shameful deed in order to protect the organization's prestige.

Kachoui, the prison director, and the Evin judges knew well enough that Sa'id had only been following orders but that his instructions forbade him from admitting this. Be that as it may, they could not forgive either him or the Mojahedin for flouting the law of a newly established regime.

The prison director represented a group of Islamists who had fought the Shah's regime just as fiercely as the Mojahedin, but by peaceful means. The two groups belonged to quite different schools of political thought, whose disputes, ironically, dated back to their shared years in prison before the revolution.

The Islamists with whom Kachoui was involved were a small group of strict orthodox Muslims who were disciples of the exiled Khomeini. They belonged to the traditionalist section of the population, and to them the Mojahedin, with their Marxist-Leninist ideas, were no better than atheists. The Mojahedin, for their own part, considered themselves to be intellectually superior and held the Islamists in contempt. The two groups regularly engaged in a battle of words accusing each other of being "soft" toward the imperialist regime.

It is not too surprising, then, that the Islamists, who had just managed to remove the Mojahedin from the top posts in the Evin tribunal, were pleased to have in their clutches, barely a year after the revolution, someone like Sa'id, the son of a well-known Mojahedin family, charged with theft. They were obviously not about to relinquish easily such a case, behind which lay a whole history of Islamo-Mojahedin feuds.

These feuds between the Islamists and the Mojahedin were to weigh heavily on the course of events after the revolution. The first executions, the debates of a council of Islamic experts as they prepared the constitution, the hostage-taking at the U.S. embassy in 1979 and 1980, and the instability of economic life all arose partly as a result of this rivalry. This is why I found my conversation with Sa'id particularly revealing, because even though he was consciously aware of the ambivalent attitude of his leaders and their double-dealing, he did know what was being said at the highest levels of the organization. Publicly the leaders gave every impression of being keen to help Khomeini and Taleghani, but privately they were saying, "We should exploit them for our own ends and try to aggravate their differences." And in connection with the summary execution of the former regime's officials, Sa'id told me things which showed that without the influence of the Mojahedin the number of executions would not have been so high.[6]

6. For example, Sa'id told me that the "hanging judge," Ayatollah Khalkhali, was during the first months of his appointment to the revolutionary tribunal heavily influenced by the Mojahedin who prepared the prosecution files for many of the prisoners brought before him.

Well and Truly in Prison

Although the man at the airport had said that I would be sent to Evin to "answer a few questions," I had been in the infirmary for twenty days. Convinced that my detention would continue for some time, I asked Kachoui to give me "nonprivileged" status so that I could join the rest of the prisoners. He accepted my request, and I was transferred that same day to Section 3.

Section 3 was a two-story building looking onto a square court measuring twenty meters on each side. The rooms were situated along two sides of the court, and there were seven on each floor. The toilets, communal bathrooms, and showers were at the end of one of the corridors. There were twelve to fourteen people in each room, which measured six meters by six. Each prisoner had a mattress which he placed along the wall each morning to use as a backrest during the day. During mealtimes an oilcloth was spread out in the middle of the room and we ate "Iranian style," sitting around the cloth on the floor. The domestic chores—sweeping the synthetic floor covering twice a day, cleaning and laying the oilcloth (and on occasion preparing the salad), washing the dishes, making the tea—were carried out in turn by one inmate each twenty-four hours; he was known as "mayor of the day."

One person appointed by the prison director was responsible for each section. The person in charge in each room was chosen by its occupants. New arrivals were assigned to a room by the section head.

On my arrival the person responsible for my section declared, "I'm going to put you in a room full of politicians and intellectuals. They've laid a claim on you, and they've been waiting to see you since they heard that you were in the infirmary."

There I found a number of my old friends and one in particular whom I liked very much. Amin Riahi was a man of letters who never played any political role other than to serve as minister of education for thirty-seven days in the Bakhtiar government (1978–1979). Another occupant was the eminent jurist who had been the president of the Supreme Court under Hoveida. He was very worried about his ultimate fate; in view of the executions already carried out, he could not rule out the possibility he might be one of the next to go. Every detainee was allocated a specific area on which to spread his mattress, and I was given a place between these two friends. The prisoners used the twenty-five centimeters of space between one mattress and the next to put the boxes holding their personal belongings. Each person could also hang, on a nail located over his head, a nylon sack in which he could keep his clothing. It was possible to guess from the size of the sack how long an inmate had been in prison.

I was informed about our section's regulations right away. Members of our immediate family were allowed to visit us once a week for ten minutes. We were separated from them by a glass partition, and we spoke with the aid of intercoms. We were allowed to receive 200 tomans (the equivalent of £10 at the time) per week as well as a bag of fruit which our relatives had to buy at the prison itself. Our breakfast consisted of tea, bread, and cheese. We also had an electric hotplate on which we could make tea whenever we liked. We had access to a shop where we could buy sugar, eggs, sardines, biscuits, and dates. The food was edible and, at any rate, wholesome. In the mornings the prisoners did physical exercises in the courtyard or walked for two or three hours. The program was more or less the same in the afternoons, but we were also allowed to stay in our room to read the books our visitors had brought us.

There were about 160 prisoners in my section. Apart from high-ranking army officers and Savak officials, among us were ministers, senators, parliamentary deputies, and businessmen; in other words, all of imperial Tehran's fine society. In addition, since the Islamic Republic did not recognize the category of political prisoners, there were also a few common law offenders in our section, bringing a bit of diversity to a building that was otherwise very select.

Apart from a number of Savak officials and two or three Baha'is,[7] who were awaiting certain execution, the others were not on the whole threatened by the death sentence, because the great wave of executions which had reached its peak in 1979 had now abated.

During the first few months of the revolution, in the winter and spring of 1979, the revolutionary tribunals in Tehran and the provinces sentenced to death and executed about five hundred to six hundred people, including high-ranking officers, leading officials of

7. A syncretic religion founded in Iran in the nineteenth century which is not recognized by Islam; hence the persecution to which its members are subjected.

the police and Savak, and politicians. The survivors of these groups now in our prison had nearly all been arrested at the very beginning. Having watched their colleagues go to their death, they believed they had been spared and now hoped they would be released. In the meantime their main occupation was to help with the preparation of defense speeches for prisoners whose fate seemed more uncertain.

As for myself, bearing in mind what I had learned about my Savak file during the first detention, and in view of the fact that I had been taken to Evin's infirmary after my second arrest, I had reasons to believe that the authorities were not at all certain that they had good grounds for holding me. I was therefore convinced that not only did I not risk being executed but that I would soon be set free.

My trip to Europe and the publication of my book had been put back. But I had in return the opportunity to meet and talk to many men who had played important roles in the deposed regime. Of course I already knew many of my fellow prisoners, either directly or indirectly, but I had not been close enough to them to have spoken to them openly and frankly. Now, in the wake of the political upheaval, people who had formerly been reticent were more than willing to talk to someone whom they saw neither as an adversary nor as a rival but as a confidant.

Nearly all of them expressed amazement at the collapse of the throne because they had had great faith in a regime which had seemed, in Jimmy Carter's words, like "an island of stability in a turbulent sea."[8] They could not begin to understand how the Shah, who had had the support of practically all the world's great powers, could have been so easily and brutally overthrown; nor could they comprehend where the "handful of mullahs" who took power had come from. As far as they were concerned, the sudden overthrow of the regime and the emergence of an Islamic force could only be explained in terms of the activities of certain other countries; they were not prepared to accept that the revolution could have arisen out of a spontaneous movement within Iran.

8. "Iran under the leadership of the Shah is an island of stability in one of the most troubled areas of the world. This is a great tribute to you, Your Majesty, and to your leadership, and to the respect, admiration, and love which your people give you." President Carter, Tehran, December 31, 1977.

Two Opposing Mentalities

The trials of former officials accused of financial misdeeds or complicity with foreigners were so hasty and badly handled that they did not really serve to enlighten the Iranian people. The overblown charges carried no conviction. Every day there were fresh reports of political and financial scandals, though no substantial evidence was ever brought before the tribunals. And at the tribunals themselves, trustworthy witnesses and qualified experts were sadly lacking. The whole process was so absurd that the responsibility of the alleged offenders was totally obscured by the sham justice.

The haste of the revolutionary tribunal was a result of an unremitting battle between heterogeneous, not to say antagonistic, revolutionary forces which had nothing in common but their hatred for the Pahlavi regime. Incapable of recognizing the differences between their adversaries, the Pahlavis had always lumped them indiscriminately together, thus uniting the otherwise disparate forces. The moment the dynasty collapsed, these forces turned on one another, leading in two years to what was in effect a civil war new to Iran.

In the meantime my fellow prisoners were living in a state of complete uncertainty, not knowing which tendency their judge might belong to. One evening I was present when some of them were discussing the preparation of the case for the defense of a Savak officer accused of counterespionage. Throughout his career the duty of the accused had been to counteract Soviet penetration into Iran, and he had to his credit exploits which from a patriotic point of view were perfectly justifiable.

In order to persuade the judge-mullah of the merits of his service to the nation, he had prepared a very convincing plea, of which everyone approved. All of a sudden one of the prisoners reported that the deputy prosecutor was an implacable pro-Soviet communist and exclaimed, "If he hears you talking like this he'll insist on a death sentence, and he's influential enough to destroy any good opinion the mullahs may have of you." It was therefore agreed by everyone present that the Savaki should not speak about his past.

This is just one example of the sense of confusion that prevailed among the prisoners faced by a politically ambivalent tribunal. This confusion was compounded by the fact that, in view of their total unfamiliarity with Islam's ethical and legal rules and values, the defendants were entirely out of their depth before the Islamic judges. Often extremely "Westernized" in their life-styles, they had practically no knowledge of Muslim law and usage. They were usually amazed to learn that in Koranic law there is no separation between the private and public life, between economic offenses and political ones—in a word, between ethics and law. So when they were arrested on political or economic charges and when the tribunal subsequently found their pleas convincing, they could not understand why the simple discovery of a case of whisky in their houses led to further charges.

I tried to explain to them that according to Islamic law the notion of responsibility is indivisible and that legality arose from a conception at once moral and juridical. The relations between a man and his wife, in just the same way as his relation to his property, must have overall legitimacy, because for Muslims they are both equally based on an all-encompassing outlook. I tried at the same time to explain to the judges that this "integral" viewpoint was unrealistic. I would say to them, for example: "When a highly placed professional maintained his honesty throughout his career, regardless of the opportunities for personal enrichment presented to him, it's clear that he obeyed his conscience and in his own light protected the interests of the country. Therefore, even if a photograph shows him bowing before Farah and kissing her hand at a reception where champagne is flowing, you should exercise some lenience."

Another discovery made by these high-society prisoners was that in a system which was otherwise extremely male-oriented, their wives could play a helpful role in the outcome of their cases. Paradoxical though it may seem, there was a simple reason for this. The Islamic tribunals did not recognize the right of the accused to be represented by a lawyer, so they were forced to fall back on the relatives who visited them once a week. The judges tended to be more favorably disposed toward wives or mothers, because in the cases in question the weaker sex seemed to them to be less suspect. Added to this was the fact that despite their own unfamiliarity with Islamic law, women had maintained one advantage in a secularized society which had drifted away from its religious roots: even in high society they had remained through grandparents, servants, shopkeepers, and so on in daily contact with tradition, whereas their husbands lived wholly Western life-styles in their self-contained technocratic and cosmopolitan environments. It was also not unheard of for wives to flout all the regulations forbidding outside contact with the revolutionary tribunal and to get in touch, if only by phone, with the judges dealing with their husbands' cases. Once contact had been established, they knew how to speak a language comprehensible to the mullahs. In brief, they were more convincing than their husbands. Unfortunately for them, many of my companions had sent their wives and children abroad a year or so earlier, particularly to Europe and the United States.

Economic Detainees

Besides officials of the ancien régime there were prisoners in Evin who had been arrested because of their fortunes; they were called "economic detainees." The tribunal was empowered to confiscate that part of their property which was considered to have been gained through "their collaboration with the cursed Pahlavi regime." They were therefore expected to draw up an inventory of their fortune inside and outside the country. At first the judges were mostly interested in the valuations of property held within the country, but after a few months they realized that the lion's share of Iranian high society's fortunes had been invested in property on the Côte d'Azur or in Paris, London, or California, or, quite simply safely deposited in a Swiss bank account.

The judges, that is to say, the mullahs, who had studied in religious schools, often in the provinces, had never before come into contact with this newly rich class which had risen some twenty years earlier, and they had no clear idea about the possible size of their exported capital. In any case, since these fortunes had been amassed through questionable means, even experts would have had difficulty evaluating them. The mullahs knew at best that such and such a prisoner was a "big fish," but they had no substantiating evidence.

In the end the tribunal succeeded in recovering only a tiny fraction of the money the elite had sent abroad. During their cross-examination, economic detainees knew they could conceal their holdings abroad, since there were no official documents that could give them away. The Swiss banks which offer numbered accounts and safety deposit boxes, where all documents and correspondence relating to the accounts could be kept, guaranteed absolute confidentiality. Furthermore, the more money a prisoner had abroad, the more he would be inclined to declare his holdings in Iran and even to make a gift of them to the Islamic Republic in exchange for his freedom. Indeed, I knew people who, as soon as they were arrested, supplied impressive lists of their assets and declared themselves ready to surrender everything, while swearing at the same time that they had nothing abroad. Their cases were settled in record time by judges who treated them with great civility, and a year or two after their release they would receive a kind of financial discharge which enabled them to obtain a passport. They can be found today living in luxurious apartments in London, Paris, Geneva, or Los Angeles.

On occasion the judges imagined that by holding a detainee for a long time they would manage to uncover some new evidence. But this was a somewhat forlorn hope. Personally I know of only one case where a detainee was forced to repatriate several hundred thousand pounds sterling from the United Kingdom, and in this instance the judge was helped by the tireless efforts of the man's first wife, determined to wreak vengeance on him and his new wife. In the end she forced him to remain in prison for eighteen months. I heard later that after his release they were reconciled and that she came to accept the status of second wife and remarried her ex-husband. . . .

One of the men I became acquainted with at Evin was Houshang Ram, director of the Omran, the Shah's private bank, established in 1960. In the course of many walks in the courtyard he provided me with interesting information about the flight of capital abroad. According to him, transfers of capital increased considerably from 1974 onward when, under a liberal banking regime, they were authorized by the Central Bank. But it was in the Islamic Republic's first year that they reached their peak, despite the restrictions imposed by the government. During this period the abundance of disposable capital, the dramatic drop in investment, and the uncertainty resulting from the sensational announcements being made in some Islamist and left-wing radical circles suggesting an imminent nationalization of the economy and the transfer of all foreign trade to state control, gave rise to a large-scale emigration of people (especially skilled technicians) and of capital.

While this massive transfer, of the order of several million pounds sterling per month, was going on under the very noses of the "excellent judges" of Evin's revolutionary tribunal, they were engaged in their tortuous efforts to ensure the return to the country of a bit of foreign currency—with scarcely any effect other than the aggravation of the flight psychosis.

At Evin the economists and accountants who served as expert witnesses on the revolutionary tribunal had created their own economic section. The Islamic judges kept away from it at first because of their unfamiliarity with the ins and outs of a modern economy. Here again one found examples of that same category of stand-in deputy prosecutor who, with their Marxist tendencies and ambiguous political identities, were pursuing their own objectives. They felt no loyalty either toward the religious judges of the Islamic Republic or to the Bazargan government which was following the same liberal economic policies as the monarchy. They seemed to be in no hurry whatsoever to set back in motion an economy paralyzed for months by strikes in the course of the revolution. They too played a role in encouraging the flight of people and capital.

Under the Shah private banks had had an extremely liberal credit policy, allowing entrepreneurs to carry on their business thanks to loans whose value far exceeded their entire assets. One of the first decisions of the revolutionary government had been to nationalize the banks. During this period the economic section of the revolutionary tribunal was arresting industrialists and demanding that they settle their debts with the nationalized banks. Since industrial plants had been lying idle for the preceding two years and all transactions had been suspended, their detention at Evin had no other effect but to increase their debts and to delay the resumption of work at their factories. It was only several years later that the Islamic judges realized that they had been manipulated by the deputy prosecutors who had completely different objectives. Having behaved like the man who kills the goose that lays the golden egg, they decided to make do without the assistance of the so-called specialists and to take matters into their own hands with the aim not of repressing but of encouraging businessmen to restart their businesses. It was, alas, too late!

Another question with which we were all preoccupied—and which was of an immediate topicality because it had been one of the reasons behind the occupation of the U.S. embassy by students—was that of the Shah's fortune abroad. I spoke with many experts about this, including Houshang Ram, and I have concluded that the Pahlavi family's fortune was of the order of £500 million or £600 million. The Shah himself did not own the largest share; this position belonged first to Ashraf and her son Sharam, and to Fatemeh, the sovereign's younger sister, whose husband had been commander of the air force.

Ram maintained that the Shah himself had been neither as greedy nor as eager to accumulate wealth as his family. On those occasions when he stepped in to override regulations, he often did so as a favor to someone else, whereas Princess Ashraf and the other members of the family were completely preoccupied with their own interests.

An Iranian Oufkir

Another subject about which I learned much in prison was the inner workings of Savak, especially its most secret aspects. I spent a great deal of time speaking to the functionaries of that "organization" which had remained shrouded in mystery, not only for me but for many officials of the deposed regime.

Responsible for intelligence and the security of the country, Savak was established by the Shah in 1957 with technical assistance from the Americans and logistic support from the Israeli intelligence service, Mossad. Its director, who held the title of minister of state, fell on paper under the authority of the prime minister. In reality he was appointed directly by the Shah and was answerable only to him.

Savak had four operational departments and four departments for logistic support. The responsibilities of the operational departments were divided into foreign intelligence, internal security (the most terrifying branch), the analysis of intelligence gathered abroad, and counterintelligence.

The first Savak director was General Teymour Bakhtiar, who was from the line of the tribal Bakhtiari chiefs. Although he was a cousin of Soraya, the Queen of Iran at the time, the main reason for his appointment had not been this family connection but his past record. As a junior officer Bakhtiar had organized a network of partisans in the mountainous regions of Azerbaijan with the aim of fighting the short-lived democratic republic put in place by the Red Army in 1945. After the fall of Mosaddeq in 1953 he was appointed military governor of Tehran, and in that capacity he carried out a ruthless suppression of people refusing to submit to the Shah's regime—above all members of the communist Tudeh party but also supporters of Mosaddeq. In the course of three years of terror he managed to dismantle all the channels of resistance to imperial policies and thus became a bulwark of the regime. Once installed as head of Savak, he did not change his methods and oriented the organization toward political intelligence. Surrounding himself with old hands, officers who had gained their experience on the job, he created a powerful security force which was omnipresent throughout the country. Through his henchmen he also initiated a system which invited members of the Tudeh party, once their resistance was broken, to collaborate with the regime. Some of the army's intelligence officers were also transferred to Savak, but it was principally through this method—adopted from the start—of installing his own men in key positions that he set about turning the force into a state within a state and an instrument of personal power. Once his agents had been implanted everywhere, he developed an ambition to become master of the country, gradually reducing the Shah to a figurehead. But the Shah was quick to spot these ambitions, and Bakhtiar was dismissed in 1961 and sent abroad where he became an open opponent of the regime. Very confident about his intelligence network within the country and thoroughly familiar with the monarch and his weaknesses, Teymour Bakhtiar went so far as to hatch a plot to assassinate the Shah in the course of an official visit to Berlin. In the end the Shah got the better of him and had him assassinated in 1971 in Iraq, at the hands of Savak itself. The story of Bakhtiar has often been likened to General Oufkir of Morocco, eliminated by King Hassan II, whom he had served loyally for many years.

A General Unlike Any Other

After Bakhtiar, the head of Savak was Hassan Pakravan. A highly cultured man who was well versed in international life, in many ways he could not have been more different from his predecessor. His father was a diplomat and his mother, Ameneh Pakravan, was a talented French-speaking Iranian writer. His family's position had given him the opportunity to acquire a good education in Europe during his youth.

While his father was posted in Egypt, Pakravan was a pupil of the French lycée in Alexandria. Afterward he studied engineering and eventually ended up at the French military schools in Poitiers and Fontainebleau. Back in Iran he joined the army, where he spent many years as a gifted instructor at the officers' school before becoming Iran's military attaché in Pakistan.

At the time of Mosaddeq, Pakravan was the head of the army's intelligence service. As he saw relations between Mosaddeq and the Shah deteriorate, he chose to remain on the sidelines and used a military mission as an excuse to go to France in early 1953. He was later to explain this period in his life to me as follows: "As an officer I had sworn an oath of loyalty to the Shah, and I also believed that we had to respect our constitutional monarchy. Nonetheless, as a patriot I could not bring myself to join in the conspiracies which the officers in the Shah's entourage were hatching endlessly against Mosaddeq. I preferred therefore to withdraw from the scene and to leave Tehran."

Pakravan's appointment as head of Savak in 1961 came as a big surprise, because he seemed a refined and tolerant man who did not exactly fit the frightening image the people had of the secret police. At the same time everyone knew that the Shah was trying to win the approval of John F. Kennedy, who had just arrived in the White House and was demanding a degree of liberalization in the so-called "allied" countries.

Pakravan tried to curtail Savak's repressive methods; he did not think twice, for example, about leaving his office door open to the regime's opponents or the intellectuals whom the Shah could not tolerate. It was he who in 1964 managed to arrange Khomeini's exile to Turkey—and later to Iraq—instead of trying to imprison him in Iran. I myself came to know Pakravan well, and I can attest that he always responded favorably whenever I turned to him on behalf of any intellectual friends or any student in trouble with Savak.

This was notably the case when I interceded on behalf of the president-to-be, Bani-Sadr, and Hassan Habibi, the current vice-president of the Islamic Republic. At the time they were both young researchers at the Institute which I headed, and I had obtained scholarships for them from the French government. But because they were Mosaddeq sympathizers, Savak refused to grant them passports. So I went to see Pakravan, who declared, "Don't worry, they'll be allowed to leave!"

Bani-Sadr's case was the more difficult of the two, and I described to Pakravan the harassment to which he was being subjected by low-ranking Savak officials. The general replied: "You can rest assured that he'll leave within forty-eight hours. But tell me—judging by what I know of French university life—don't you think foreign students may remain there for years without finishing their studies? Have you heard about the possibility?"

I said by way of answer, "I've spoken to my friend Georges Balandier, who's a professor at the Sorbonne, and he told me that he would personally supervise Bani-Sadr's Ph.D. thesis in sociology."

Pakravan contented himself with saying—and I've never forgotten his words—"When you mentioned the problem to me, I asked my staff, 'What's so special about Bani-Sadr?' They said his name was on the list of people whom the military tribunal deemed should not be allowed to leave Tehran unless they were granted permission specifically by the Shah. So I presented his case to His Majesty with the suggestion that it was preferable to let opponents become well educated rather than remain narrow-minded and ignorant."

But Pakravan's tolerant disposition was in many ways not to the Shah's taste. It is therefore not very surprising that the sovereign did not accept his program to reform Savak.[9]

When things settled down a bit on the American side (for after Kennedy's assassination the Shah had no problems with Johnson), the Shah got rid of Pakravan, using as an excuse Prime Minister Mansour's assassination, which in his eyes was a sign of insufficient vigilance on the part of the secret police. To replace him, he appointed General Nassiri, the former commander of his guard, who possessed neither the refinement nor the learning of his predecessor. As to myself, the

9. Pakravan had, for example, asked for advice from Jean Stoetzel and the French Public Opinion Institute with a view to establishing a small public opinion study group, independent of Savak. A few years later he confided in me that he had wanted to accustom the Shah to such surveys, even if the results were never published.

new head of Savak reproached me for having gathered together, in order to create my research institute, all the Shah's opponents. I sensed that the vise was tightening around me, and in 1969 I seized the opportunity offered me by René Maheu, director general of UNESCO, to work alongside him as director of the youth division.

Some time later Pakravan was appointed Iran's ambassador to Paris. I used to see him now and then. Our relations were frank and trusting, without there being any need to stand on ceremony. One day I said to him, "I don't understand the Shah. Why did he deprive himself of your services? You could have been an excellent political adviser for him."

He replied, "In the first place, the Shah doesn't want advisers. He only wants people who carry out his orders. Second, we didn't have the same idea of an intelligence service. Quite often when he asked me to prepare a report about a certain person or situation, I'd tell him that I'd look into it and submit a report as soon as possible. But when I eventually presented it to him, I had the impression that the report never matched his expectations. What he really wanted to see were arguments in support of a decision he had taken about a prime minister, ambassador, or member of his own family, or an indication that the director of Savak could read between the lines and know what the Shah wanted without having to be told. So I know why Nassiri makes a point of only presenting the Shah with those reports whose tone and content he knows will meet with his approval. You'll see that he'll remain in his post as long as the Shah does not feel compelled by exterior forces to replace him."

And that in fact was to be the case.

Whenever I asked my Savak co-detainees, "Why didn't you inform the Shah about the extent of financial corruption among officials and many members of the imperial family, when you knew very well what was happening?" they would reply, "Nassiri repeatedly told us that he could not present any report to His Majesty which he had not expressly asked for."

The "People's Dissatisfaction" Bureau

In the course of my conversations with these former agents I learned that there had existed, within Savak's department of internal security, a section known as "the people's dissatisfaction bureau." The former head of this bureau and I were in the same section in Evin, and I had the chance to speak to him on a number of occasions. He had a law degree but had never been involved in arrests, interrogations, or other operations of that nature. He told me that he and his associates had carried out investigations into such issues as the rising cost of living, inflation, and the scarcity of certain foodstuffs, problems that were often deliberately exacerbated by speculators. He also told me of the extensive studies they had conducted into the housing problem. In the years before the revolution this was a frustrating, near impossible task. The more progress the investigator made, the more likely he was to come up against "big shots" who were totally protected. They were the ones who had to be tackled, but without the Shah's support the administration was impotent. The reports prepared by the investigators always had to be vetted by Nassiri.

The same Savak bureau chief also told me: "One day Nassiri called me into his office. He was very friendly at first. Then he said, 'While very much appreciating your research efforts, I must tell you that His Majesty doesn't like it at all when I submit reports to him on topics he has not asked me about. So what use are your reports when I don't know what to do with them and when they're the source of embarrassment? What I'm trying to say is, why prepare documents which I'm obliged to bring to His Majesty's attention when I know that he's not the least bit interested in them? So let me advise you: carry on with your studies. Always be prepared, but if I haven't asked you, don't send me your reports.'"

The moral of this story is that the Shah did not wish to be kept informed of his intelligence service, at least not about such decisive matters as public opinion. I was able to confirm this on other occasions. In the course of one of my cross-examination sessions, the Islamic judge, who had a thick folder before him—my Savak file together with a fairly critical report from 1968 on the Institute of Social Research—showed me the comment the Shah had made: "Why do reports of this institute focus on our weak points instead of highlighting our great achievements?" He displayed, in other words, some irritation and amazement in response to the reports of a scholarly organization as he did to those of his own intelligence services.

In short, the Shah was a typical example of a leader who becomes incapable of tolerating open criticism in the press or in Parliament, and simply sinks into a megalomania that cannot cope with negative remarks, no matter how trivial, even in the form of confidential reports prepared by his own intelligence-gathering agencies.

Some intelligence specialists, such as Alexandre de Marenches in a book published in 1986,[10] have argued that the blame for the Shah's fall lies with his intelligence services. But in the light of everything I learned in my conversations with the Shah and later in prison, it is clear that such an analysis is principally a product of a misunderstanding essential to the nature and inner workings of the Pahlavi regime.

To assume that intelligence services are purely mechanical and interchangeable units, which can function in any sociopolitical circumstance, is to overlook two factors: one, the sociological context of regimes under which liberty is kept on a tight rein and in which intelligence agents are subjected to the same processes of terror and self-censorship as all other citizens; and two, the behavior of an autocratic ruler who, through a convoluted process of deception and self-deception, ends up molding, over a period of years, an intelligence service that does nothing but flatter his fantasies.

Everything points to the fact that no autocrat can tolerate for long an intelligence apparatus which tells him the truth. In his hands the most efficient police force in the world becomes a useless instrument—useless, that is, for him as well as for everyone else. There are those who have suggested that things would have turned out better—in the Shah's Iran and in Saddam Hussein's Iraq—if the heads of the intelligence services had been more courageous men. They maintain that if this had been the case, the Shah would not have fallen and Saddam Hussein would not have attacked Iran and Kuwait. But such theses fail to take into account the particular conditions in which secret services operate in authoritarian regimes.

A functionary's courage is a human quality which his superiors must constantly try to nurture; he in turn must be able to generate this quality in his colleagues by example. This is hardly possible in a system based on personal power. In other words, if an intelligence service is to function properly, it is not enough simply to grant it

10. *Dans le secret des princes*, which he wrote with Christine Ockrent, 1986.

purely formal authority to reveal the truth; it must in addition be actively encouraged to seek it out, even if the information it is instructed to gather is destined for only one man. In a regime in which every man in office owes his position to his ability to circumvent rules and regulations and to conceal embarrassing facts, it is difficult to see how an intelligence service and its head can be expected to dedicate themselves to the truth without incurring the wrath of the autocrat in power.

One other example will help to show that the Shah did not really wish to know how the country was being run. Overstepping his prerogatives, in 1958 the Shah established an Imperial Inspectorate which was answerable only to him. The organization was made up of former ministry officials who were often selected from among the most competent and honest civil servants. It had the task of bringing to an end the negligence and corruption rampant at every level of state. Despite its extensive investigations into various issues, it failed to improve the Pahlavis' method of management and administration.

Abdollah Entezam, a one-time minister of foreign affairs, had known the Shah since 1936, when the future king was a student at the College de Rosay in Switzerland. A long-standing diplomat in the League of Nations in Geneva, Entezam had been a close friend of the Shah for many years. He confided to me that the Shah had often told him that he would have liked Savak to become an organization like the British intelligence service. In Entezam's opinion this admiration could be attributed to two factors: one, the Shah had grown up at a time when Britain's power in the world was uncontested and the quality of its intelligence service universally acknowledged; two, the Shah always kept in mind that the 1953 Anglo-American coup against Mosaddeq had been a product of collaboration between the CIA and British intelligence, although he himself had at first not believed that the operation could succeed. According to foreign journalists, on August 19, 1953, while the Shah was having lunch with Soraya in the dining room of the Hotel Excelsior in Rome, he was brought agency dispatches which he kept reading and rereading, holding them in his trembling hands, trying to establish for certain that he could return to Iran. In reality he admired and feared the Anglo-American services at one and the same time.

According to Entezam, later, when he was on an official visit to

Great Britain, the Shah was asked by British protocol if he wished any changes to his schedule. He replied that he would like to see the intelligence service archives in Sussex. Although surprised by this request, his hosts granted it and organized the trip with the utmost secrecy. There they showed him the classification system and information contained on countries, events, and politicians contained in the archives. The imperial guest then asked to see his own file as well as that of his father. No one knows exactly how much he was allowed to see of his own file; what is known, however, is that he spent a long time looking at his father's, and he was able to see, in the reports of successive intelligence agents, that they had had him in their sights since the time he was serving as a captain in the Cossack division—in other words, long before he became General Reza Khan. The Shah retained a terrifying image of that visit to Sussex. It reinforced his apprehensions about British policy as well as his admiration for the British intelligence service. But it should be said that as far as the intelligence service is concerned, the Shah totally overlooked the fact that it is an organization that is quite distinct from the police; that is to say, it is a service whose agents take scrupulous care to avoid the use of force as much as possible. Savak, on the other hand, operated under conditions in which its agents were constantly tempted to resort to force to extract information.

Moreover, the British intelligence service operates in a political and juridical system in which the Parliament, the press, and the judiciary have every right to criticize it when they believe it has overstepped its powers, something which inevitably makes it exercise great prudence.

It should finally be noted that despite their historical renown, the British intelligence service and the CIA, which were regarded as infallible in the 1950s and 1960s, proved incapable of foretelling a number of decisive events.

Underinformed or Overinformed?

In my conversation with former officers I also learned that in addition to the reports from Savak the Shah received briefings from the intelligence services of the army's land, air, and naval forces as well as from the gendarmerie's intelligence department. The police, for its part, submitted reports to him on the activities of political groups in bazaars, universities, and working-class areas. Next it was the turn of the radio/television organization to send him political briefs every day. The minister of information too prepared bulletins known as "untransmitted news" for the benefit of the sovereign and a few high-ranking officials. These contained facts and comments about Iran reported in foreign media but prevented by the censors from publication in Iran itself.

While pursuing my studies after the Islamic revolution, I would occasionally consult the archives of the Ministry of Information, and there I stumbled upon the last series of these bulletins, which immediately before the overthrow of the Shah had become extremely thick (fifty to sixty pages).

In other words, the Shah would receive an average twenty political reports each day, three-quarters of which were prepared specifically for him. Such reports were brimming with details—in which the Shah took particular delight—relating to every sphere, including the private. It could not therefore be said that he was underinformed; he may even have been overinformed in some ways. But, excessively sure of himself, he felt no need to discuss or to analyze this information with anyone else.

Even this flood of information could not provide him an overall picture, because he himself selected specific and partial areas for investigation. As long as the country was not in a state of crisis, access to this information gave the Shah an edge over his entourage and made him seem the true master of the situation. At first hint of crisis, however, this apparent advantage rapidly turned into a handicap. The real facts about what was happening in the kingdom were not reflected in the reports which, as the crisis set in, became increasingly irrelevant.

The Shah lacked a complete picture because he preferred to feed his own fantasies rather than mend his ways. I can cite an example of this: About two years before the revolution, when I had just returned from a trip in Europe, I said to Hoveida, then the prime minister, that I increasingly sensed the existence of two separate images of Iran: one was the official Iran, prosperous, making progress at a staggering rate, a place where everything was perfect; the other was the Iran of discontent, which was particularly pervasive outside the country. This view depicted Iran as an underdeveloped country where an exploited nation lived totally gagged and muzzled by Savak. The media and intellectuals in the West were increasingly convinced of the accuracy of the second image. More worrisome still, the 200,000 Iranian students abroad, who should soon be returning to run the country, were also falling under the influence of this negative image. We were, in other words, in a dangerously unstable situation, and it was absolutely imperative to overcome this national schizophrenia.

Hoveida asked me what I proposed to do. I said, "There are research institutes which study this kind of problem. We could turn to them for assistance on the condition that we give them a completely free hand to carry out their work."

The prime minister replied, "That's an excellent idea! I'd like to start consultations right away to find the best communications center and to get the studies under way as soon as possible."

Then and there he telephoned Reza Ghotbi, the director of radio and television, and asked him to cooperate with me and to deal with all the expenses. Two months later, in Paris, I went to see Michael Bongrand, who was one of France's leading communications specialists, to discuss the practical details of carrying out the appropriate research.

Bongrand immediately set up a team of experts to investigate, as objectively as possible, the internal and external reasons for Iran's negative image. Reza Ghotbi and I provided them with all the facilities they needed, and we organized as many meetings as possible between them and Iranian specialists. They traveled extensively throughout the kingdom and submitted a report to us in the spring of 1978. It is true that by then Hoveida was no longer prime minister, but he was court minister nonetheless. The Shahbanou had been aware of the study and had taken a keen interest. The fact remained, however, that no one dared to put the report before the Shah, quite simply because its conclusions did not accord with his views about the way things stood in Iran.[11]

It is therefore not surprising that, according to accounts of the two

11. The report's conclusions include the following passages: "We have come to realize that the fantastic rise in Iran's revenue in 1973 destabilized its growth process and multiplied its problems. It is impossible to move with impunity from the carving of ivory miniatures to the acceleration of particles."

or three meetings he held toward the end of his reign with top military and civilian officials, the Shah was completely disoriented and unable either to direct the discussions or to draw any conclusions from them.

When the crisis surfaced, the Shah's entourage and all of high society were eager to absolve themselves of responsibility and to shift the blame onto foreigners or Savak. This was particularly absurd where Savak was concerned, because its fate was so closely tied to that of the throne that it could not betray the Shah. What is true, however, is that Savak literally fell apart, both on the theoretical level and organizationally. At Evin my companions informed me that when the Americans helped set up Savak in 1956–1957, they established three fundamental principles: the Iranian regime was threatened by communist ideas; communist propaganda was disseminated by an organization; danger always penetrated into a country from without.

"In other words," they used to say to me, "all our attention and all our expertise were focused on these three elements. Now, contrast this to the facts that the Islamic movement was totally domestic in origin, propagated its ideas through traditional mechanisms, and had no need for an organization. . . ."

They also told me that they took part regularly in the conferences of top American and European intelligence experts and specialists in political agitation, and that at no time were they warned about the possible threat posed to the throne by Islamists. "All our reflexes, all our activities," a former Savak officer said repeatedly, "were directed for twenty years toward the same point: the red peril." Western experts—including Israelis who, it should be said, were in constant contact with Islamists—never mentioned that religion could be a revolutionary force.

Official Savak functionaries, who numbered about five thousand,

---

"The shock is enormous. It is traumatizing the elderly, creating upheaval in families, shaking institutions, calling hierarchies into question, overturning taboos. . . ."

"Be it a crisis of identity, a moral crisis, or a crisis of faith, in Iran all symptoms are there, and despite all these difficulties it is from now on that the regime should consolidate its power by granting new liberties. . . . There exists, in effect, a kind of 'censorship by assumption' which consists of prohibiting information which it is thought may displease the Shah. This type of unformulated principle can lead to the worst kinds of abuse."

relied on the service of about 100,000 paid and unpaid informers who were known as "sources." Taking into account the fact that these officials were allowed to associate with only a limited number of people, including their close relatives, they were all the more isolated from the people because their terrifying reputation turned them into the most-avoided people in any neighborhood, mistrusted even by their own family.

My informants explained to me that their closest relatives, even their parents, refrained from saying anything remotely political in the presence of Savak agents. This isolation meant that Savak officers were increasingly dependent on informers. But from the summer of 1978 when the country sank into a state of crisis, the informers began to distance themselves from Savak officials. Rendered ineffective in this way, Savak was virtually out of the game well before the Shah left the country. . . . At the beginning of 1978 Nassiri, Savak's director for the preceding thirteen years, was removed from his post by the Shah and appointed ambassador to Pakistan. A few months later, when the Shah recalled Nassiri and had him arrested in the hope of mollifying public opinion, many functionaries of the political police felt they had been abandoned by the monarch.

The reason for the change was clear to everyone. Since Jimmy Carter's arrival in the White House in January 1977, the Democratic administration had been expecting to see tangible signs of liberalization in Iran, and the Shah, who knew that Savak was the main target of the opposition, was simply trying to demonstrate his good intentions to the Americans.

In the field of intelligence and counterintelligence Savak did in fact provide important services to the state and its foreign policy. Thanks to the assistance of American, British, and Israeli experts it gathered not just military but also political and economic intelligence. The main targets of these activities were communist states and the Middle Eastern countries which surrounded Iran. Perhaps the area in which the Shah reaped the greatest benefit from these activities was with OPEC. He maintained personal control over Iran's policies within OPEC, and he was able to operate from a position of strength because of the high quality information he received from Savak agents about the oil policies of the Arab countries, particularly those of the Persian Gulf. Savak also established such an effective network in Afghanistan that it succeeded in predicting the Soviet invasion of that country thirteen months before the event—though its intelligence was ignored by the CIA.

Chinese Tea

My fellow prisoners told me that in the ruthless war between intelligence services the KGB was always Savak's main adversary, frequently thwarting its activities. Savak, for its part, tried to make up for lost ground in the Soviet satellite countries. According to my cellmates, diplomats from Eastern Europe posted in Iran systematically received counterintelligence training before leaving for Tehran. Savak agents assigned to keep an eye on them found evidence of this from following their movements, or as a result of searching their homes, or while listening to their conversations by means of microphones secreted in their rooms.

Some of the stories they told me were quite instructive. For example, when the first embassy of the People's Republic of China opened in Tehran, Savak discovered, by tapping their telephones, that the Chinese diplomats had received a list from Peking of Iranians they should contact. So even before the diplomats made a move of any kind, Savak had easily identified the Iranians they would be seeking to talk with. They also found out that the people concerned were all descendants, two or three generations removed, of Chinese tea cultivators whom local entrepreneurs had brought to Iran at the beginning of the century to introduce tea cultivation there. The Chinese intelligence services were apparently hoping that blood ties would prove sufficiently strong to induce these people to become their agents.

All this indicates the eagerness with which foreign intelligence services operated as well as the range of their activities. It should nevertheless be emphasized that agents from communist countries did not on the whole take much interest in the political activities of Iranian organizations; they were mainly after economic, technical, and military information. This was especially the case from 1972 onward, when President Nixon decided that Iran could purchase the most sophisticated American weaponry without any restrictions. Western services in Iran, on the other hand, the most pervasive of which was the British, were above all interested in the commercial contracts between Iranians and foreign companies, and they basically tried to help their own industrial firms.

When it came to evaluating the efficiency of the different intelligence services, Savak agents put the KGB at the top. Next, in descending order of efficiency, came the British, followed by Israel's Mossad, and finally the CIA—even though the CIA was closely linked to Savak's own activities. From 1972, the year in which Irano-American relations were set fair, the Shah had made it clear to the Americans that as far as Iranian political life was concerned, especially with regard to the undercover activities of left-wing extremist groups allied with the Soviet Union or otherwise, they could count on Savak. Nixon assured the Shah, in return, that the CIA had stopped recruiting agents in Iran. This gave enormous satisfaction to the monarch: his subjects (army personnel in particular) no longer risked being recruited as "spies for a foreign power," albeit Iran's closest ally.

The ex-Savak agents never tired of telling us stories about their exploits in dealing with the different foreign intelligence services. They said that during one period there were more than ten thousand Soviet citizens in Iran, working, for example, in Isfahan's steel complex, in silos, dam construction, or in a very well-known hospital run entirely by them. Added to this were many experts from other Eastern European countries. The Savakis took great pride in the fact that Western intelligence officers, who had been their instructors during the early years of Savak's existence, often came to them for information which they could not obtain anywhere else.

As I listened to them I came to know a type of character which until then had been entirely unknown to me. I realized that in their stories imagination played as large a part as reality. They reminded me of the amateur pigeon hunters in the countryside who used to tell us tales when, as a child, I spent summers in the mountains with my family. In their yarns, truth and fantasy were indistinguishable. The hunter who after hours of walking had not shot a single pigeon could easily recount, by the evening light of the village square, how he had shot fifty. And in a way he would not really be lying, because there may even have been a wonderful day in the past when he *had* killed fifty. There was an element of exaggeration, of course, but I chose to view it merely as a natural extension of their adventure.

In the case of many intelligence agents I rediscovered this tendency to give the imagination a free rein. They would view every political and military phenomenon from the intelligence angle, trying to find mysterious explanations for events which seemed perfectly straightforward to everyone else. Even when the case involved friends or allies, the idea of a conspiracy always lurked in the backs of their minds.

An Enigmatic Figure

An important personality from the former regime who was to turn into something of an enigma was General Fardoust. According to my fellow prisoners, Fardoust had worked energetically in Savak, particularly in its counterintelligence department. He was a former classmate and close friend of the Shah and for many years deputy director general of Savak. He continued to work with intelligence even after he had left his post. I was told that during one of his visits to the United Kingdom, the Shah had asked Queen Elizabeth what she did with the various briefing reports she received. The queen had replied that a section in her secretariat dealt specifically with such documents, and she was given a synopsis of them every day. Having decided to adopt the same system, the Shah established a special bureau, at the head of which he placed General Fardoust.[12]

From 1973 onward, however, this bureau lost much of its importance because, as I noted earlier, the Shah preferred to receive information direct from the relevant intelligence department; the business of coordinating and summarizing information was therefore somewhat redundant. Nevertheless, in the last years of his reign the Shah appointed General Fardoust to head another organization—the Imperial Inspectorate which prepared reports on corruption, red tape, and maladministration.

12. In his *Memoirs*, published in Tehran two years after his death, General Fardoust says that the British, who realized that the Americans had become the chief advisers to the Iranians since the establishment of Savak (1957), offered to put their own services at the Shah's disposal in order to gain access to him. They organized a three-month training course at the intelligence service for General Fardoust to help him set up, on his return to Iran, a special office for analyzing the data provided by the various "services." He says that 200 to 250 pages of information were summarized in a report each day and sent to the palace in a briefcase to which only the Shah had the key.

After the revolution Fardoust agreed to cooperate with the Islamic Republic, and the Shah was profoundly disillusioned with his old friend. We know very little about the role played by the general in the early days of the revolution. There are those who maintain, however, that at the time when left-wing extremist groups turned specifically on the army and Savak with a view to dismantling them, the general tried to preserve the useful elements of the former regime. There can be no doubt that he put at the disposal of the Islamic Republic large quantities of information which proved extremely useful in establishing its own security "services" and in ensuring the smooth functioning of revolutionary tribunals. In addition, his knowledge must have proved very useful to the leaders of the Islamic Republic when it came to sizing people up and judging them. He may well have played a role in sending some people to their deaths before the firing squads, but it is equally possible that the information he provided allowed others to escape execution or imprisonment.

For the time being the true facts about the personality of this figure, who belonged to the Shah's innermost circle, and the role he played, remain unknown.

The Eagle That Was Lost on the Ground

While I was a prisoner I had long conversations with the last commander of the air force, General Mahdiyoun, who was about fifty at the time. Tall and very sporty, he had been the operational commander of aviation for many years, before being appointed as commander of the air force immediately after the revolution.

At Evin the prisoners spoke of Mahdiyoun as an accomplished pilot with four thousand flying hours to his credit. Trained in prestigious American flying schools, each time a new combat plane had come into use he had gone to attend refresher courses in the United States. He explained to me the system used for training Iranian combat pilots. After entering the army the young pilots were first trained at home and then sent to the United States to receive more extensive training lasting twenty months. During this time they had to fly a minimum of 250 hours in fighter planes. At the rate of $4,000 per hour, this training cost a total of $1 million. If one were to add all other expenses, one could easily imagine the sort of outlay this represented for the army, which in 1985 was training about five thousand pilots. On the eve of the revolution the army had no less than 2,500 single-seater fighter-bomber pilots who could assume sole responsibility for all the operations involved in an air sortie. Mahdiyoun proudly informed me that the Iranian air force ranked third in the world in mobility, after the American and Israeli forces; 80 percent of its total force was involved in flights each day,[13] and Iranian pilots carried out seventy to eighty sorties a day, even venturing into the airspace of neighboring countries.

In the course of long walks with Mahdiyoun in the prison courtyard, where our discussions sometimes lasted two or three hours, I became aware of two very basic points.

First, I understood the extent of the air force's vast technological and logistical dependency on the United States, to the point where Iranian bases were virtually integrated into theirs. For example, thousands of spare parts were sent directly from the United States in a kind of endless airlift, and their use was supervised by American experts. Supplies were ensured on the basis of a computerized system which worked with virtually no human intervention. Before stocks were exhausted at an Iranian air base, the required parts were automatically ordered at a base in Texas which was twinned with the one in Iran. The cooperation included the purchase of the most sophisticated aircraft and equipment for communication and detection from the ground or in mid-air (AWACS). As a result, the Iranian air force could at times achieve a better technological performance than the American air force itself.

Second, General Mahdiyoun's accounts of life on the airfields enabled me to see that a new type of man had come into existence in Iran. It was as if the courage, the mental agility, the excellent physical condition, and the self-discipline that these pilots displayed in aerial combat all became dull and faded once they were back on the ground and in contact with human beings. Their near religious devotion to ever more advanced technology and the fact that they were constantly flirting with danger and death transformed these men into creatures

13. The ratio of daily aerial sorties to the number of operational planes reveals the preparedness of the pilots and ground crews, the rapidity of servicing capabilities, and the efficiency of logistical support.

completely different from other human beings, if not to say into some kind of superbeings. They harbored a sense of superiority and condescension toward ordinary mortals, and this played a large part in their sociopsychological maladjustment. While acutely sensitized to all things technical, they were impervious to their compatriots' cultural, civic, and sociopolitical sensibilities. They could not therefore understand the motives of their fellow countrymen or grasp the reasons behind a revolution which had run roughshod over the values they held so dear. They were extremely nostalgic for the Shah's regime which had consistently supported the air force for twenty-five years, as well as for the United States which by virtue of its technology was master of the sky. They thus displayed a tremendous political naiveté, and it was not surprising that after his release from prison General Mahdiyoun was implicated along with some 150 pilots in an attempted coup. Directed from afar by the Iranian opposition in Europe, the plot, known as the Nozeh conspiracy, was discovered; the pilots achieved nothing. A number of them, including General Mahdiyoun, were executed by firing squad in August 1980.

Only a few weeks after their deaths Iraq attacked Iran, precipitating one of the longest and most deadly conflicts since World War II. The response of the Iranian air force stunned the Iraqi high command because they had imagined that it had been completely dismantled. The survivors of the Nozeh conspiracy who had been sentenced to long prison terms were quickly pardoned by Khomeini, whom they had earlier planned to assassinate, and were immediately called upon to defend their country by commanding its fighter-bombers. There were no refusals. Many of the pilots showed great bravery, and a number of them were killed in aerial combat. Saddam Hussein had awakened nationalist sentiments in these "renegades," sentiments which the Islamic leaders of Iran had themselves been unaware of or had underestimated. A similar phenomenon occurred in the case of the navy.

Persia's Freemasons

At Evin I also had occasion to come into contact with another secret realm, that of Freemasonry. For reasons which will become clear, Freemasons constituted a perfect prey for the Islamic revolutionaries, who could use them to strike a direct blow at the previous regime by discrediting it morally and spiritually. Immediately after the victory of the revolution, known Freemasons were removed from all public posts. In cases brought against the officials of the ancien régime, the tribunals considered membership in the Freemasons to be proof of conspiracy with the Pahlavi regime, connivance with foreigners, and so on. There was no shortage of prisoners held on such charges at Evin.

Freemasonry is widespread throughout the world. It is a secret association whose members subscribe to the idea of fraternity and solidarity on the basis of certain rites of initiation. Initially Masonic associations were a kind of builders' guild. Real "practicing" masons traveled around Europe in the seventh century and mainly built churches. They kept the tricks of their trade to themselves and passed them on to their apprentices through a series of initiation rites. (It is as a souvenir of this past that Masonic associations still maintain the apron, the angle iron, and the compass as their basic symbols today.) Starting from the seventh century there emerged in Great Britain, and especially in Scotland, the modern theoretical version of Freemasonry, which propagated liberal ideas while maintaining respect for the powers that be and for existing traditions, including the church and the monarchy. In France the Grand Lodge was established in the eighteenth century and in the nineteenth century served as a vehicle for republican and democratic ideals based on a kind of positivistic philosophy. Throughout this period French Masonic lodges upheld the ideals of the revolution of 1789 and propagated them throughout Europe and the Middle East, notably in Egypt, Turkey (then the Ottoman Empire), and Iran under the Qajar dynasty. For this reason a significant group of enlightened politicians became members of Masonic lodges or were inspired by Freemasonry. They played an important role in the struggle against despotism and notably in the revolution of 1906,[14] which was to lead to the establishment of a constitutional monarchy. In those heroic days, Iranian Freemasonry played an important part in secularizing

14. The first Masonic lodge established according to the movement's rules was set up in Iran in 1907. Affiliated with France's Grand Lodge, the new lodge, called "Iran's Awakening," was created by the professors of the Alliance Française and was based in the residence of a progressive prince, Zahir al-Dowleh.

the state apparatus and in partially breaking the omnipotent power of religious figures, particularly in such spheres as justice and education. Religious leaders thus developed an enduring grudge against Freemasonry.

Starting from World War I, Masonry of French origin, which was intellectual and democratic in nature, began ceding its place to Masonry imported from Great Britain, which was seen simply as a kind of British influence. Iranian Masons nevertheless continued to be influential until Mosaddeq—whom they did not on the whole support—became prime minister and nationalized Iran's oil in 1951. After the fall of Mosaddeq and the strong return of Great Britain and America into Iranian political life, Freemasons burst back onto the political stage. They occupied many seats in the two chambers of Parliament as well as key posts in the state apparatus; but this time they completely put aside their predecessors' democratic ideals. The Shah imposed Sharif-Emami, one of his trusted lieutenants, as the grand master of Iranian Masonry, thus shattering the organization's long-standing procedures.[15] The Masons were now at His Majesty's service and given access to all the best posts. With the rise in oil prices and the subsequent launch of huge investment projects, Iranian businessmen began to join Masonic lodges, and there was a corresponding rise in the number of secret monthly dinners, where ministers and other government officials mingled with other Masons, addressing each other as "brother."

Nearly three thousand "neo-Masons"—on whom, it should be said, the original rules of Masonry imposed the strictest discretion and reserve—thus became docile and unswerving servants of an autocratic regime which required obedient and unquestioning technocrats. The moment they came into power in 1979 religious figures saw an ideal opportunity for settling old scores with the Masons, who from the turn of the century had opposed them in the name of "progress" and secularization. The Masons were driven out of office, and many were arrested without a murmur of protest from the public in whose eyes

15. Ahmad Houman, a former president of the bar in Tehran, with whom I spent several months in prison during my third detention, summed up his own view for me in this way: From the moment when Iranian Freemasons themselves jettisoned the candidate favored by their lodges—Dr. Loghmanol Molk—they decisively abandoned their autonomy vis-à-vis the powers that be and in effect surrendered to the Shah's policies.

they stood discredited. Were the Freemasons I saw in jail guilty or innocent? Had they betrayed or served the nation? For the time being it is impossible to know for certain, but the statements and confessions of a large number of Masons, recorded by the revolutionary tribunals, will perhaps allow this mystery to be solved in the future.

The Corridor of Fear

(Third Detention, July 1981–September 1983)

After my release in April 1980 I moved away from academic life and the state apparatus in order to prevent any possible misunderstandings with the new regime. My prison experience had taught me that the radical factions of the regime had no time whatsoever for independent intellectuals, and that no matter which path the regime eventually took toward moderation the intelligentsia would be the last group accepted into the fold. So I decided to take up offers from publishers to edit books for them. This work suited me well and I dealt with a large number of manuscripts, mostly translations on a variety of contemporary issues.

Fourteen months passed in this way. Then the conflict between Bani-Sadr, who was by now president, and the clergy close to Khomeini came to a head resulting in Bani-Sadr's dismissal. This decision had to be sanctioned by a parliamentary debate and a vote condemning the head of state's incompetence. The debate took place on June 20 and 21, 1981, and was a heated affair in which old allies openly attacked each other for the first time. Bani-Sadr had apparently forgotten that a year before his election as premier in January 1980 he was unknown to the public, and that it was only thanks to the support of Khomeini and the Shi'i leadership that he had won nearly twelve million votes. As first president of the republic in a country where even kings had been unable to reign without the blessing of the representatives of God, Bani-Sadr should have been conscious that his success was largely due to influential clerical support. Naively imagining that he had been granted power by the people, he had tried to exercise it as he pleased. He rapidly clashed with the mullahs, who in the end removed him with a simple wave of the hand.

In the parliamentary debate my name was mentioned twice by deputies who wished to compound the charges against Bani-Sadr and had no qualms about exploiting my association with the Shah's government to cast aspersions on him and to present him as an element injected into the revolution by the ancien régime. They knew well enough, of course, that, by helping a young militant nationalist twenty years earlier and by allowing him to leave the Shah's Iran to study in Europe I had acted in accordance with my conscience and had gone against the political mainstream. That particular student's time abroad had, moreover, ultimately proved very fruitful for the revolutionary cause. Although he had broken his agreement with me and had not pursued his studies with Professor Georges Balandier, he had worked extremely hard to unify the opponents of the Pahlavi regime living outside the country and to establish a kind of bridge between them and Ayatollah Khomeini, who at the time resided in Najaf.

On the day of the debate I was at home lunching with friends while listening to the proceedings on the radio. When my name was mentioned a friend who lived about twenty kilometers outside Tehran suggested that I go and stay with him for several days. Despite the reluctance of my wife, who would not allow herself to be unduly alarmed by the ferocity of the debate and felt that the revolutionary tribunal would not arrest me again now that it had become thoroughly familiar with my past, I decided it would be prudent to leave.

After spending a few days away from the capital, an irresistible urge to see my youngest son, who was then four years old, drew me to Tehran where I stayed with my nephew. It was during that time, on June 28, that a bomb exploded at the headquarters of the Islamic Republican party, killing more than eighty high-ranking officials, including Ayatollah Beheshti, president of the Supreme Court and the most influential religious politician after Khomeini. A few days later, on July 1, I was arrested.

The pasdars had probably been following my every step. That day I moved to my niece's house in the north of Tehran where I had finally decided to take refuge. Less than half an hour after I arrived, I was in the kitchen with my niece who was busy cooking one of her specialties, Shirazi-style shrimps exquisitely prepared with pickled onions. Suddenly I sensed an uninvited presence and turned my head in the direction of the living room. My eyes came to an abrupt halt on the figure of a man who was looking directly at me, silently and with the merest hint of a strange smile. I realized at that moment that the house and garden were surrounded by armed men who had blocked every exit, from the cellar to the roof. I was their captive.

Adopting a rather cordial manner, the man in the living room approached me, took me gently by the arm, and said, "Come, they only want to ask you a few questions."

Then, with the same affected cordiality, he led me to the door where more pasdars and a Mercedes-Benz awaited me.

I had no illusions: the "discussion" I was being invited to would probably last for quite some time—a long time, even. It was therefore best to be prepared. I asked the head of the pasdars if he would be kind enough to go back into the house and fill an overnight bag with a few basic necessities: pyjamas, a book, a pencil, and my toothbrush. He concurred without argument, thus betraying his true intentions: he had not come to take me for a brief conversation; he meant instead to throw me in jail.

During the ten minutes or so that I sat in the car, surrounded by guards and awaiting his return, my mind raced uncontrollably. Troubled thoughts and disturbing memories tripped over each other. I recalled in particular the story told me by close friends about the trial of the Hungarian leader László Rajk, and I remembered how he had been forced by the police and the party to confess to crimes he had not committed and had been sentenced to death and executed in 1949. It was only seven years later, in 1956, that he was exonerated from all these charges and rehabilitated . . . posthumously.

I was horrified at the thought of coming to a similar end: sullied by senseless accusations for the sake of a cause; crushed underneath the crazed machinery of a blind power hell-bent on destroying all individuality; sacrificed for the good of a state which justified itself on the basis of an infinite number of what it regarded as sacrosanct arguments. In short, what I feared above all else was that I would be subjected to an Iranian version of a Stalinist trial.

Had I already been selected by someone as an ideal scapegoat? When the pasdar returned with my bag and the car set off, I could not wait to ask him question after question, trying to understand why I had been arrested. He said they believed I had been one of Bani-Sadr's advisers. I protested vehemently, arguing that I had not seen Bani-Sadr since he had become president of the republic two years earlier. "Well, then," the pasdar returned, "you can present evidence to this effect and you'll be released right away!"

Could I believe him? Probably not. His reply came as a relief, nevertheless, because it made me think that my arrest was not part of a premeditated plan.

After five days of provisional detention I was finally transferred to Evin, which I believed I knew well as I had already spent four months there. I naively imagined that I would be able to resume the way of life I experienced after my second arrest, and in all honesty the idea of making new and interesting acquaintances was not altogether displeasing to me.

I rapidly realized, however, that things had changed. In little more than a year Evin had turned into something of a concentration camp, characterized by a climate of arbitrariness, fear, and violence. A guard whom I knew from my previous detention had been assigned the task of "welcoming" me. As if to dissociate himself from the orders he had to carry out, he apologized for having to put a blindfold over my eyes. Then he led me to the central building which housed the public prosecutor's section of the revolutionary tribunal.

Still blindfolded, I was ordered to sit on the ground. I took advantage of my guard's temporary departure and discreetly raised the corner of my blindfold. A terrible spectacle confronted me: fifty or so young men and women, all blindfolded, sat lined up next to one another along the entire length of the corridor. The image was one of utter powerlessness, of absolute submission. We were all disoriented by the uncertainty of waiting and the fear of the unknown. This was rendered all the more distressing because it had to be endured in darkness. At regular intervals a guard walked past us, shouting,

"Don't raise your blindfolds! Pull your knees tight against your chests!"

The Power of Prayer . . .

From time to time a pasdar would come to fetch a prisoner and lead him or her to the judge's office. At noon the oppressive silence was suddenly broken when a pasdar announced, "Anyone who wants to pray can come with me to carry out the ablutions."

About twenty people, including me, responded and were led to the washrooms. A guard took off our blindfolds and gave each of us a piece of paper—a symbolic representation of Mecca—on which we could place our heads when we prostrated ourselves in prayer.

To all appearances, prayer had a salutary effect on our guards. The atmosphere suddenly eased noticeably. Brought together momentarily by the religious ritual, guards and prisoners shared a common experience.

Afterward I was taken to the examining judge. He happened to be the man who had also cross-examined me during my previous detention. I was allowed to take off my blindfold, whereas the Mojahedin detainees had to keep theirs on even at this stage. The judge seemed surprised to see me before him once again. His gestures and words suggested that he could not understand why, when I was liberated fourteen months earlier I had not tried to leave the country along with so many other figures associated with the imperial era.[1]

He went straight to the point and asked me to reply to three questions: In what circumstances had I been arrested? What had I been doing since I had been set free? And to what political organization did I belong? The manner in which the cross-examination was conducted reassured me. First, it was clear that my arrest had not been instigated by Evin Prison's judicial authorities. Second, the examining judge did not appear to be bent on concocting an imaginary reconstruction of my political past and specifically of my rela-

1. Despite all the opportunities I had to leave the country secretly, there were two reasons why I decided to stay in Iran: first, I wanted my situation vis-à-vis the Islamic regime to be perfectly clear and unambiguous; second, despite the reigning climate of anarchy and insecurity, I was persuaded, in my heart of hearts, that Islamic justice would not go so far as to claim my life.

tions with Bani-Sadr, which is what I had most feared. And, finally, the fact that the judge was already familiar with my case made me particularly optimistic. In the volatile climate of the time and the virtual state of panic which had seized the country, it was easy to fear the worst—hasty and arbitrary judgments, a settling of scores, and possibly even summary executions. . . .

When I returned to my place next to the other prisoners, who were still sitting side by side on the floor in that corridor of fear, I felt more confident. An hour later a pasdar ordered us to form a single file so that he could take us to join the "flock" in the cell blocks. And so, still wearing our blindfolds, we shuffled along, one behind the other, weaving our way through the prison. At one point a pasdar led us up a narrow spiral stairway. I was at the head of the line, and when I reached the top of the stairs I lifted my blindfold slightly to try to make out what was happening. The scene I witnessed at that moment will never be erased from my memory. For me it was a symbolic image, a striking snapshot of the penitential world of Evin: about forty blindfolded men, immersed in the silence of the dead, were winding their way up a staircase suspended in mid-air like an unending coil.

It was an infernal spiral, like those that haunt the chiaroscuro etchings of Piranesi's "feverish constructs." This was prison: a world which never ceased twisting around itself! We had all been condemned to shuffling around in circles. But for how long?

I was taken to a cell and the door was locked behind me. I realized yet again that Evin was no longer the prison I had known a year earlier, when we had been entirely free to wander in and out of the different sections throughout the day. Now a guard arrived just four times a day to take us to the toilets, and this was always done with the greatest haste.

Because of the current political crisis, which had intensified to the point of armed clashes between the Mojahedin and other extremist groups and the Islamic regime, the cells were also far more crowded. Evin had been designed under the Shah for about two thousand to three thousand detainees and had housed only a thousand when I was released from prison in 1980. But after the start of the Mojahedin's armed uprising and Bani-Sadr's flight from Iran, up to three hundred people were arrested every day for a year, and by the end of 1981 the prison held up to twelve thousand people. On the night I arrived there were about thirty inmates in each cell, rising later to fifty or sixty and eventually to seventy.

My first observation was that my fellow prisoners were extremely young—at the most twenty-one or twenty-two years old, with the exception of two engineers who were in their thirties. After about an hour's conversation I realized that these young people represented a new generation which had emerged from the lower middle class. Thanks to the rapid growth of education under the Shah and to a certain improvement in living standards, they had been able to complete secondary-school education, although their parents had been illiterate. The steps the Shah had taken to develop the economy and create a new educational infrastructure had clearly brought about an improvement in the social standing of an underprivileged class. This was an undeniable achievement, but the regime had not matched the material and social well-being it offered with moral or intellectual satisfaction. Possessed of a deep idealism that could not be gratified by material gain alone, my young cellmates had grown up in an ideological vacuum and without the kind of moral leadership that might have given their lives meaning. In these circumstances they had turned to extremist ideas, whether Islamic or Marxist, which pushed them into vehement opposition both to the imperial and the postrevolutionary regimes.

The Sleep Architect

And so I began my communal life with these youngsters, who struck me with their strange mixture of idealism, innocence, warmth, and candor. Once they had overcome the initial mistrust which arose from social standing, notoriety, and age, they treated me with casual friendliness.

It was the pasdar's business to bring us food, to fetch us for interrogation sessions, to lock up the newly arrived prisoners, and, on occasion—although this was rare at the time—to release one or other of us. In order to organize our own lives in the cells we had divided the daily chores among ourselves.

First there was the prisoner in charge of meals, whose role was crucial since our food had to be distributed equitably. Although certain dishes were brought to us in portions, others were served in bulk, in huge pots, and had to be divided up. When the dish for the day was announced as chicken with rice, this meant that there would be a single chicken for sixty people. We would watch the person in charge with amusement as he cut it up into "portions," with painstaking precision and an absolute determination to be fair. Like a good mother looking after her children, the prisoner responsible would take into account each person's physical condition, age, health, and capacity for endurance. He would set some things—usually bread, cheese, and dates—aside for new arrivals, who had undergone long and exhausting interrogations at the prison tribunal without being given anything to eat. In each cell there was a water tank containing about twenty liters. In the summer, when it was very hot, we had to limit our consumption, and in any case we had to take care not to drink too much in order to avoid putting excessive pressure on the system.

There was also a prisoner responsible for deciding where each person would sleep at night. His task was not easy either. We were given a number from 1 to 60 and allocated a space each evening. As long as there were at most forty-five prisoners in a room measuring six meters by six meters, it was possible to sleep alongside one another in three rows. But when numbers rose above forty-five we had to be arranged with the legs of some between the legs of others. The "sleep master" also needed to take the height of each person into account, and because of departures and arrivals he had to reorganize the room each day. His task sometimes lasted two full hours, which is why I gave him the honorary title of the "sleep architect."

In the summer we did not need blankets. But from the first days of autumn the weather became cold. We had only a few small cushions and an insufficient number of blankets, which we had to use in turn. In our cell there was a single goose-feather pillow—a remnant of Evin Prison under the Shah—which had been allocated to me out of consideration for my age; but I used to reserve it for people who had been mistreated during their interrogation.

At eleven o'clock at night the lights were switched out at the central control; we were awakened at seven in the morning by the guard, who brought us bread and cheese but no tea. Because of the acute pressure on the prison's resources, for five months we were not allowed any hot drinks. In a prison so overcrowded everything was in short supply, not only blankets, pillows, dishes, and plates (during the first few months we had to eat four to a bowl) but also sanitary facilities and cells.

Although we were provided with vital necessities, we had the distinct feeling that the prison authorities were not going out of their way to ensure our well-being. This was undoubtedly a reaction against Bani-Sadr who, while president of the republic, had denounced the Islamic judiciary's ill treatment of prisoners, most of whom belonged to his Mojahedin allies. Relations between the pasdars and the Mojahedin in the prison were consequently very strained. Under Bani-Sadr's presidency the Mojahedin were self-confident and had given their jailors a hard time: they would sing revolutionary songs, cover the walls with graffiti, and at times go so far as physically to threaten the guards. But the president's removal and their armed insurrection had turned the Mojahedin into outlaws, at war with the state, and from June 1981 their living conditions in prison deteriorated noticeably: locked doors, the loss of the right to roam about freely and to have visitors, mandatory blindfolds, and so on. The situation was further aggravated by the fact that pasdars were regularly assassinated as they traveled back and forth between Evin and the city.

The Mojahedin were at this time convinced that the regime would soon fall under the blows they were inflicting. All the young people who were arrested, weapon in hand, seemed certain that the Islamic government would not survive for more than a few weeks. Whenever I asked them how they could be so sure, they would reply, "Because of our scientific analysis." One could see in them a combination of revolutionary romanticism and a thirst for danger as well as an absolute cult of an organization. Having broken away from the dominant values of their society, history, and families, they were totally dependent on the movement. Every decision and every instruction emanating from the organization was seen by them as a divine edict, which they followed as a zealot follows the command of God. I also came to understand during my confinement with them just how devoted they were, as an organization, to their weapons.

This attachment to weapons was of particular importance in binding their intensely hierarchic network together. Most of the weapons had been acquired in the early days of the revolution when they and other political organizations raided army barracks. Since then, despite the excellent relations they had maintained with the leaders of the Islamic Republic for a short time after the revolution, they had never agreed to hand in their arms. This fact had remained incomprehensible to me. I could not understand why an organization which was accorded great prestige by the public and the political leadership refused to assume a legal role in the political life of the newly established regime. It was only during this particular term at Evin, when the conflict between the Mojahedin and the Islamic regime reached its peak, that I finally understood their devotion to weapons. In the years before the revolution they would measure the loyalty and dedication of their fellow members by the number of submachine guns, grenades, and pistols they were prepared to hide. To the Mojahedin, weapons constituted moral and material credit. They were the organization's lifeblood and a key component of its members' political mentality. Even though they risked being killed in the hundreds in the course of commando operations, they were happy to go, clutching their "secret weapons" just as the Crusaders used to march to their deaths cross in hand.

The Debris of a Civil War

During the first two years of the revolution the Mojahedin played a game of hide-and-seek with the authorities, but they did not use their weapons, nor did they present themselves openly as rebels. My cellmates explained to me that at the time they had been under orders not to confront the hezbollahs—members of the Islamic party—or the pasdars, and to remain calm when attacked. This tactic succeeded in winning over public sympathy. Seen by the general public as a disciplined organization which abided by the rules of society and the state, the Mojahedin gained thousands of supporters. At the same time they tried to recruit very young people for political and military training. Mojahedin prisoners told me that during this entire period their most important order was to infiltrate the administration and especially the new institutions that the regime was establishing.

All these young people, who had spontaneously followed an organization whose goal was the creation of an egalitarian society, suddenly found themselves in the middle of a movement of a completely different order when in June 1981 the Mojahedin's leaders called for armed insurrection against the religious authorities. Needless to say, the majority of the organization's members and sympathizers, who were between eighteen and twenty-two years of age and had had no previous experience of armed struggle, were caught like sitting ducks in the first few days of the insurrection.

One evening in July 1981, a month of fierce clashes, the pasdars brought to our cell a young man who was from Sirjan in southeastern Iran. I took him aside the following day and asked him about his life and how he had been caught up in the movement. He told me that he had been a primary schoolteacher and that the ten Mojahedin comrades with whom he had been arrested had also been teachers. When I asked him how the pasdars had managed to catch them, he said:

"Nothing could have been easier. Everyone in the village knew that we were activists belonging to the movement; we, on the other hand, were not even aware that an armed insurrection had been declared. But we were arrested in Sirjan after the organization in Tehran announced that a demonstration would be held on June 20 to underline its determination to oppose the regime by violent means. Since there was no revolutionary tribunal which could pass judgment on us in our little village, we were put on a minibus and sent off to Tehran. The journey took two days and one night. The four pasdars who were guarding us were from our area, and they knew us well."

The young man went on with his story and described a moving scene to me: "At one point during the night I realized that the pasdar sitting next to me was asleep and that his submachine gun was pressing against my leg. I looked around and I saw that the three other pasdars were also asleep. My eyes suddenly caught those of one of my comrades, who had also remained awake and clearly had the same idea: we could overpower the four pasdars, seize their submachine guns, and escape into the night rather than end up in Evin, that terrifying prison where we could be sentenced to death by the revolutionary tribunal. But scarcely had the thought crossed our minds when we both lowered our eyes in shame. We had known those pasdars since they were children, and we couldn't imagine killing them in cold blood in the name of armed insurrection whose logic we didn't understand. The pasdars, for their part, didn't see us as enemies they could just shoot at. During our journey to Tehran, whenever the pasdar next to me wanted to relieve himself, he would leave his submachine gun with me."

This simple story clearly illustrates the absurdity of the fratricidal war that had just begun. The pasdars and the Mojahedin were youngsters from the same generation and the same section of the population, with identical religious and cultural backgrounds. Some of them followed Khomeini and the clerics while others belonged to a Marxist organization which was also supposed to be Islamic. The Mojahedin spent their time setting bombs and assassinating, at point-blank range and without discrimination, anyone considered to be a supporter of the regime. But given the fact that the regime was itself a product of a religious and popular revolution which had taken place only two years earlier, how was it possible to judge who was for it and who was against it? The distinction was totally arbitrary. There were young people with "pure" sentiments on both sides of the divide. In reality it was their leaders who, as a matter of vanity, seemed incapable of sparing the Iranian people bloodshed. Members of the Mojahedin organization and other Marxist groups following their lead in the civil war behaved, in their own country and in the face of people with the same cultural and religious backgrounds as themselves, in exactly the same way as the Vietnamese behaved toward American invaders or the Palestinians toward the Israeli occupiers of their territories.

Let me offer another example of the unnecessary loss of Iranian youth during the armed clashes which tore their country apart. At about two o'clock in the morning a young man of twenty, who possessed great dignity and courage, said to me as he lay down to sleep by my side after returning from an interrogation session: "If they come for me tomorrow, I'll be executed."

Noticing my surprise at his certainty, he explained, "This is the first time that the three judges questioned me without making me wear a blindfold. I realized they weren't afraid any longer that I might recognize them."

That night was in fact his last. He spent the time whispering his life story into my ear and telling me why he had become involved in political activity. He also asked me—if I emerged from prison alive—to give his yellow jumper to his brother as a final souvenir. The next day marked the start of large-scale executions. They would usually take place after midnight. The prisoners would be awakened by the rattle of submachine gun fire followed by a final bullet for each victim, which we counted, sitting up and holding our breath. There were up to eighty executions a night, and in the cells the prisoners felt closer to death than to life.

Since assassinations were also taking place on a daily basis in streets and public places, the tension at Evin increased dangerously.

During the first few weeks of my imprisonment my cellmates seemed quite optimistic, because, as I said earlier, they believed the Islamic regime was about to collapse. But when they learned that their young leader, Massoud Rajavi, had managed to escape to France on July 28, 1981, accompanied by Bani-Sadr on board an army Boeing 707, their faith in rapid victory declined noticeably. Although the escape of Rajavi and Bani-Sadr seemed like a show of force, it also proved that the fall of the Islamic regime was not as imminent as the Mojahedin had seemed to believe when they had issued the internal circulars suggesting that all that was needed to overthrow the government was a few bombs and assassinations.

Hassan-Gestapo's Speeches

When the radio announced Bani-Sadr's escape I came in for a beating. In the style of the times the pasdars had given me the title of "Bani-Sadr's teacher"; and there was one particular illiterate, simple-minded pasdar who liked to hit prisoners. His name was Hassan, but the prisoners had given him the title of "Hassan-Gestapo," which was all the more appropriate as he wore his hair closely cropped.

Whenever he unlocked the door to conduct us to the toilets, Hassan-Gestapo would launch into a speech meant to "put us straight" and to cleanse us of our evil "Western, capitalist, Marxist, Zionist, or Masonic ideals." My companions would listen to his declamations with great pleasure and delight, because the longer he spoke the longer they could stay in the toilets. Normally the time allocated for sixty to seventy prisoners to use five cubicles was no more than eight or ten minutes. . . . But we also liked to listen to him because he would often tell us quite unintentionally about what was happening elsewhere. For us prisoners, totally cut off from the world and forbidden to exchange information about the arrival of new detainees, the situation in the tribunals, or the comings and goings of well-known personalities, Hassan-Gestapo's statements, although bordering on the ludicrous, were often very revealing.

He was proud of being a fervent disciple of Khomeini and would boast that a pasdar who worked at the Imam's residence was a friend of his. This friend could hear the Ayatollah's voice every evening through the door of his prayer room when he spoke to the Hidden Imam who "revealed" all the secrets of the world to him and advised him what to do. In this way Hassan-Gestapo would give us what information he had. The young detainees liked to listen to his hysterical rantings and ravings despite his brutality, because once they were locked up in their cells again they would have new topics to discuss. The other pasdars, who were more disciplined, more self-restrained, and less sadistic, did not allow Hassan to speak for long outside our cells and used to call him back to order, shouting, "Hassan, you talk too much. Get on with your work!"

"The Resistant Liberal"

It was Hassan who gave us the news on the day of Bani-Sadr's departure. His comments on the subject reflected the displeasure with which all the prison staff had received the information. As far as Hassan was concerned, since I was Bani-Sadr's "ideological mentor," I was to a large extent responsible for the former president's machinations. He was obviously of the opinion that when Bani-Sadr had been an assistant at my institute, at the ripe old age of twenty-two, I could have put different ideas into his head. On that day, after rehearsing one of his standard speeches, Hassan pretended to leave but came back a few moments later to reprimand us, supposedly because the young people in my cell had spontaneously started to sing. Hassan yelled at us through the keyhole: "You're singing? Very well, you'll see what happens to people who sing!"

The song was harmless, but as far as he was concerned singing could only be interpreted as politically subversive behavior. He came into our cell and cried, "Who started the singing?"

Since there was no reply, he pointed at me and said in his most authoritative voice, "You, Bani-Sadr's teacher, out!"

I rose and walked out into the corridor.

"Tell me who started the singing," he ordered.

He started to give me a thorough beating. But another pasdar, a nice young man called Sabzeh Ali, whom I had known since my previous detention and to whom I had given English lessons, spotted us from afar and rushed toward us. In a very firm voice he told Hassan-Gestapo to stop hitting me, and he led me back to my cell. I heard Hassan mutter vengefully, "Your punishment is not over!"

Two days later Hassan was on duty early in the morning. He unlocked the cell door and made me step out into the corridor. He put a blindfold over my eyes and tied a cloth over my mouth. I had just enough time to ask him what he was doing, but he gave no reply. (He confessed to me later that among the tricks he had learned from the other wardens, there were a few dozen techniques for making a prisoner believe that the moment for execution was nigh. One of these was not to respond to a prisoner's questions and not to tell him where he was being taken.)

On that morning he made me walk blindfolded for some time. Then he tied me to a metallic door and beat me severely on the head, chest, and stomach. When the beating stopped he removed his blindfold and exclaimed, "Now your punishment is over." He took me—reeling and in a very bad state[2]—back to the cell.

I sensed that my cellmates were in a solemn and anxious mood. They had suspected that I was being ill treated, but when they saw me they realized that despite my lengthy absence I had not denounced anyone. They greeted me kindly and warmly and offered me a glass of water and a sugar cube.

As I said earlier, most of the young people I knew at Evin were under the influence of Marxist ideology. Regardless of the particular tendency to which they belonged—Islamic Marxists (Mojahedin), pro-Soviet or anti-Soviet communists, Maoists, Trotskyists, and so forth—they all had a dominant Stalinist streak, an incredible gullibility, and a remarkable political immaturity. This Stalinist left systematically described any religious person who disagreed with them as a "phalangist" and any secular opponent as a liberal. The term "liberal" was used indiscriminately to describe anyone educated in the West or

2. After receiving these blows I suffered for months with sore ribs.

in domestic universities, that is to say, all the country's skilled professionals. In this way the Stalinist left threw into the "dustbin of history" everything that Iran had learned and acquired as a result of its contacts with the West during the preceding fifty years. This "antiliberal" campaign created a vacuum in universities, the administration, factories, banks, the diplomatic service, the cultural sector, and elsewhere which was difficult to fill.

Even more treacherous than this naive and inexperienced left was the pro-Soviet communist Tudeh party, whose leaders had returned to Iran in 1979 after twenty years of exile in the Soviet Union. Back in Iran they pulled out all the stops in their bid to make up for lost time, adopting the opportunistic tactic of trying to convince the people that they had been unconditional supporters of the revolution and the Islamic Republic during the preceding three years. The leaders of the party, completely discredited as far as the public was concerned, put their "wisdom" at the disposal of the new regime, which had no experience of how to manage a revolution or a country. The business of driving out the liberals, cunningly conceived by the Tudeh, was taken up by a number of groups on the extreme left. Later on this game was also entered into by that faction of the Islamic regime which was worried about being outmaneuvered by the extreme left.

Later still, especially after the death of Khomeini in 1989, the members of this same radical Islamist faction were to revive the idea in a struggle for power with the religious moderates. As for myself, no sooner had I arrived at Evin when my cellmates labeled me "a liberal intellectual" (with all the connotations I just described).

One day as I lay on the floor, hurting all over from my thrashing by Hassan-Gestapo, I heard five or six boys who claimed to be pro-Soviet communists (although they were not Tudeh members) whispering among themselves. I called out to them and asked them what they were saying. Smiling, but with a solemn tone, their spokesman said to me, "So far, we've been calling you 'the liberal,' but from now on we've decided to change your title to the 'resistant liberal'!"

I pulled myself up as best I could and addressed my sixty companions: "Let me ask you this: is it better to be a resistant liberal or a spineless revolutionary? You were the ones who started the singing. But did you have the courage to tell Hassan that I was not to blame?"

They all replied in one voice, "Yes, you're right. We behaved badly and we ask for your forgiveness."

From then on, despite our differing political views, I was no longer held at arm's length by my cellmates, and whenever the prison administration asked for a spokesman on our affairs I was selected by my companions as their representative. The anathema imposed on the "liberal" had been lifted.

The Miracle of Doctors

Early one morning a pasdar came to inform us that a doctor would be visiting our section at nine o'clock and that he would be able to see four or five prisoners. We therefore had to select those among us who were most in need of medical attention. Given my condition at the time I was put at the top of the list. When they led us to the end of the corridor I had no idea who the doctor would be, but as soon as I caught a glimpse of him, sitting next to a small trolley holding his medications, I recognized an old friend, Professor Mofidi. An eminent scholar, he had headed Tehran University's Institute of Malariology and Tropical Medicine for years. Unlike other well-known medical professors in Tehran, he had given up his own private clinic in order to devote himself to research. He was always well informed about developments in the rest of the world and was a highly regarded member of the World Health Organization. For many years before the revolution we had worked closely together to promote scientific research and higher education, and in 1968 we had collaborated on drafting a bill on the administration of universities and the careers of lecturers and researchers. As I write this the law remains in force. I had all the more respect for Mofidi because he was a modest man always prepared to cooperate with others.

Professor Mofidi was a prisoner at Evin because he had practically been forced, at a critical moment of the revolutionary crisis and under pressure from friends, to accept the post of minister of higher education in the government of General Azhari, which lasted only three months. During this period about a hundred professors laid siege to his ministry, purportedly to press for the reopening of universities; in reality they wanted to maintain the revolutionary momentum. Despite all the tolerance and understanding Mofidi himself showed toward the disaffected academics, the military cabinet decided to ban the presence of crowds outside the ministry or on its balconies. The strikers ignored the ban, and the soldiers in the street opened fire on a sixth-floor balcony, fatally wounding one of the protesters. After the revolution Mofidi was held responsible for the affair and arrested twice, although he had really played no part in it. He was condemned to three years' imprisonment after his second arrest.

Our chance encounter at Evin was charged with emotion, though we tried to conceal our feelings from the pasdars who were watching us carefully. There were tears in our eyes, and we were so moved that we could not bring ourselves to speak. One of the two pasdars, a young villager, began to suspect that we might know each other, although we had not said anything to this effect. He looked at the doctor and said, "Do you know this one?"

The doctor lowered his head and mumbled, "I'd heard his name before."

Professor Mofidi examined me and established that my blood pressure was very high and my heartbeats irregular. Since I could not say anything in front of the pasdars about being ill treated, he could not understand why I had these symptoms. As I was answering his questions I quickly slipped in a few words in English to let him know that I had been beaten up, so that he could make the correct diagnosis. He gave me some medication and vitamins and announced to the pasdar: "This prisoner has a heart problem. I'll need to see him every Tuesday."

And so I was taken to be checked by Mofidi each week, and thanks to him I was able to create a veritable "pharmacy" in our cell. I was not in the habit of taking much medicine myself, but I noticed that the younger generations of Iranians consumed considerable quantities, and stimulants in particular. That was why, on the morning of my weekly visits, I had to memorize a list of a dozen or so medications which were for my cellmates but which I had to pretend, in front of the pasdars, were a part of my own medical treatment. . . . The good doctor entered into the game, and when the pasdars expressed surprise at the amount of medicine I was receiving, the doctor used to tell them that I was extremely ill. In any case, the subterfuge helped boost my newly acquired popularity as the "resident liberal."

Professor Mofidi was to spend another year in Evin Prison before being released; throughout his detention he provided valuable services to the prisoners. He would spend his days, from seven o'clock in the morning until late into the night, going from section to section, accompanied by his medicine trolley; he used to see about a hundred patients every day.

As for Dr. Sheikh, whom I mentioned in connection with my second detention, I learned that in the course of the past eighteen months he had taken a more important role and was now head of the entire medical service. Since he was an orthopedist/surgeon, he spent most of his time carrying out operations. He had acquired such a reputation that when Ayatollah Ghodoussi, the procurator general of the revolutionary tribunal, was severely wounded by a bomb explosion in his office, the pasdars had taken Dr. Sheikh to the victim's bedside—but too late.

Such work carried out by doctors constituted a first step toward the rehabilitation of people who had been highly placed under the former regime and who were known as *taghoutis*.[3] The fact that uncompromising Islamists, such as the pasdars, allowed "establishment" doctors into their world could be seen as an initial breach in their purist vision which demanded that they be totally self-sufficient. Their conviction was particularly shaken in the course of the Iran-Iraq War, during which doctors rendered a service as great as another category of *taghoutis*: the army officers and the fighter pilots who gave their lives. The purists were forced to admit then that not all *taghoutis* were bad.

Let us return, however, to life in our cells. At seven o'clock in the morning a pasdar would open our door, which remained locked at night, and give us bread and a piece of feta cheese. The person in charge of meals would slice the cheese into equal portions with his usual painstaking precision, using a length of string. On those occasions when the pasdar brought us dates, these were also distributed equitably.

3. *Taghouti* is the adjective corresponding to the substantive *taghout*, a Koranic term indicating one who, like the pharaoh, was not prepared to submit to the will of God. For Islamists, "taghouti" was the equivalent of "Westernized," suggesting a different kind of appearance from them: clean shaven, dressed in the Western style, wearing a tie.

At noon another pasdar would come with a huge pot of rice, and he would give, to the person in charge in our cell, one ladleful for each prisoner.

The evening meal usually consisted of potatoes and a few vegetables; once a week we were instead each given two hard-boiled eggs. We considered this to be a real feast. We were rarely given meat, but on the whole the food was adequate.

A state of isolation, like that imposed on us in Evin, inevitably produces certain psychological symptoms, most notably a longing for contact with the outside world. From our cell window we could just about make out the branches of a tree situated on top of a hill. One day one of my cellmates decided to climb onto the shoulders of another prisoner in order to see the entire tree. When his feet were back on the ground, he declared triumphantly that he had seen not just the tree but a dog under the tree as well. All at once half the cell was clambering up to see the dog and the tree; it was an important event for the inmates, not only because it provided a break in the monotony of their daily lives but also because it represented a link with a world from which they had been totally cut off.

It was much the same whenever there was a new arrival who could tell us what was happening outside the prison. Some of the young people, who were completely under the spell of one of the variety of Marxist ideologies, were still expecting the Islamic regime to fall at any moment. The young Mojahedin, captured while carrying arms during demonstrations or because they had been denounced by previously arrested friends, were convinced that Massoud Rajavi (then in Paris) would return to lead a massive insurrection. They pleaded that the insurgents would break open Evin's gates and free thousands of prisoners. The poor Mojahedin who refused to repent were doomed to be sent to their deaths by firing squad, their heads filled with dreams of a brighter future. Throughout their unswerving march toward death, they remained blinded by a propaganda which made them think, for example, that in the course of an armed attack in which two hundred of them had been killed, three hundred members had been spared, because the organization had counted on losing five hundred. . . .

At times like these I thought about all the harm that could be caused by "revolutionary ideologies" exported from the West during the past few decades, first to Latin America and then to Africa and Asia. If autocrats like the Shah, who ruled over these regions, used the sacred formula of growth as an excuse to imitate the West mindlessly in the economic domain, revolutionary elites were no less blindly obedient in the realm of ideological concepts. Much like their counterparts, the economic technocrats, these elites tried to apply, just as they stood and without any reference to the specific historical and sociological features of their countries, revolutionary equations formulated—but never applied—in the West.

The Spirit of Henry Dunant

Another of the prisoners' concerns was the inadequacy of dental care. In that summer of 1981, when the number of detainees rose by several hundred each day, the medical service included only one dentist. He received prisoners in the morning and pasdars in the afternoon. For this reason he had been given instructions not to treat teeth but to pull them out. . . . As for myself, after spending several sleepless nights suffering from terrible toothache, I was at last authorized by a pasdar to see the dentist. I will always remember how privileged I felt as I took my place in that dentist's chair. Gazing out of the window at the snow-peaked Mount Damavand and put completely at ease by the reassuring smile of the young dentist—who had barely finished his studies before being sentenced to ten years' imprisonment as a repentant member of the Mojahedin—I felt that, in a way, all was well with the world after all, and that the common civilities and decencies of life would survive and continue to protect us.

During my session with the dentist I recalled the discussions I had had in Geneva in 1950 with a university friend. At the time I was preparing for my history of philosophy exam in the company of the granddaughter of Henry Dunant, the founder of the Red Cross. Like all her compatriots, she was very proud of the organization. Coming from a country that was the object of the greed and covetousness of colonial powers (notably Britain and Russia), I myself regarded all international organizations with considerable mistrust. I dreamed of the attainment of universal peace without worrying too much about what was to be done in the meantime with the ills that arose from war. As far as I was concerned, Henry Dunant's brainchild was no more than a palliative intended to salve the conscience of the good burghers of Geneva. My university friend, who had been brought up in circles where there was considerable skepticism about the goodness of humanity, maintained that people would always be motivated by egotism, that they would never respect their fellow human beings, and that wars and human rights violations would always be the order of the day. The best thing to do, therefore, was to be realistic and try to help the inevitable victims by alleviating their suffering.

Reflecting on this old debate with a fellow student, I remembered a morning some two months after my arrival at Evin when we heard some very strongly worded remarks against Amnesty International on the prison radio. I explained to my cellmates that this probably meant that the humanitarian organization had criticized the conditions in which prisoners were being held in Iran. That afternoon Lajevardi, the tribunal's procurator general, walked past our cells for the first time and asked us if we were short of anything. Since I had been nominated spokesman by my cellmates, I told him that we needed better-quality bread and more frequent hot showers—for the thing we missed most was the possibility of cleaning ourselves properly: we were allowed only one hot shower per fortnight. That same evening the pasdars took us to the shower rooms, where we were allowed to stay under the lukewarm water for as long as we liked—something which had never happened before.

Now, in that dentist's chair, I thought to myself, "If I ever get out of here, I must seek out my friend, offer her my *mea culpa*, and pledge to do my utmost to increase support for international organizations such as the Red Cross." For the mere establishment of regulations which compel states not to abandon sick prisoners to their fate is of great humanitarian value. I benefited from this idea myself when, having bestowed his expert care upon me, the good dentist declared, "You will not suffer any longer." During my previous sleepless nights it had seemed unthinkable that I would ever again be free of pain.

With my treatment over, the pasdar slipped the blindfold over my eyes and took me to sit in the corridor where I waited with the other blindfolded prisoners until everyone's dental session was finished and we could be led back to our cells in a single file. At one point, as I was sitting there, I felt someone touching my beard and hair. He said, "What? Still here? What a terrible business!"

And so the pasdar would not understand, he added gently in English, "You're always on the side of the losers."

I recognized the voice of Dr. Sheikh. He was, of course, referring to the fact that I had been arrested once because of my alleged support of the Shah, and now I was out of favor again on the suspicion of having helped Bani-Sadr.

Dr. Sheikh's remark plunged me deep into thought. Sitting blindfolded in that Evin corridor, I had plenty of time to reflect, and it occurred to me that aside from the Shah and Bani-Sadr, with whom I had in any case never really been associated, the fate of losers had in general always held greater interest for me than that of winners. After all, I mused, were losers not people who had not let glory—or the illusion of glory—slip through their fingers? And once they had overcome the bitterness of defeat, were they not in a better position to understand the factors which raised people to the heights as well as those which plunged them to the depths?

Giving Lessons to a Mullah

Precarious though our own circumstances were in prison, we also spent a lot of time worrying about our families, with whom we had lost all contact. We were conscious of the fact that as they read daily reports in the newspapers about executions at Evin, they must be living in a permanent state of fear. We tried to reassure them by any means we could. We took advantage, for example, of any prisoner's release to send messages to our relatives. But this was not as simple as it may sound, because at the moment of their release prisoners were carefully searched by the pasdars,[4] who were particularly keen to find any telephone numbers they may have hidden on their person. We had invented a technique of tattooing telephone numbers with the point of a needle on bank notes which we hid in the hems or belts of prisoners' trousers. But we had to prepare things in advance, carefully and secretly, choosing those of our companions who we

4. During these times of merciless confrontation, the pasdars were very conscious of the fact that obtaining the smallest bit of information or just a telephone number could help stop a bomb attack or assassination.

suspected would soon be released. There were times when we were wrong. But on the whole our predictions were accurate, and despite the risk they were taking, the messengers usually did all they could to convey news of us to our families. Nonetheless, as the civil war continued to rage, the atmosphere in Iran was so tense that isolated telephone calls were never enough to put our relatives' minds entirely at rest and could on occasion arouse suspicion.

Three months after my arrest at the beginning of autumn, the Evin authorities agreed to allow our families to send us winter clothes—we had all been arrested in the heat of summer with no more than the shirt on our backs. The mere fact that our relatives could send us clothes and possibly a bit of money served as confirmation for them that we really were in Evin. All the same, they were never fully reassured until they could hear our own voices on the telephone. I was allowed to use the phone for the first time five months after my arrest. It was in fact on the day of my first cross-examination that the judge-mullah gave me permission to telephone my wife and tell her, quite simply, that I was at Evin; this was at least a confirmation that I was still alive. My wife's highly emotional reaction revealed the great strain my entire family was under. I managed, all the same, to ask her in the course of our brief conversation to bring in a few of my books so that the judge could see for himself that, contrary to the claims of an ignorant and overzealous young examining magistrate, I had not been an ideologue of the former regime. And since the mullah himself appeared to be calm and restrained, I said to him—once I had regained my composure after the emotional telephone call: "Your honor, you're acquainted with my ancestors who were all eminent theologians."

"Yes, of course!"

"You're willing to grant, then, that I am well versed in the principles of Islamic justice."

"Certainly!"

"You'll be able to see for yourself that in one of my books, entitled *Liberty, Ethics and Law*, I have sung the praises of Islamic justice as opposed to European justice. But the way in which this justice is being applied today bears no resemblance to the principles on which it is founded. Even if we accept that you're dealing with groups that are inspired by nihilistic and suicidal ideologies—and I'm very familiar with them since I've been living with their members for the past five months—that still doesn't justify the tribunal's severity. The fact that you've become so harsh indicates that your adversaries have managed to drag you down to their own level. You'll see later, your honor, that my own detention, for example, was groundless. Since I've never been an opponent, my imprisonment is of no benefit to the Islamic regime. In addition to myself, I know that a number of prisoners in my cell have been arrested on the vaguest of suspicions, and I have no doubt that a simple verification of this would allow them to be released. Islamic justice requires, above all else, enormous restraint and the greatest possible serenity. The biggest danger threatening you today is that the extremity of your adversaries' actions will make you abandon this restraint and serenity."

To which the judge-mullah replied: "You're perfectly correct, but you also have to remember that Islamic justice has not had enough experience in dealing with the strange phenomena we're facing today. Our adversaries' acts of violence compel us to arrest every possible suspect, and we don't have enough examining magistrates and judges to cope with the influx. That's why so many prisoners are held here in a state of uncertainty."

I should add that the revolutionary tribunal was working in a rather ambiguous environment. For example, one morning one of our guards, called Ali, who was usually hard and unhelpful and constantly scolded us and threatened us with punishment, came to stand in our doorway and, clearly embarrassed and uncomfortable, made the following announcement: "Following Bani-Sadr's removal, the authorities are holding presidential elections. Four candidates have been approved by the supervisory council. The Tudeh and the People's Fedayin have declared their support for Mr. Raja'i, the current prime minister, who has been nominated by the clergy. The election will be held the day after tomorrow, and there will be a ballot box here. You can vote for whomever you like."

After this democratic and peculiarly convivial declaration, he resumed his usual arrogant tone: "One, you should know that you're under no obligation to vote and, two, the Islamic Republic can manage very well without your vote. Do whatever you please!"

Then he slammed the door shut and left. His partly gentle, partly aggressive speech left us a little bemused, all the more so because there were a number of Fedayin (pro-Soviet communists) in our cells whose organizations had been mentioned by the guard.

The Philosophy of the Sun

Another activity organized by the prison administration consisted of "guidance" classes. This involved bringing mullahs, usually from the Qom seminary, to the prison to speak to the prisoners and, in accordance with the words of the Koran, show them "the right path." On the first such occasion the mullah was a man of about thirty. He entered our cell and launched into an hour-long rhetorical discourse about the virtues of Islamic justice. My cellmates remained unresponsive and silent. All at once I broke the silence and said to our guest speaker:

"You speak to us about the principles of Islamic justice, but you say at the same time that you haven't come to hear our grievances. The people you should be talking to are not prisoners but those who sit in judgment on their cases. To explain what I mean, I'll repeat a story my father used to tell me when I was a child. Once upon a time there was a quarrel between the sun and a cloud, with each claiming to be stronger than the other. In reply to the cloud's claims about its apocalyptic and destructive powers, the sun suggested that they put their strengths to a test. The cloud accepted. The sun pointed to a man who was walking in a forest below, wearing a coat, and said: 'Since you're so strong, do something to make that man take off his coat.' The cloud then unleashed a violent storm, but the harder the wind blew, the heavier the rain fell, the more tightly the man clutched his coat to himself. Then the sun said to the cloud: 'Now that you've proved that your violent methods are ineffective, let me show you what I can do.' The sun set to work, and in a few moments the man was suffused with warmth and took off his coat."

For our speaker's benefit I added, "To overcome violence you must preach the philosophy of the sun to the tribunal."

He thanked me and left. As soon as he had gone, my companions turned to me and said, "You must not speak to people like that. Under the Shah our older brothers, who found themselves in prison, always kept quiet in front of Savak agents."

I had to argue with them for two hours to try to persuade them that most of the people working for the Islamic regime were different from Savak agents, and despite their aggressive approach and their ignorance, they were not mercenaries.

"Don't forget," I said to then, "they go off to the fronts voluntarily, and they're willing to give their lives to push back the invaders. There's a sense in which they come to us as emissaries to open a dialogue, and we must embrace them with open arms to try to break the cycle of violence."

Did I convince them?

The Torment of Terrorism

Barely a month after Mohammed Raja'i's election as president of the republic, the guard Ali came to open our cell door early one morning and told us in tears that President Raja'i, Prime Minister Bahonar, and a number of other officials had been killed in a bomb explosion. An attack of this kind, carried out by the Mojahedin against the country's top officials as they were trying to organize the defenses of the nation in the face of an Iraqi invasion, could not fail to arouse the profound indignation of the general public.

Invoking "religious duty," Khomeini called on the nation to denounce the Mojahedin and their sympathizers. The circumstances of the explosion (the bomb was placed in the president's briefcase by the Supreme Defense Council's executive secretary) demonstrated the extent to which the Mojahedin had infiltrated the regime and the sense of insecurity they had created at every level. The Mojahedin organization had inculcated the notion of sacrifice into the minds of its young adherents so successfully that young girls of sixteen felt driven to tie grenades to themselves and, during the Friday prayer ceremonies that were held throughout the country, throw themselves into the arms of the ayatollahs. The resulting explosion would tear both aggressor and victim to pieces. Antiterrorist measures were initially ineffective in the face of such kamikaze operations. Khomeini and his lieutenants clearly did not intend to succumb to such formidable enemies.

During the summer, autumn, and winter of 1981 my cellmates and I could not help noticing that it was easier for the regime to deal with the Iraqi invasion than with these adversaries. For since Khomeini's return to Iran in February 1979 the Mojahedin had worked systematically to spread their influence and had succeeded in bringing under the banner of an equivocal Islam, which did not openly declare its Marxist affiliations, a generation of youth that had remained completely apolitical under the former regime and that had felt helpless in the wake of the revolution. Their recruitment centered on religious families, and it was not unusual for Islamic officials suddenly to discover that their sons or daughters had joined the ranks of the Mojahedin. Each day from August 1981 onward we used to see in the newspaper lists of people who had been executed, the names of a number of mullahs' children.

Be that as it may, Khomeini's charisma and his countrywide network of Shi'i clergymen succeeded in gaining the people's involvement in the hunt for the Mojahedin. Although they lived in hiding, emerging only occasionally to attack supporters of the regime, the Mojahedin could not in the end escape the vigilance of a population which on the whole supported the Islamic revolution. The extent of loyalty to Khomeini was such that families would even denounce their own children to the committees of pasdars. In choosing to apply in Iran the methods of Latin American Tupamaros and Palestinian guerrillas, the Mojahedin underestimated the people's dislike for ideologies that were alien to Iranian culture.

Liberty Forgotten

One evening we saw among the newly arrived detainees a man of about forty who was charged with belonging to one of the extreme secular left-wing groups that was supporting the armed insurrection. He was an electronic engineer and had spent twenty-odd years in the United States, where he had been a fierce opponent of the Shah and very active in the confederation of Iranian students. Like all opponents of the former regime who had returned to Iran en masse from the summer of 1978, he had come back to swell the ranks of the revolutionaries. He presented us with surprising details about the number and variety of small Marxist-Leninist parties. Sharing with us his own attempt at self-criticism, he acknowledged that the methods of intimidation, denunciation, and calumny practiced by the extreme left-wing parties in the two years immediately preceding and following the revolution (1978–1979) had had such a negative impact on the political climate of the country that the Islamist parties had been encouraged to adopt similar tactics for fear of being swept away by the left. He also admitted that the left-wing parties had not taken the Islamists seriously and had been convinced that power would come to them automatically. Having preached popular revolution, they had not envisaged for a moment that "popular" could be taken to mean "religious" by the population. Moreover, since some of the more vocal left-wing secular groups did not in practice respect individual liberty and human rights, they were in no position to demand these rights in the aftermath of the Islamic revolution. Had they themselves not sought to overthrow the Shah's regime through terror alone?

The remarks of the new arrival perplexed our young companions and gave them much to think about.

Siamese Twins

During the five months I spent in that cell I also met a type of prisoner very different from the Islamic Marxists. Arrested on various charges (economic offenses or collaboration with the former regime, for example), they belonged to an older generation and had a totally different mentality. They embodied the values of the monarchic era as well as its ways of thinking and behaving, and they proved incapable of adjusting either to the spirit or the rhythm of our new austere and communitarian life-style. They were prepared to violate every rule of harmonious coexistence in order to obtain for themselves an extra share of something, be it a single date or a vitamin tablet.

One day I took a few of the detainees in this category to a corner of the cell and said to them, "If you carry on behaving like this, you'll find you'll be doubly imprisoned. Here in the difficult conditions of our cell we're so dependent on one another that it's impossible to pursue an individualistic existence. In reality we're like Siamese twins."

By way of example, I spoke to them of how the newspapers were shared out and read collectively. But their incomprehension was so total that I realized no argument would persuade them.

Whenever we had collective discussions in our cell I could see that there was an enormous gap separating the two generations of prisoners. It was obvious that the obsessive concern for personal interest and individualism animating the older men could never be reconciled with the spirit of generosity and idealism the younger generation had gained on the crest of the revolution. Outside the prison walls it was precisely because the older generation did not serve as a model for them that the young people became involved in what were frequently suicidal activities.

On the other hand, whenever the tension subsided a little—for example, when we did not hear about the assassination of hezbollahs in the street or about executions at Evin—one could sense the emergence of a kind of sympathy between the younger prisoners and the pasdars of the same age. It was quite clear to me that the former had more in common with their jailors than with their older cellmates. For the pasdars, who more often than not were from rural areas or from southern Tehran, were no less animated than young people from better-educated circles by the great winds of change that were blowing through the country.

I could not help but think that the Shah's regime, despite its economic and technological achievements, had alienated the young en masse, and in the end this had been the cause of its fall. Unfortunately these young people who were prepared to accept any sacrifice—which they had proved now beyond any doubt—had fallen into the clutches of politicians who had exploited their idealism and dedication. I vividly recall the many times I awoke in the middle of the night to see, in the darkness, a number of my young cellmates standing on their feet in order to allow the others to sleep more comfortably!

Since these young boys were a mine of information for me on the mental universe and the behavior of Iranian youth, I tried to offer them something in return by always being prepared to organize debates or language classes, with, it should be said, the minimum of facilities, because we were not allowed writing materials. To help me organize my thoughts I used to rely on a *tasbih* (Muslim prayer beads), which a former cellmate had given me as a present when he was released. I would awake well before seven o'clock each morning, and in the silence of the cell I would mentally recall all the subjects I wanted to mention, with one subject per bead. At the end of the five months I was counting up to ninety-eight beads. At that point, however, it was decided that detainees who were over forty should be transferred to another part of the prison, Section 6, where the use of pen and paper was permitted.

Section 6

Section 6 was a kind of villa with four rooms on the ground floor, three rooms on the first floor, one bathroom, and several showers. That winter there were twenty-eight to thirty people in each room, and some prisoners even had to sleep in the corridors. We were privileged to have at our disposal a yard containing a number of plane trees, a little flowing stream, and a small swimming pool. In truth the yard was not unlike a summer garden in one of Tehran's better quarters. Coming as I did from the closed environment of a cell, to be free to roam around the yard and in and out of the different rooms was an unbelievable luxury. Furthermore, there were no pasdars on guard in the villa, and the prisoners were allowed to organize their daily lives for themselves. My fellow prisoners were mostly people who had held high posts under the Shah's regime, principally in the army or in the business sector, and the majority of them were held on suspicion of carrying out anti-Islamic activities.

Not surprisingly I found a number of former acquaintances among the two hundred people held at the villa, and it was very interesting to be able to speak with them. On the first night I was so excited about my sudden near magical transfer to a "dream" villa that I could not sleep a wink. The sense I had on that night of the possibility that I might eventually escape this nightmare was even stronger than on the day I was actually released twenty-three months later.

It was not only the freedom to wander about at will that transformed our life after the move to Section 6 but also—why not admit it—the freedom to go to the toilet whenever we liked. We found these new privileges immeasurably precious, even though in many other ways our conditions had not improved.

From a psychological point of view, two factors play an important part in the daily life of a prisoner. First, the constant struggle to understand the reason for one's arrest and to prepare a defense; and second, the endless worry about one's nearest and dearest. In my own case I still did not know why I had been arrested, and apart from the brief telephone conversation with my wife, I had had no contact with my family.

In our new section the anxiety and tension was all the more intense because some of the prisoners held there were threatened by the death sentence. This was true, for example, of a former top Savak official who under the Shah had headed the counterterrorism committee. He was charged with ill treatment of the Mojahedin and members of other guerrilla movements. Other detainees in this category were accused of having organized, as royalists, abortive military coups against the Islamic regime. Diverse types of prisoners were all thrown together, and National Front members could be seen calmly mingling with officers of the Shah's army and Savak officials as well as with Bani-Sadr's allies and other Islamist or Marxist revolutionaries.

The discussions and debates among these different groups were inevitably interesting and poignant. There were even occasions on which some detainees would find themselves recalling and commenting on armed clashes in which they had faced each other at the time of the Shah. In the two years I spent in Section 6 I witnessed the gradual emergence of a new set of values from the confrontation between opposing ideologies. With the slow passage of time the prisoners began to judge one another not according to political affiliation or past record but on the basis of the human characteristics they displayed: what counted more than anything else was the way the individual treated his fellow prisoners and how one behaved—with courage and dignity or with cowardice—before the tribunal.

For example, in our room we had a general from the Shah's army whose behavior in prison was modest and good-natured. A great sportsman, he used to lead, with indisputable authority, gymnastics sessions in which fifty-odd prisoners took part from six to seven o'clock each morning. The group of four prisoners with whom he shared food and living quarters included a notorious and longstanding opponent of the Shah and a communist engineer. The latter was particularly amazed by the general's good manners and concern for others. He told me he would never have believed there could be men like this in the Shah's army!

There was, on the other hand, another former general, in one of the other rooms, whose behavior was totally different. Several months after our transfer to Section 6 we were allowed a daily ration of cigarettes, which consisted first of one cigarette per person, then two, and finally three. In order to derive the maximum enjoyment from this meager allotment, the smokers had organized themselves into groups of five or six, known as "smokers' collectives." Instead of each person smoking his own quota, the members of each "collective" would prolong their pleasure by sharing one cigarette at a time, several times a day. And if a cigarette was ever offered to them in addition to their "official" quota, they would as a matter of course put it into the communal kitty. But in this general's room the members of his "collective" discovered that whenever he had such a windfall he would go and smoke it by himself in the toilet. He was immediately ejected from all the collectives.

The quality of existence is even more important than existence itself. Although long-term detention has negative effects on human beings, it can also be positive, for it suppresses certain social conventions and allows the true characteristics of each individual to emerge. The detainees end up learning about their strengths as well as their weaknesses. This is why, as far as I am concerned, no judgment of character is more accurate than that passed by one prisoner on another.

Although our life in the "villa" offered certain advantages, it also had one significant drawback, namely the permanent presence of a prisoner responsible for the group who was selected by the pasdars—a "kapo," in other words. We were allowed to organize our own days, and the pasdars would simply come to check up on us from time to time; the kapo was thus in a way "answerable" for us. Our kapo was a "common-law" prisoner who had been arrested in western Iran in the course of an armed robbery. With the help of a few frustrated and uneducated pasdars of rural origin, he had become a petty tyrant. To begin with, he had taken over one of the rooms on the ground floor, supposedly to set up a cooperative store; in fact he used it to sell things at exorbitant prices. Surrounded by a retinue of dubious moral caliber, he had formed a kind of gang which spread fear throughout the section. For my own part, contrary to the opinion of most other prisoners, I was convinced that this situation had not been planned but was the result of a combination of accidental factors. I was to be proven right by subsequent events.

Prison Lessons

A few days after my arrival in Section 6 one of my former assistants, Takmil-Homayoun, who had been close to Bani-Sadr and had helped him hide before escaping to France, joined our community after spending six months in solitary confinement. During those six months his guard, an elderly pasdar, had gone to his cell every evening to study the Koran with him, and a friendship had developed between them. Being older than the others and having lost his son in the war, the pasdar was highly regarded by his younger colleagues. A real guardian angel for Takmil, he had followed him to our section. Through Takmil we let him know that the kapo in our section was not a very nice man and that it would be better if he could be moved to a section reserved for common-law offenders. Not only did he grant our wish, but he asked what other changes would make our lives easier. He accepted our proposal that we should be allowed to choose our own section head, and we elected a printer named Davoud, who was extremely courteous to everyone.[5] We also suggested that the room previously used by the section head be turned into a classroom which could be used both for lessons on Islam and courses on topics of general interest, especially language classes. I was selected to be in charge of these lessons, and in keeping with the advice of the man we had come to call our "good pasdar" we made every effort to avoid giving our classes any political overtone—for the pasdars would not tolerate any signs of rebellion. In fact, they did not even permit us to discuss or comment on the Koran,[6] the reading of which is considered to be sacrosanct by Muslims.

In our villa we had people from a wide variety of professions, among them a first-rate geologist who had worked for twenty years in Iran's mining industries. I invited him to speak to us about gas, oil, iron, lead, silver, and so on. When the pasdar saw that our lecturer confined himself to nothing more harmful than the formation of the earth's crust and the ice ages, he brought us a blackboard and chalk.

5. There were at this time a considerable number of printers at Evin who were charged with having prepared illegal newspapers and publications.

6. They were afraid we would take the same path as the Mojahedin, who in the name of an Islam strongly tinged with Marxism had turned into an Iranian version of the Khmer Rouge.

A dozen or so days went by in this way, without any interference from the pasdars. When our geologist had exhausted his subject, I invited a geographer to talk to us about Iran's flora and climate. After our lessons in geomorphology and geography, I asked a historian to tell us about the first people who had migrated from the cold northern steppes (of Russia) to settle on the Iranian plateau. By the end of a month of daily lectures we had convinced the pasdars (who would knit their brows together whenever they heard unfamiliar technical terms) that we were not conducting political or politically motivated discussions, and they left us entirely to ourselves. When our historian completed his lectures in prehistory and moved on to an examination of early and then contemporary Iranian history, the pasdars did not say a word. In the course of these lessons, which lasted almost a year, we managed to go over many aspects of historical, artistic, economic, and even political life in Iran. Since the secretary general of the hunting association was also with us, we even had lessons in the different kinds of game indigenous to the country. We also had a number of lectures about transport and traffic delivered by a former police colonel who had studied these subjects in a range of urban centers, from San Francisco to Tokyo. I even invited an editor to speak to us about the question of censorship, both under the Shah and under the Islamic regime; he did so without our encountering any difficulties or problems.

At the end of the lecture series one of the detainees, who had beautiful handwriting, wrote a twenty-page report for us to present to the procurator of Evin Prison. When I handed over the report to the head pasdar, Haji Reza—a young man of about thirty with a secondary-school education—and asked him to pass it on to his superiors, he skimmed over a few paragraphs with obvious interest and said earnestly, "Your report proves that holding people like you, whose education has cost the country a fortune, is sheer madness, especially on such tenuous grounds. You were absolutely right to prepare this report. It will give my superiors something to think about. May God protect you!"

I can only assume that Haji Reza's views were not shared universally by the prison administration, otherwise the detainees in the villa would not have remained in Evin for months and even years.

The Magic of Technology

Although they did not share Haji Reza's admiration for the Section 6 detainees' level of education and expertise, whenever the need arose the judges, deputy prosecutors, and pasdars at Evin showed that they understood the value of the prisoners' talents.

During my first period of imprisonment a big restaurant owner told me the story of how, the moment he arrived at Evin, he had put forward proposals for improving the food quality. The prison director, Kachoui, had given him a free hand, and he had taken over every aspect of food preparation, from the purchase of provisions to food distribution and preservation. In this way he had become the prison director's principal adviser. I also became acquainted with an eminent civil engineer, Siamak Farzad, who had been sentenced to life imprisonment on various charges, ranging from membership in a Masonic lodge to giving bribes in order to win major construction contracts. At first he had been sent to Sorkheh-Hessar Prison where he had noticed that the prison hospital was in a dilapidated state. The director, a very sensible merchant from the bazaar, had entrusted Farzad with the task of carrying out the necessary repairs on condition that they be done at the prisoners' own expense and using their own technical expertise. So Farzad had embarked on a large-scale project which took two years to complete and entailed constant trips between the prison and Tehran. Later he was to benefit from an amnesty and was set free.

Although the prison regime was at its most severe during my third detainment, the technical expertise of the prisoners in our villa was no less appreciated by the prison authorities. We had among us a construction engineer named Neshat who was about fifty years old and had been educated in the United States. Totally devoted to advanced technology, he viewed America's achievements with near reverence and could not stomach the pasdars' anti-American slogans. He made no secret of the fact that he intended to return to the United States the moment he was allowed to leave Evin, even if this meant slipping out of the country illegally.

He would explain all this to the pasdars with astonishing frankness. Indeed, he was completely lacking in any political awareness in an environment where everything was, ironically, highly political. Nevertheless, Neshat was seen as a kind of "technical wizard." Although he had a bare minimum of resources and equipment, he could repair anything, from spectacles and watches to the bathroom boiler. As soon as the pasdars discovered his talent, they viewed him with great respect and frequently took him without a blindfold—a sign of absolute trust at the time—to any part of the prison where something needed to be repaired. In return for his work he had been given a hammer and a set of pliers, which he used to great effect to solve all our daily problems; one moment he would be setting up extra shelves for storing provisions and the next he would be making us a coat stand or putting up a line for us to hang our washing on. He worked ceaselessly, day and night, and the pasdars considered him to be a kind of "superman." In reality he became Evin Prison's chief engineer. He was released after a year and, just as he had announced to the tribunal, left immediately for the United States.

There was also, among the people detained in the villa, an artist from the traditional school of painting, whose arrest had not been for political reasons. Naturally cavalier in attitude, he proclaimed himself to be libertarian and openly mocked anything remotely political. But his character was molded by popular Iranian notions of gallantry, and he had a great talent for friendship. It was a strong friendship indeed that linked him to an old army general, a former deputy minister of defense and armaments, whom he had met in prison. The general was a highly cultured man and beyond all reproach, but he was also very introverted and hypersensitive. He had attempted suicide in prison and spoke to no one except the painter, who was skillful at drawing portraits. The pasdars often asked him to draw portraits of the Islamic Republic's leaders, including Khomeini, from their photographs. These drawings were destined to grace the walls of Evin's sports hall, which was also used as a mosque and lecture room. As the artist worked, the other prisoners would watch the pasdars with surprise and amusement, seeing them in a new light, for they were enchanted by the artist's magic. The pasdars were so taken with his talent that they provided him with everything he needed to practice his art and were willing to do anything he asked of them. In that time of high tension, when the pasdars' mistrust of the prisoners was never greater, the mere fact that a prisoner could ask the pasdars for favors was an unusual phenomenon. But our artist was so uninterested in worldly matters that it never occurred to him to derive any personal gain from the situation, and he used to ask the pasdars only to make life easier for the general.

As to our appearing before the tribunal, we knew that as long as the cases of the prisoners charged with involvement in armed attacks had not been heard by the judges, ours would not be either. In reality I was not too unhappy about the delay because the mere fact of being cross-examined or sentenced in a tense and highly charged climate carried certain risks, especially in my case where everything revolved around my reputation and the image that the judges and examining magistrates might have of me. I had sensed from the first few days that the examining magistrate dealing with my case, who had a degree in law (this was quite unusual in Evin at the time), had tried, without saying anything, to send me to an out-of-the-way part of the prison so that I would be forgotten. This man, like others of his kind, did not welcome the tense climate which had been reigning over the tribunal since the start of the Mojahedin's armed insurrection. They tried to have themselves transferred to other posts, leaving the unappealing task of interrogation to the pasdars who had already "dirtied their hands"—if one can put it this way—in the course of the bloody clashes with armed groups.

While I am filled with admiration for all those people who work for organizations such as Amnesty International or who sign petitions against repression in different parts of the world, I believe that one cannot condemn the acts of violence perpetrated by a ruling power against people who resort to blind terror without at the same time condemning terrorism. Regardless of the qualities of those who use it, terrorism will only compel a judicial system, of whatever kind, to adopt in turn exceptional and repressive measures to destroy the armed aggressors. Mindless violence is always to be condemned. We Iranians are unfortunately in a good position to know, both from our experience under the Shah and under the Islamic regime. Armed groups forced Savak to become more repressive, and the same thing happened again under the Islamists. Horrifying though the repression may be, how can one be surprised at the behavior of a judge who, faced with an accused who knows the location of a cache of arms, cannot put out of his mind the fact that if he does not extract a confession, people, including innocent people, will be killed? This was the appalling situation which existed when prisoners appeared before the courts in Evin during the summer, autumn, and winter of 1981.

Each morning the names of seven or eight prisoners were called over the speakers. They had to present themselves at the back door of our building. A pasdar would come to lead them, blindfolded, to the tribunal. Once there they had to wait, sitting along a corridor wall, for a deputy public prosecutor to take them to one of the offices in which either the preliminary investigation into their case or the passing of sentence would take place in the presence of a mullah.

As I have said earlier, the judge-mullahs tended to be more lenient than the deputy prosecutors or examining magistrates. But during times of high tension the judges were so dominated, not to say terrorized by the deputies that the sentences were often very severe. When the accused were sentenced to prison terms there was a possibility their sentence might later be reduced—a life sentence could, for example, be reduced to five years—by the amnesties which were granted regularly by Khomeini to mark occasions such as the anniversary of the revolution on February 11, or the Iranian New Year on March 21. This was not possible in the case of death sentences; here no recourse was available.

Men like the first prime minister of the postrevolutionary period, Mehdi Bazargan, or moderate members of the clergy, like Beheshti and Motahhari (who were close to Khomeini), succeeded, two months after the revolution, in reining in the revolutionary tribunals and limiting the application of capital punishment. But after the Mojahedin's armed uprising the pendulum swung back again. This was why my fellow inmates were fully aware that they risked execution if they were implicated in guerrilla operations. Of course the judges always left room for hope that their lives might be spared if they agreed to provide information, and furthermore the inner workings of the tribunals remained eternally mysterious.

"The Dustbin Master"

One afternoon, two months after my arrival at the villa, the names of about fifteen prisoners were read out over the public speaker system;

they were told to "present themselves with all their belongings."[7] A few felt very optimistic and thought they were about to be released. We said goodbye to them, and for the next few days we did not know what had become of them. Soon after we read in the papers that they had been executed.

Despite our leisurely walks and physical exercise, our lecture series, our afternoon teas, after-dinner visits to other prisoners' rooms, none of us ever felt really safe. The smell of death was always in the air. In addition to the prisoners who were sentenced to death in Evin itself, we also saw a procession of condemned prisoners arriving from other prisons; they were forced to spend a few days with us because all executions were carried out at Evin. In this way we used to hear about trials conducted behind closed doors, and we would learn about the existence of other prisons—and there were many in Tehran at that time—the most important of which was Jamishidieh, where the military tribunal sat in judgment on cases of soldiers and civilians implicated in the attempted coup d'état against the regime.

In view of the news blackout imposed in Evin and other prisons, any contact with outsiders was a precious source of information. What gave a political prisoner the greatest satisfaction was to be able to piece together a picture of what was really happening politically from scraps of information gathered here and there, because he was then in a better position, cut off though he was from the outside world, to judge in general how things stood and in particular what his own chances were.

A kind of obsession with news took hold of my coprisoners, and it made them keen to volunteer for any chore that would allow them to move about in the prison. This could consist, for example, of accompanying the kapo to fetch the huge pot of food, or even of offering to empty the dustbins, although there was already a prisoner in the villa who was specifically responsible for emptying the bins twice a day. In fact, only three prisoners were allowed to leave the villa on a regular basis: the kapo, the doctor (who stayed with us), and the "dustbin master." This was considered to be a privilege because the people in

7. For the prisoners the formula "present themselves with all their belongings" could mean a transfer to another prison, liberation, or execution. The guards made a point of leaving the meaning unclear.

question not only brought themselves to the attention of the prison authorities, who came to regard them as a kind of community service employee, but could also obtain bits of news and information.

The question of information in the prison was one of my pet subjects in my discussions with fellow prisoners. I would make the point that as far as information was concerned, Evin was a microcosm of modern-day society and that information had become the real source of power in our age. For example, when the Shah was at the height of his power, he used to receive roughly twenty confidential reports a day in addition to the reports he received from international contacts. The United States, for its part, had lost its all-powerful image and its credibility when it had emerged that the CIA did not know about everything that was happening in Iran. Much the same phenomenon can be seen in other industrialized countries where, despite the profusion of information available and apparently free access to information, people are less and less informed, especially about the inner workings of economic and political decision-making. This is why every little scrap of information about the public or private life of politicians takes on enormous significance when it comes to light.

As for myself, I found a chance to roam by volunteering to do work on a new prison building close to our villa. Soon after I was transferred to Section 6 I was told that the administration had asked younger prisoners to lend a hand to the construction workers for two hours a day. Each day a large number of prisoners would volunteer for this manual labor, not only because it gave them a chance to leave their cells but also because the physical activity was a boon to people otherwise forced into inactivity. In fact there were so many volunteers that the pasdars were unable to use them all and had to be selective. One day I too decided to volunteer. As I was pushing a wheelbarrow full of bricks, the prison director (a bazaari who, according to Haji Reza, claimed he had read my books and who always treated me with a certain deference) came up to me and exclaimed, "My dear professor, why are you pushing this wheelbarrow? We have instructed the pasdars repeatedly that they should select the youngest people. Just imagine our disgrace if the authorities find out that we've forced an intellectual of your caliber to work like a convict. . . ."

To which I replied, "My dear man, let me tell you, first of all, that I myself offered to help because physical activity in this beautiful weather and lovely mountain air is a real pleasure, and very healthy as well. Second, is there not a popular adage that says, 'Others have sown so that we may reap; let us sow in turn so that others may reap after we're gone'? Aren't you glad that others worked before us to construct Evin with its beautiful grounds? Without their efforts you and I would have ended up in hovels and sheds instead of a well-equipped prison. Since regimes come and go and prisons remain, should we not work for the well-being of future prisoners?"

The director returned, "I know that you're joking, Mr. Naraghi. But you know very well there are no prisoners in Islam. At the beginning of the revolution there were even enthusiastic young people who wanted to destroy Evin, but we stopped them. If the Mojahedin hadn't embarked on their absurd armed insurrection, neither you nor I would be here."

A Renegade's Morale

Besides organizing daily lectures and language lessons, I continued to take a keen interest in the fate of my companions. As we walked together in our section's courtyard, we would share confidences and grievances and try to help each other to analyze our problems. For example, I remember walking more than an hour a day, for a whole month, with a young butcher, originally from the town of Saveh in central Iran. He had been thrown into prison because he had tried to protect one of his friends who had been involved in a drug-related incident. Very warmhearted, the boy had a carefree attitude, a good sense of humor, and a vivid imagination. Although passionately devoted to life, he was prepared to brave the most difficult situations. For me he was the archetypal Persian depicted by Gobineau 150 years earlier; that is to say, he was the product of an ancient and refined civilization which did not allow people to take themselves too seriously or to launch into grandiloquent speeches. And in fact his wit and sarcasm never left him. Although he had never studied Omar Khayyam, Hafez, or the other great Iranian poets, he was entirely at one with them. I saw him as a model of what social mobility could achieve, far better than any modern education, in terms of culture, humanism, and a general philosophy of life. I never tired of his company, and I learned a great deal from him about life in small provincial towns, particularly about the problems of young drug addicts—an issue which was completely covered up by official puritanism.

In one corner of our yard, near the swimming pool, there was a fallen tree trunk which served as a bench. The prisoners would go there to sit by themselves when they were traumatized at the thought of appearing before the tribunal, by anxieties about their families, or for other reasons. People went there whenever they could not bear to be in the company of others. The trunk was known as "the bench of despair." Often when a man was spotted there the others would come and ask me to speak to him. I never turned down such a request, for I knew that, at least in the short term, conversation would help alleviate the sorrow.

The business of comforting a distressed prisoner essentially consisted of listening to him and making him see, as far as possible, that solutions did exist for problems over which neither he nor I had any control. Cast out of the everyday world and unable to affect it in any way, our only hope was to try to imagine, and to believe in, the best possible outcome to our predicament. It was also important to point out that experience showed that the passage of time, the interminable waiting endured by many of us before our cases were dealt with, was a positive factor. Furthermore it was important to persuade a distressed man that the situation of our families—a constant source of anxiety to all prisoners—was often less difficult materially than we imagined. For in a traditional society such as Iran people have numerous informal channels of support, and this could be seen, for example, in the help the prisoners themselves received in various forms from people in the outside world.

Conditions in our villa began to improve after a few months. Haji Reza used to give me about a dozen cigarettes a week as a token of gratitude for my efforts to educate the prisoners and to help our community in general. This made my task easier when I had to deal with a depressed prisoner if he happened to be a smoker; not a smoker myself, I could offer him a cigarette all to himself, to help soothe his nerves.

I also used my extra cigarettes to help maintain people's morale by keeping them occupied. I had the idea of offering a cigarette to any prisoner who could bring me three new words or phrases from the revolutionary Islamic speeches regularly disseminated by the media. To them this may have seemed a pointless activity. But by the time I left Evin I had collected about a thousand expressions which came in part from the Koran and in part from Western and Marxist revolutionary terminology—precious material I could exploit later in linguistic and sociological studies.

Yet despite the tricks we used to "kill time," we were all deeply concerned, between the summer of 1981 and the winter of 1982, about the distress our families were suffering because of uncertainty over our fate. I learned later that throughout this time my wife and my second son, aged fourteen at the time, would wait impatiently every day for the evening papers to appear, to go over the names of the executed prisoners in fearful silence. My parents followed exactly the same procedure at their house, and each day as soon as my mother was certain that my name was not on the gruesome list, she would ring my wife to express "their pleasure," without ever mentioning the newspapers. The fact of the matter was that my family remained completely in the dark about my case for fifteen months, and neither my relatives nor I knew exactly what charges the tribunal intended to bring against me. The Islamic regime, threatened by the Mojahedin, was in the grip of panic and had fallen into the trap of responding to violence with violence. It also tended to treat all the suspects under arrest as implacable enemies. A nagging suspicion that I might be executed was therefore ever present, and it was felt not only by my family but also by many of my friends.

That was why Marc Kravetz, the *Libération* journalist, put me down as "lost" in his book *Irano Nox*. Then there was Walton Gelhoff, secretary general at the Foreign Ministry in Bonn, with whom I had formed a friendship twenty years earlier when he was beginning his diplomatic career in Tehran. He had tried to bring about some movement on my case by contacting Iranian officials through the German embassy—all to no effect. He too interpreted his lack of success as a sign that I was under a sentence of death.[8] Some of my

8. He was, needless to say, totally stunned when he saw me alive and well in Paris in the spring of 1986, when he was a member of UNESCO's executive council. In November 1987, in a speech addressed to the farewell banquet held to mark the ending of the mandate of the organization's secretary general, the Senegalese Amadou-Mahtar M'Bow, Walter Gelhoff thanked him for the discreet and persistent contacts he had made with "a UNESCO member state to obtain the release of an imprisoned friend."

fellow prisoners also confided to me later that in the winter of 1981 they too thought I was likely to be executed. They had been even more convinced after a visit paid to our section by Mousavi-Tabrizi, the revolutionary tribunal's procurator general, who had a particularly severe attitude toward prisoners. When I tried to explain to him that I had been arrested on suspicion of collaborating with Bani-Sadr, although I had not seen him at all since his election as president of the republic, Mousavi-Tabrizi looked very irritated and pronounced the words—tantamount to a death sentence at the time—"You are a renegade!" I thought he was particularly annoyed because he knew he could not justify my detention, but as far as my companions were concerned, from that day onward I was a dead man.

In that same winter of 1981, when Prime Minister Mir-Hossein Mousavi was presenting his budget for the following year to the Parliament, he delivered a speech in which he was at pains to establish the socioeconomic originality of his budget. He declared, "Our budget bears no resemblance to those which used to be prepared by the theoreticians of the former regime, such as Naraghi." Mr. Mousavi's statement notwithstanding, I must say that throughout my entire life I have never played the smallest role in drawing up a budget! The accusation made by the head of government simply revealed the extent of ignorance which—I was to realize later—aroused great amusement among the judges at Evin.[9]

The Mystical Brotherhood

Worrying though the direct and indirect threats made against me were, they did not succeed in disturbing my peace of mind, and throughout my detention I refused to abandon my congenital optimism. In the first place, for reasons I have already mentioned, I did not personally believe that the tribunal was seriously contemplating my execution. Second, from the very start of my third arrest until my release twenty-eight months later, I stuck to the essential belief that execution was one possibility among others which I had to be

9. Since the revolutionary tribunal claimed to be independent vis-à-vis the executive, the judges at Evin missed no opportunity to show their superiority over the government. They were also keen to suggest that the detainees were under protection while at Evin. . . .

prepared to accept—because I subscribe to the notion of destiny. I felt that death, even when premature and brutal, was one of the given factors of existence. One of the sayings of Iranian mysticism often came to my mind: "Life is something which is briefly entrusted to your care; the day when it is taken from you, you have no right to complain, because it never belonged to you." The same idea animated the Sufi brotherhood, whose writings were commented on in a book by the renowned French Iranologist Henry Corbin. When I was fortunate enough to find it in the Evin library, I immediately set about translating it into Persian for publication after my release.

In short, I accepted my detention as an unavoidable reality, and because I had not been surprised by either the revolution or its subsequent vicissitudes I felt less bitter than many others. To the officials of the former regime I could justifiably say that I had always criticized their excessive zeal on two fronts: mindless and haphazard Westernization, and a scandalous enrichment of the top layer of society. And to the revolutionaries belonging to any of the different tendencies (Marxist, nationalist, or Islamist) who had collaborated with the religious figures to overthrow the Shah but who had tried afterward to seize power themselves, I could put the following question: "You exploited the great strength possessed by religious leaders to mobilize the masses against the Shah. But how did you imagine you would be able to take over and run the country without them? Did you really think that they would just go back to their mosques and hand everything over to you? Very well then! The religious figures were stronger than you. They didn't let you have your way, and you've no right to cry foul now."

Personally I felt not so much a prisoner of the system as a victim of a complex situation from which the authorities themselves were suffering. And I believed that if the tension did begin to ease, there was a distinct possibility we could be released.

It had been announced that in February (1982) our families would be allowed to visit us, an event hundreds of prisoners were anxiously awaiting. The pasdars whetted our appetites by telling us that the prison authorities were building a new reception room for that very purpose. The great day arrived at last! Everyone was dressed and waiting at the crack of dawn. We paced up and down the courtyard, waiting for our names to be called on the loudspeakers. At eight o'clock the first group of twenty prisoners heard their names called. Blindfolded, they were led to a minibus and taken to a building recently constructed near Evin's main gate. Before entering the room, which was divided in two by a long glass partition, the prisoners were allowed to remove their blindfolds. During the first few months of family visits we could do nothing other than stand by the partition without speaking to the visitors. We had to wait until May before the intercoms were installed, making communication possible.

When my turn arrived I spotted my wife and two of my children. The little one, who was only five at the time, spontaneously rushed toward me only to find there was a glass partition between us. Although deeply disappointed at not being able to throw himself into my arms, he regained his poise right away and communicated with a smile. Afterward, when I told my companions about my son's reaction and his nice smile, one of them wrote a poem about it.

After a few months the prison authorities granted permission for the pasdars to bring children aged less than seven to us so that we could embrace them. The pasdars performed this task with considerable gentleness and even affection. The visits took place once every three weeks, and they were granted only to prisoners who were not likely to exchange information which might affect their cross-examination. The visits were never more than ten minutes, which obviously seemed much too short to us and forced us to be as concise as possible. Because we were not allowed to have any paper, many of us would scribble a few brief phrases in the palms of our hands so we would not forget the important things we wanted to say. For my own part, I would run quickly through any essential points in the first few minutes so that I could speak to my wife more calmly in the remaining time. It is vital for a political prisoner that his visitor tell him about any political developments that might affect his case, and I was fortunate as my wife not only followed current events but was able, because of her Islamic upbringing, to make sense of many developments which remained incomprehensible to others.

Sometimes my companions would return from the visiting sessions completely perplexed by the conversations with their wives, for the simple reason that these women were incapable of stepping out of their own mental framework enough to understand their husbands' situation. Moreover, unless the meeting, which lasted no more than ten minutes, had been carefully "planned" by the two sides, it often left more of a negative than a positive impact. Having been locked up for considerable lengths of time in a prison cell, a prisoner would often end up behaving like a child who was accustomed to a very specific rhythm of life and felt that the world belonged entirely to him. Any change from without, which disturbed this rhythm unexpectedly, risked upsetting him. It was in fact not unusual to find that the prisoners who had been in the best of spirits earlier in the morning as they eagerly waited to meet their families, returned later in the day depressed and traumatized. Seeing their loved ones for a brief spell only served to exacerbate their frustration. But this kind of trauma was unheard of among the revolutionaries—whether Mojahedin or communists—who had already spent a number of years in prison under the former regime and were adept, as were their families, at drawing the maximum benefit from the visits.

One way or another the visits were the most important events in the prisoners' lives. In the afternoons and evenings of the great day we would exchange the detailed information we had gleaned from our visitors, trying to understand what was happening outside and piecing together the "psychopolitical puzzle" of a regime which many of us found incomprehensible. Carefully composed, these tiny bits of information from across the political spectrum, depending on the prisoners' links, helped shed some light on our immediate prospects.

Since I was viewed as an incurable optimist, my companions used to let me know the minute they had any news which they thought might lend itself to a favorable interpretation—pointing to our imminent release, in other words—and overnight I would construct a theory to encourage them. Even my most skeptical companions would frequently accept my analyses. They seemed to feel, deep down inside, that it was better to take account of all the indications—which according to my assessments suggested our not-too-distant release—rather than constantly to dwell on the possibility that we might be executed or have to spend the rest of our lives in prison.

Eventually the prison administration gave permission for us to hug our children. This development was so significant to my companions that many of them turned into stone carvers! They would spend days by the swimming pool where they would polish small granite stones in order to turn them into medallions. Then they would carve out the name of their child on one side of the stone and a flower on the other. One morning, on a visiting day, I was delighted to be given a medallion in my youngest son's name. Later, close to the date of my release, my sculptor friend also made me a gift of a rosary fashioned from date stones; I have carried it with me ever since.

The celebration of religious and national occasions also helped to improve morale in our section. The historian Takmil-Homayoun proved a very capable master of ceremonies, and the presence among us of academics, poets, singers, and other artists made our celebrations so memorable that the pasdars often preferred to join us rather than go to Evin's great hall where the prison authorities held more official ceremonies attended by several thousand detainees and addressed by speakers from the Islamic Republic's hierarchy.

Devotees of the Same Martyr

The great hall was also used for weekly prayer meetings on the eve of the Muslim sabbath. Starting from the autumn of 1981, before my transfer to the villa, on some Thursday evenings the pasdars would tell us that we could, if we wished, attend the prayer meeting—under close guard, of course. The first such occasion I attended left a deep impression on me. Lajevardi himself, the frightening procurator general of the tribunal and the governor of Evin, greeted the crowds of prisoners and ushered them one by one along the many rows of seats. He performed the task with the type of skill and, more significantly, friendly cordiality he might have shown in more peaceful times in one of the traditional ceremonies popular in Tehran's southern districts. His polite and unassuming manner left the prisoners totally bewildered. It was difficult to accept that this was the same man who a few hours earlier had arranged the execution of twenty, forty, or even eighty prisoners!

I could not help but be struck, in the course of that first prayer meeting, by the electrifying atmosphere when, with the entire gathering on its feet, several thousand prisoners and a few hundred pasdars joined Lajevardi to chant their devotion to the martyr Hussein. Beating their chests rhythmically with their hands, they all shouted in unison: "Hussein! Hussein!"

Prisoner and jailor thus sang the praises of the same saint: the pasdar perhaps because he had just that morning lost a brother, a cousin, or a friend, assassinated in a public place by Mojahedin guerrillas; and the prisoner because he had possibly lost a brother, cousin, or friend executed that very afternoon not more than two hundred meters from the hall. Both invoked the same martyr Hussein as a symbol of the world's injustices.

Islam and the Shi'i martyrology provided the leaders of the Islamic Republic with a powerful weapon. Cleverly mixing the temporal with the nontemporal in their speeches, they knew exactly how to use Islam to the best effect in order to break down barriers and draw young opponents into their camp. Invoking historic tales of Shi'i martyrology and using a language of love and devotion, they appealed easily to religious symbols embedded deep in the collective psyche and only temporarily submerged under a veneer of secular ideologies.

This was one reason why the Mojahedin changed sides so rapidly. Almost as soon as they arrived at Evin, Mojahedin prisoners would join the ranks of the "repentees" and turn into apparently fervent supporters of the regime. I was therefore not very surprised to see that evening, in the hall of Evin, the enthusiasm with which these youths supported the regime and prayed for Khomeini in spite of their previous opposition.

It is easy to believe that such a conversion was no more than a ruse by the Mojahedin to save their own lives. But although there were obviously numerous "conversions" of convenience, there were also many genuine changes of heart. Indeed, I met quite a few of these new devotees. Even if we assume they were a minority, it is worth dwelling on their cases. These were young people who had been trained, in the name of a revolutionary Islamic Marxist ideology, to submit unreservedly to a political organization which claimed to be all powerful. Now cut off from that organization, they surrendered to another which was at least as powerful but which was more substantially Islamic and furthermore enjoyed the support of the clergy. They frequently ended up becoming even more passionate supporters of the regime than the pasdars themselves.

In addition, I believe this transformation may be explained psychologically by the fact that the Mojahedin found themselves confronted in Evin by the contradictions inherent in their doctrine and their analyses of the political situation. For example, since the Mojahedin accused the Islamic regime of being in the pay of foreigners, the judges at Evin took great pleasure in demonstrating to the young prisoners that in fact it was their own organization which, with the firm support of the West, was gradually moving its base to Iraq, a country at war with Iran.[10]

Our Library

Yet another source of distraction for some of the prisoners was the creation in our section of a small library, thanks to the help of our resident doctor who had free access to the main building and hence to the central library. On Haji Reza's request, I was given the task of running the library with the help of two young prisoners. The books there had obviously been selected with great care. Books on the Koran and Shi'i theology naturally took pride of place, but there were also philosophical and political works which had been deemed acceptable by the Islamic regime. Much to my amazement, I also found a number of my own books—though only those in which I had criticized the haphazard Westernization pursued by the Shah.

I used to encourage my companions to read some of the theological books so that they could familiarize themselves with a world from which their secular life-styles under the Shah had estranged them and thus be in a better position to face their Islamic judges. Among the other works of a political nature, there were also fifty or so volumes of the documents found by the Khomeinist students in the American embassy in 1979, when they had occupied it and taken the diplomats hostage. The volumes brought together reports prepared over a period of two decades. They were at once a reflection of American policy in Iran and of the tenor of relations between the Americans and the officials of the former regime. Most notably they revealed that the political intelligence of the Shah's "protectors" had not been superior to the regime's own intelligence. One was given the impres-

10. The Mojahedin had repeatedly obtained declarations of support from Western bodies. In 1989 the European Parliament once again adopted with extraordinary naiveté and a two-thirds majority a resolution calling on the UN to expel the representatives of the Islamic Republic and to recognize the Mojahedin organization as the representative of the Iranian people.

sion, in effect, that the American embassy staff had often been quite content just to maintain friendly relations with the regime's public figures, to meet them at dinners accompanied by their wives, and to be on first-name terms with them, imagining that this would ensure their being kept informed about the country's political developments. With one or two exceptions, the reports did not contain any deep analysis of Iranian society.

Neither religion nor the potential of Shi'i Islam to mobilize an entire nation for a cause had apparently held any interest for the embassy analysts, any more than they had, for that matter, interested Iran's own secret agents. For the American embassy as well as for Savak, religious personalities were seen as nothing more than a barrier against the spread of communism. One of the notable characteristics of the reports, which were after all about aspects of Iran's political, social, and economic life, was that they rarely mentioned the problem of corruption, even though during the final years of the Shah's regime it was one of the most fashionable topics of conversation in high society circles.

About a year after my transfer to Section 6, when the threat posed by the Mojahedin was abating and tension was diminishing at Evin, we were allowed a little more freedom. This gave us the opportunity, with the cooperation of Haji Reza and a number of well-educated pasdars, to collect some money to buy books. In this way we managed to obtain *The Story of Civilization* by Will Durant, an American historian whose humanistic vision reflected the progressive optimism of the Roosevelt years. The work, which had been translated into Persian at the time of the Shah, consisted of twenty heavy volumes to which the author and his wife had dedicated their lives. The work's arrival was a source of pleasure to many in our section. From the very first day prisoners would line up outside our library to borrow one of the volumes which they would then read in the shade of a tree.

This appetite for history had, in my opinion, two sources: first, in the face of the implacable official line, carried by all the media, reading accounts of past events allowed our own situation to be put into historical perspective; second, these travels through time served as a reminder, as we endured our distressing isolation, of the eternal battle against oppression and injustice which, despite many setbacks, always triumphed in the end. For a person who is placed in a situation of impotence, history in this sense suggests the possibility of future vindication and provides a kind of consolation; for the person can at least see that his fate is not unrelated to that endured by many others throughout the centuries.

In reading the section of the encyclopedia on the French Revolution, I was struck by two dominant ideas. In the volume in which Will Durant analyzed the thinking of Rousseau and Voltaire, who played a fundamental role in triggering the revolution, he showed that between the forces of passion and those of reason, the revolution ultimately allowed itself to be carried by passion; between the ideas of Rousseau, taken up by Robespierre, and those of Voltaire, embodied in Condorcet, the former won the day. Even if later, as passion gradually subsided, Voltaire's ideals triumphed, it was at first Rousseau who had the upper hand. The second point I found interesting in Durant's analysis concerned the link between religious and societal change. When Christianity emerged under the Roman Empire, existing institutions continued to function despite the spiritual transformation. During the Renaissance the reverse was the case: spiritual values held fast while economic and social institutions changed and developed. The French Revolution, on the other hand, attacked both spiritual values and social institutions at one and the same time. This, in Durant's view, was why France experienced several decades of turbulence. The same observation can be made about the Iranian revolution, in that it called into question, in the name of religion, the spirit of secularism on which all the reforms undertaken since the start of the century were based, and it overthrew the monarchy and its entire administrative system. Small wonder, then, that Iran also had a difficult time regaining its equilibrium.

The Tattooed Crown

In the spring of 1982, when a slowdown in the number of executions created a rather less tense atmosphere and when we were happy to be reading our history books, one day we witnessed the arrival of a most peculiar person. He was about fifty and had a very thick black beard. The whites of his eyes seemed to reduce his pupils to black dots, and his glum and mistrustful glance gave him an incredibly taciturn look. His frightening appearance was thrown into even greater relief when the detainees learned that the man, who answered to the unusual name of Shourjeh, had—or so he claimed—been commander of a firing squad and that he had executed five hundred "renegades" like us. Claiming to have been the assistant of the "hanging judge" Khalkhali, he told us with great pride that he had started with the execution of the former regime's officials in the first few months of the revolution and then moved on to drug traffickers. In full view of a number of pasdars, he had shot a bullet into the hand of a man who had been instructing him, through the intermediary of the tribunal, to evacuate his house. He had been locked up on instructions of Evin's chief judge, Ayatollah Gilani. Despite his offense he continued to behave aggressively as if he had the right to sit in judgment on everyone else. After the arrival of Shourjeh, Haji Reza did everything he could to avoid him and never came near our section because he felt that such people tarnished the image of the revolution. The less-educated pasdars, on the other hand, seemed quite impressed with Shourjeh. Claiming to be "the voice of the people," he harangued us endlessly, ostensibly to show us the right path but in fact to prove his Khomeini credentials to the pasdars.

Although he was illiterate, he hid the fact so well that we did not discover it for quite some time, and thanks to his intelligence and incredibly good memory he could talk nonstop for two hours each morning and two hours each afternoon in a pure and relentless revolutionary fashion. He would denounce, at one and the same time, imperialism, Zionism, Freemasonry, Marxism, nationalism, and the like, directing his words at specific individuals and threatening them with the firing squad. He refused to leave in peace those prisoners who wanted to read quietly in a corner of the courtyard because he felt certain they were only studying in order to be of better service to the interests of imperialism and the CIA. As usual, the skeptics were convinced that he had been sent deliberately by the prison administration to make our lives hell, whereas I believed that the authorities were themselves embarrassed by the presence of such an insolent person—whose son was, to top it all, himself a pasdar. My companions were even more irritated by the insults of this "preacher of revolutionary Islam" when they learned that a few years earlier he had been a member of a gang of crooks in southern Tehran.

This sinister companion of ours seemed to have an incredibly strong constitution: he hardly ate and could sleep virtually anywhere. Exhausted by his diatribes, we were desperate to make him stop. A dentist who found him particularly unbearable had tried to confront him directly on a number of occasions, but I advised him against this and persuaded him to wait for a suitable opportunity to get rid of him. One day someone told me that he had noticed a tattooed royal crown on Shourjeh's left forearm, although it was normally well hidden by his sleeve. I immediately let my companions know that the day of reckoning was approaching, but first we had to confirm the existence of the tattoo. After all, here was a man who lectured everyone, including the Islamic authorities, about revolutionary rectitude and who claimed to have executed a hundred or so officials from the Shah's regime, but who had preserved his royal tattoo throughout his revolutionary zeal. It was clear that he lacked the courage to inflict a few days of pain on himself in order to remove it with sulfuric acid.[11]

I decided to take personal charge of the situation and to draw maximum advantage from the opportunity provided by the month of Ramadan, during which we performed our ablutions at about two o'clock in the morning. On three successive nights I rose in the hope of seeing the famous tattoo, and finally succeeded in spotting an imperial crown framed by two swords on Shourjeh's left forearm. I said to the dentist, "Without picking a quarrel with him, just say, 'With such a tattoo I would keep my mouth shut if I were you!' "

The dentist, who had been waiting for this moment, lost no time in carrying out my instructions. Typically, Shourjeh's immediate reaction was to start hurling all manner of abuse at the dentist. Nevertheless he stopped gracing us with his speeches, and a few weeks later Haji Reza managed to have him transferred to another prison. What became of him, I wonder?

11. In our section there was a prisoner who had been a frogman under the former regime. His body was covered from head to toe with scars and blisters because he had used sulfuric acid to remove the tattoos which had formerly covered his body: images of naked women and inscriptions unacceptable to the Islamic regime.

Victory Against Saddam Hussein

On May 24, 1982, Iranian troops recaptured Khorramshahr, the big Persian Gulf port which had been taken by the Iraqis during their surprise attack in September 1980. The victory was received with great joy by the prisoners and jailors alike. From the beginning of the Iran-Iraq War a great many Iranians who were otherwise hostile to the Islamic Republic had fallen in line behind Khomeini with the aim of pushing Saddam's troops out of southwestern Iran.[12]

It is not surprising then, that at the time of the liberation of Khorramshahr virtually everyone allowed himself to be carried along by the spirit of patriotism, with a large majority of the people supporting the policies of the regime. We were at that moment within an inch of attaining national unity, because all those professionals, civilian or military, who had previously considered the clergy to be an anachronistic body and who had refused to believe in its mobilizing power during the revolution,[13] could now see clearly that they were extremely effective in the battle against invaders. At the same time the young pasdars, more of whom were working class and to a man were Islamists, had to acknowledge the moral strength and efficiency of the secular classes. To cite an example: one of our companions, Ali Ardalan, who had been Bazargan's finance minister and who was arrested at the same time as me for having protested, in the name of the National Front, against some of the regime's repressive measures, was now entirely behind the policy of legitimate national defense and would declare to anyone willing to listen that Saddam Hussein had to be put in his place. He also condemned without reservation his former National Front ally, Shahpour Bakhtiar, who from Paris maintained rather ambiguous links with Saddam.

At any rate, the joy of the Khorramshahr victory was reinforced by the prospects of peace presented by Saddam's offer to withdraw his troops behind internationally recognized borders. All the necessary conditions for a cease-fire were there, and Iran was within sight of

12. It was for this reason in particular, as I say earlier, that the Mojahedin's armed rebellion had no chance of success.

13. Nationalists, Marxists, and Islamists alike all claimed sole rights to the ideas and impetus which had caused the revolution (whereas it was in fact a result of the symbiosis of all these tendencies).

peace. In the meantime we prisoners managed to put together some proposals for the reconstruction of the war-damaged areas of the country. We pooled all our professional resources—soliciting the assistance of specialists, such as construction engineers, agronomists, economists, and former officials who were familiar with Khuzestan—to prepare a report setting out our conception of how urban and rural life might be revived in the ravaged area. When we called Haji Reza over to give him the hundred-page report and ask him to whom we should send it, he said, "You've performed a very useful task here. It's absolutely essential that it be brought to the attention of the president of the republic. I'm going to see to the matter personally."

We were in for a letdown a few weeks later when the Iranian forces continued their advance and pushed into Iraqi territory for reasons which completely escaped us. The cease-fire we had been looking forward to never materialized. Not only through this act did Iran squander a precious opportunity to claim war reparations, but also, more tragically, it lost a historic chance to reestablish national unity. For on the day when Iranian troops crossed into Iraq, the universal support for what had been a defensive war was shattered.

This was in fact the second time that the Islamic regime had allowed the opportunity to create a large-scale national consensus slip through its fingers. The first, of course, had been immediately after the victory of the revolution, on February 11, 1979. An entire nation had risen up to overthrow a monarchy which had ceased to represent it, but the extremism of some Islamist circles, influenced by Marxism, helped antagonism to prevail over the will to national unity and fanned the divisions in society. This schism was to lead to the removal from government posts of experienced officials and professionals, for which the regime is still paying the price.

From the summer of 1982 onward, opposition to the war began to gain ground to such an extent that Bazargan and his allies moved to publish open letters addressed to Khomeini and to circulate pamphlets demanding an end to the hostilities. As I write this nine years later, one can see that many of the problems that the Islamic government now faces are the result of a conflict which was imposed on us but which we could and should have ended earlier.

Some Islamic leaders, many of them young and inexperienced, were convinced that the Muslim people, and especially the Shiites of

Iraq, would rise up against Saddam Hussein. They were, however, committing a mistake similar to that of officials in Baghdad who had counted on disorder in the army and a rebellion of the Arab-speaking population of Khuzestan when Iraq attacked Iran. In a word, if Iranian nationalism made people deaf to Iraq's Arabism, Iraqi nationalism, in turn, did not succumb to Iran's Islamist appeal. Many analysts believe that had the war ended in 1982—that is, before Iranian troops advanced into Iraq—Saddam Hussein's regime would have collapsed. In fact the Iranian attack provided Saddam with an undreamed-of opportunity to arouse his people's nationalism and suppress the opposition. One way or the other, the Iranian people continued to support the war effort, but they did so without the enthusiasm they had shown in the first two years of the conflict.

The Gynecologist's Refuge

In the winter of 1981–1982 new arrivals in our section included not only members of organizations involved in armed insurrection but also members of various professions—the so-called "liberals" whose arrest could be explained by the extensive powers given to the revolutionary tribunal. For example, when the Iranian bar was disbanded because the revolutionary tribunal did not recognize its legitimacy, a number of jurists who had resisted the decision found their way to Evin. Another profession which came under pressure was gynecology, for the tribunal wanted to make abortion illegal. From the moment he arrived I found one of the gynecologists detained in our villa especially interesting because he seemed to behave rather oddly for a doctor. He did everything he possibly could to appear "Islamic." Immediately on arrival, for example, he asked us to tell him in which direction Mecca lay so that he could perform his prayers five times a day—unusual behavior for a doctor who had spent twenty years in the Soviet Union. All in all, he seemed incredibly keen to adhere to the prison regulations, and he gave the strange impression that he was perfectly at home in this kind of situation.

One day he agreed to walk with me in the yard, and he explained to me that he was the nephew of Dr. Morteza Yazdi, a leader of the pro-Soviet Tudeh party, and that in 1943, thanks to this family relationship, he had been sent at the age of fourteen to the Soviet

Union to study along with about twenty other youngsters (this was at a time when the Red Army was occupying part of Iran). He had lived at first in Baku and then moved to Moscow. He told me that of his twenty years in the Soviet Union he had spent ten studying and ten working, and had but one single objective: to leave the country. But during the 1940s and 1950s it was virtually impossible to obtain a passport and permission to leave. He had therefore adopted the tactic of not saying or doing anything that could cause the slightest suspicion of him. In order to have no commitments he had never married, and he had discovered that the way to stay out of trouble in the Soviet Union was not to allow oneself any free time. He told me that leisure would itself have constituted a danger because it would have meant spending time with Iranian immigrant circles which were thoroughly infiltrated by the KGB. He had therefore volunteered to work eight hours during the night in his hospital, in addition to his routine eight hours during the day. As a surgeon-gynecologist he had spent his time in operating theatres, where he not only felt in his professional element but where he also felt safe in the knowledge that no one could really speak—the anesthetist and the nurse were gagged by their hygienic masks, and the patient was fast asleep. . . .

This silence was doubly reassuring, for he was neither in a position to speak himself nor did he risk overhearing others, in which case he might have had to report what they said. It was thanks to those long years of silence that our gynecologist managed to return to Iran during the time of the Shah, even though he knew he would have to spend a year in prison for having lived in a communist country. When he stepped off the ship at the Caspian Sea port of Enzeli, he voluntarily delivered himself to Savak agents, who were waiting to dole out his preordained punishment, without making even the slightest gesture toward the members of his family whom he saw also waiting for him on the quay.

The day after this conversation I wanted to continue our discussion and asked him about the way things were run in his Russian hospital, but he said, "I spoke a lot yesterday. For the love of heaven, please don't ask me any more questions. It terrifies me. I will only answer you this one last time, but only on condition that you don't ask me anything else. As for the hospital, well, when our names were called on the loudspeaker, it was exactly like here. We were never sure why they were calling us; it could just be a matter of someone visiting us; it could be for praise or for punishment; or it could be that we were being sent to a town we wanted to go to or, quite the reverse, to a town we didn't want to go to. Anything was possible at any moment, and no one was certain what the next day would bring. There you are, my friend, I have told you everything now, and I'm sure you've understood it all very well."

Thanks to his twenty years in the Soviet Union he adapted immediately to prison life. He never complained and he was so adept at answering questions under cross-examination that he was given the minimum sentence possible at the time.

When I met him after leaving Evin he gave me the impression of being a perfectly well-adjusted citizen. He had married a country woman from a traditional and very religious family and did not seem beset by any of the uncertainties suffered by his colleagues. Despite the upheavals that the minister of health had set in motion in the national association of doctors, our gynecologist was, unlike many of his colleagues who raised protest after protest, the very personification of serenity.

The Party of Foreigners

Apart from the gynecologist there were a number of Tudeh party members in our section, most notably ex-army officers who had sought refuge in the Soviet Union about thirty years earlier. Many of these political emigrés had returned to Iran in the wake of Khomeini's own return in February 1979. Although they considered themselves to be superior cadres, they did not measure up to their pretensions, either politically or intellectually.[14] On top of this, after spending many years in the grip of the KGB terror, their personalities were broken and they suffered from a permanent state of insecurity. In short, they bore little resemblance to the eager activists who had emigrated to the Soviet Union all those years ago.

14. In the eyes of the younger generation, which believed that the Shah had deprived them of something by concealing the achievements of communism, the intellectual mediocrity of these graduates of Soviet universities inflicted a fatal blow—especially in the field of human sciences—to the myth of "Soviet expertise."

The Tudeh was established in 1941 after the occupation of Iran by British and Soviet troops, which was followed by Reza Shah's abdication and a return to democracy in the country. During its early years the party represented for workers, the middle class, and intellectuals alike, progress, liberty, and national independence. But at the end of World War II the party's image began to change. The Red Army refused to withdraw from northern Iran and tried to establish a "democratic" puppet government in Azerbaijan. Pressured by the Soviet embassy in Tehran, the Tudeh party decided to support that government even though Iranian nationalists regarded it as a secessionist movement which could only lead to the partition of the country.

The Tudeh emerged considerably weakened from this experience and was further weakened when the party doggedly ignored Mosaddeq's popular movement for the nationalization of oil until it ended in failure in 1953. This second experience laid to rest any hope that the Tudeh could act as a defender of national interests. Despite the heroic opposition of some of its members to the acts of repression perpetrated by the Pahlavi regime after the 1953 coup, it came to be seen in the end as a party which was totally dependent on the Soviet Union and therefore devoid of any credibility.

In 1979 the party's leaders returned from exile in the Soviet Union determined to make up for lost time by opportunistically presenting themselves as passionate supporters of the Islamic upheaval. Men and women who had been shaped during the preceding forty years by the materialist conception of history and who were wholly permeated with the spirit of Stalinism turned overnight into ardent defenders of the revolution and implacable proponents of a fiercely religious system. Insensitive to the cultural aspects of the revolution, they set about trying to guide the Islamists' determination to create a less materialist society in the direction of a permanent climate of essentially anti-American ferment. They even managed to cause dissension within the ranks of the new ruling class itself.

Always careful to proclaim their allegiance to "Khomeini's line," they decided to target, in the name of a totally Islamic revolution, the moderate wing of the religious leaders whom they described as "liberals in the service of imperialism." They played a decisive role in sabotaging the Bazargan government and in pushing the Islamists (whose own ideal was to establish a truly independent regime, free of both East and West) into adopting a predominantly anti-Western position. In November 1979, when the American embassy in Tehran was occupied and the diplomats taken hostage—deeds which had been carried out with the assistance of the Mojahedin and other Marxist and Islamist extremists—they could congratulate themselves on not only precipitating the fall of the Bazargan government but also, and more significantly, on bringing to an end a brief period of multipartyism. Their sole aim was to bring about the establishment of a pro-Soviet revolutionary dictatorship in which they would have been the prime movers.

These calculations were undone by the Islamists and in particular by the revolutionary guards, who controlled the levers of power and who had trained their sights on the Tudeh from the start. When a key KGB agent supplied information to the pasdars about relations between the Tudeh and the KGB, the evidence against them became overwhelming and they were easily indicted on charges of espionage. The information was so damning that when in February 1982 the first groups of communist activists began to arrive in Evin, no one doubted the role they had played as stooges of the Soviet Union. On that day there was a mood of optimism among most of the prisoners, for they saw the operation launched against the "party of foreigners" as a significant step toward the cleansing of a regime which they had feared would be irretrievably infiltrated by Tudeh members. There were even prisoners, especially among the liberals, who declared that they were ready to forgive their own imprisonment, unjustified though it had been, now that the regime had proved itself capable of arresting communists caught "red handed." And former officers of the imperial army could not hide their admiration for the ways the Islamic government had managed to expose the party—they believed that the revolutionary guards had been far more efficient than Savak in the battle against Soviet infiltration.

Date Omelette

Another group of prisoners at Evin were people accused of transgressing Islamic morality—people, for example, arrested while holding a birthday party in which boys and girls danced together or consumed alcohol. Usually it was as a result of a neighbor's denunciation that members of "ethics committees" would enter someone's house, arrest the guilty parties, and take them to the committee building. People detained in this way were normally released the next day after signing statements saying that they would never take part in such "debaucheries" again. This did not apply to recidivists who were sometimes sent to Evin. We had among us three such men who had been prison guards and were now serving a two-year sentence for organizing "orgies" with singers and dancers they had met in Evin. To explain: Immediately after the revolution the procurator of the revolutionary tribunal had summoned comedians, dancers, and singers of all types to tell them that they could no longer put on plays and shows or act in films unless they adhered to certain rules of "Islamic decency," and that under no circumstances were women to sing in the presence of men. The three ex-guards had been accused of arranging private dates, while on duty in the procurator's antechamber, with female performers called before the tribunal, whom they later met in town. The judge-mullahs were usually not very severe in such cases. As long as they obtained a statement of contrition from the guilty parties, combined with a firm declaration that the offense would not be repeated, the accused were generally released. But because our guards had been on duty and their offense was thus considered an abuse of power, they had been sentenced to two years' imprisonment as an example to others.

Haji Reza, who knew these men very well, treated them with particular concern and even affection, and was determined to reform them. He had appointed two of them, who were serving their terms in our villa, to be in charge of our section. They were obliging in the extreme, and they did all they could to improve our conditions. Haji Reza came from time to time to have breakfast with them in their small room in the villa. He often asked me to join them on these occasions, and we would discuss the cases of some of the prisoners whose offenses were not very serious and who could probably have been released with a small administrative "push in the right direction." Believing as a good Islamist in the need to establish a fairer regime for all citizens and a more independent state in relation to foreign powers, Haji Reza did not subscribe to the view that everything inherited from the past should be systematically rejected. I sensed that in fact he was irritated by those among the Islamists who advocated a fresh start from zero, and this was undoubtedly why he never tired of asking me questions. At the end of our breakfast sessions, which tended to go on forever, he would stand up and say in a mock stern voice, "That's quite enough for today! Otherwise they [he meant the hard-liners of the regime and the revolutionary tribunal] will decide that I've allowed myself to be seduced by counter-revolutionaries."

Haji Reza's wish to converse with people who did not belong to his own circles and who were in a position to broaden his horizons was tempered with fear that he might be seen as a counterrevolutionary. This was an ambivalence that could be detected in all the officials of the Islamic Republic, at all levels. In private they were quite willing to have contact with "others," but they made a point of not doing so in public.

One of the privileges we owed to Haji Reza's kindness, and one that was particularly appreciated, was being allowed to keep, after winter had ended, the oil stove we used for making tea and sometimes to cook. Drinking tea as often as one likes is considered by Iranians to be a blessing. The possibility of making a few of our own dishes now and then to augment our regular meals was an additional boon. At lunchtime we were usually given rice (the national dish) accompanied by a sauce with vegetables, but we rarely had meat. In the evenings we were served badly cooked kidney beans or a tasteless soup.

On Thursday evenings, when many of the staff left Evin for a day at home, the authorities found it easier to serve eggs, which for us were a real treat. Each of the several thousand prisoners was allowed two; they were usually delivered already cooked but as a favor were sent raw to our section. The twenty-five to thirty prisoners in each room had subdivided themselves into groups of five to eight who always ate together. The head of each "mealtime collective" would take a turn on the oil stove to cook the eggs. But since the stove gave off only limited heat, the omelette-cooking ritual would last from five until nine in the evening. As the head of my collective of eight people, I would manage to make three omelettes from our weekly quota of sixteen eggs. The secret was to use the whole range of ingredients at our disposal: potatoes, tomatoes, onions, and even apples and dates.

In this way I could serve, according to the mood of the day, a Mexican, Russian, or Italian omelette, for which I became duly famous. A useful rule was never to turn away food offered by the prison administration but instead to try to improve it. For example, once a week our supper ration was a kind of stew. It was inedible in itself, but the ingredients were not of bad quality if taken separately. So we would take the carrots from the stew and recook the potatoes and meat on the oil stove, adding a few onions and some tomato sauce which we could buy at our small prison cooperative. In this way the stew would be transformed into a completely different meal for our collective. Then there were the awful kidney beans, which the prisoners refused to eat, preferring instead to dip into their personal stocks of butter and cheese. I was quite happy to use the rejected beans and to fry them with a "white sauce." They were consumed with delight by everyone.

My companions used to congratulate me on my culinary innovations, and when at the end of the meal they thanked me for my efforts, I would tell the radicals among them: "Unlike you, I am not a revolutionary, and I don't advocate that we reject everything and start again from scratch. Instead I try to improve what I have, using the ingredients at my disposal. But this is precisely the kind of reformist approach that fills you with horror."

Haji Reza and a number of other pasdars sometimes came to share a meal with us, and they too appreciated my culinary efforts. That was why they turned a blind eye to the source of my onions which "the person in charge of meal distribution" would hide in his pockets or under his shirt when he fetched our food in a huge pot from the central kitchen.

Cross-examined at Last . . .

After a year and a half in detention I was called at last for cross-examination. According to the established custom, the names of the prisoners, who had to stand at the ready by the door of the villa, were read out on the loudspeakers. The prisoners were then taken by the pasdars via the prison courtyard to the central building. From the villa to the magistrate's office, they had to wear blindfolds. Then it was up to the examining magistrate to decide, according to the nature of the charges, whether the accused had to keep wearing his blindfold or could be allowed to take it off; this would set the tone for the session from the very start. In my case, the magistrate asked me in a stern but polite voice to take the blindfold off.

His questions were exactly the same as those put to me in my two previous sessions in April 1979 and in March–April 1980: they centered on my general impressions of the two regimes. When I said that the answers to all his questions had already been recorded in my file, he gave me to understand that before he could release me, he had to have a few pages of questions and answers to show that he had performed his duties properly. In the course of his preliminary investigations he had interrogated Bani-Sadr's former collaborators about his relations with me and was convinced that I had not seen Bani-Sadr during the sixteen months of his presidency. So he had no reason to keep me in Evin. After several sessions in his office our relations became increasingly cordial, and in one of these he told me that Ayatollah Khamene'i, who as I write is the "leader of the Islamic Republic" but who was then president, had asked the procurator on two occasions why I was being held for so long without trial. I realized that the magistrate wanted to be in a position to answer the question, because he asked me to explain the reason. I told him, "You can say that you were kept busy with your investigations into the activities of terrorist groups and that people of my kind suffered as a consequence." After a few weeks he informed me that I was to be released the following day, and that I could ring my wife to ask her to come and fetch me at 9:30 a.m. at Evin's main gate.

On the next day, however, I was not called until 2 p.m. I was taken to the central building where an assistant examining magistrate took responsibility for me. He led me, still blindfolded, to another office. He told me that the case had "slipped out of their hands" and that others who were not part of the Evin revolutionary tribunal wanted to question me. If it had been up to "my judge," he said, I would have been released right away.

I found myself before the new examining magistrate who had come specifically to question me and in whose presence I had to wear a blindfold (for the first time since the beginning of the revolution). I sensed immediately that I was facing a person who was deeply prejudiced against me. As far as he was concerned, I had been a real *éminence grise*, both at the time of the Shah and that of Bani-Sadr. Nevertheless, as he became familiar with my case—gradually making his way through my Savak file, which he had not seen before—I had the feeling that his suspicions were diminishing. After a few hours the interrogation was suspended, and the magistrate sent me to Section 6, escorted by a pasdar. There was no suggestion that I was about to be released. For the next few days I was in a state of depression, and I understood how painful an unfulfilled promise of liberation can be for a prisoner. I was given no explanation of why the decision to release me had been annulled. I learned little by little, mostly through messages from my former examining magistrate, conveyed to me by other prisoners, that the revolutionary guards outside Evin had intervened in my case. I realized that I was once again the target of left-wing groups who had managed to poison the minds of the revolutionary guards, even though the two groups were busy fighting each other. The new examining magistrate came two weeks in succession. After the third session I was left with the impression that he would not come again, because he was so perturbed by the huge gap between the image he had of me and the facts before him. His position was all the more difficult because revolutionary pride did not allow fervent militants like him to admit that they had been wrong. So I stayed imprisoned in the villa for another six months until one day, during a visit, my wife announced that I was soon to be transferred to the central tribunal's house of detention, where the cases of prisoners considered to be nonsubversive were dealt with.

One fine day in September 1983 I was asked to present myself at the door of the villa, where a pasdar told me to get into a car without a blindfold—which was exceptional. We crossed Evin's main courtyard and headed for the central tribunal's detention building, a few kilometers away, where about forty prisoners were being held, all more or less on the way to liberation. The atmosphere at the detention center was vastly different from that of Evin. The food, to take just one significant example, was much better, and I was offered dishes which included meat. On the day after my arrival I was taken to a judge who had proper legal training and whose level of political understanding was much higher than the examining magistrates I had encountered up to then. With great deference and modesty the judge said, "Mr. Naraghi, your file was passed on to me about two months ago. I have examined it carefully, and I have not found anything in it that might justify your arrest. No charges can be brought against you, and I can certainly not see anything here that would justify a twenty-seven-month detention. That's why I've been awaiting your arrival with impatience in the hope that you could explain your adventure to me yourself."

The Judge's Mea Culpa

It took me two hours to tell him about my numerous arrests and interrogations and to establish the absurdity of pressing any sort of charge against me. The judge, whose name was Ansari, heard me out and, clearly moved, said in reply, "I have to acknowledge that for five years all Islamic activists, including myself, were misled by the reputation fabricated for you by the pro-Soviet communists. I must confess that as a student I myself mentioned your name in a political meeting in Mashad as an example of the type of intellectual under the former regime whom we were vilifying. But after examining your file and the books and articles you've published, I realized how unfair I had been. As a Muslim I solemnly plead for your forgiveness and beg that you accept my apology." He went on to say:

"My request for forgiveness obviously has no bearing on your situation as a prisoner, and as an examining magistrate I'm going to ask the procurator general to bring you before a tribunal in a way which will remove, once and for all, any ambiguity about your position. But before the procurator passes judgment on your case, I'm asking for your religious forgiveness for the nonsensical ideas I had about you. It was an example of bad judgment, which I pledge to rectify."

I naturally told him I would be only too happy to grant his wish, and in the Persian tradition I rose to embrace him.

This conversation could not be described as an interrogation and was a source of tremendous satisfaction to me. Quite apart from the judge's modesty and his heartfelt apology, his thoroughgoing familiarity with my case served to reassure me. He told me that he had tried to reconstruct my life from my early youth and that he had read all my writings carefully. In the two months preceding my transfer from Evin to the central tribunal—a procedure which always took a long time—he had not lost a moment in gathering information about me. For example, in volume seven of the documents that the Islamists who had occupied the American embassy had published in 1980, he had discovered a report about me dating from 1967 by the American diplomat Martin Herz, which was a kind of political memorandum to his successor before he left Tehran.

The document set out the American diplomat's opinion of some thirty personalities in Iran, among whom I figured. Whereas Herz attested to the loyalty of the majority of this group to the Americans, he described me as someone who was interesting to cultivate but who showed no particular allegiance to the United States.

Herz's skepticism derived from a United Nations–sponsored project I began in 1966 on the brain drain from Asian, African, and Latin American countries. Convinced that the best way to tackle this issue was to make the leaders of these countries aware of the scale of the damage inflicted by this loss of skilled personnel, I arranged an interview with the *New York Times* to ensure that the paper published extracts from my report as soon as it was submitted to the UN. A number of State Department officials offered me considerable assistance in accomplishing my task, particularly during the time I spent in Washington. There were, nevertheless, other less imaginative functionaries who were irritated by my findings. The suggestion that the United States, far from providing scientific assistance to Third World countries, was, quite the reverse, depriving them of a large part of their most qualified personnel, was a new idea at the time and one that some American officials were not terribly pleased to have brought to their attention. So when I refused to give a copy of the second part of my report to the American cultural attaché in Tehran, the embassy was doubly annoyed, since they were not used to having their requests turned down by anyone in the Iranian administration.[15]

15. This report contained the following passage: "Our experience with him in discussing the Brain Drain has been disappointing, for his emphasis seems to be so anxious to publish his book on the subject that it is almost as if he were reserving his principal points in order to make another public splash. Naraghi is an interesting conversationalist, and his disheveled exterior conceals a mind that is both orderly and imaginative. He is not, in my opinion, a 'Savak agent,' but it is normal that he should not preserve any confidences, for he owes no special loyalty. He is someone to cultivate."

When Ansari showed me the page in the volume of the U.S. embassy documents where this affair was mentioned, he confessed to me that as far as the Islamists had been concerned, anyone who had frequented the embassies of the big foreign powers had espoused their views; but an examination of the available information had shown that their assumption had not been correct and that it was possible for someone to frequent foreign embassies and to remain a true Iranian patriot.

Tapped Telephones

Another document in my Savak file which contributed to my exoneration was a transcript of my telephone conversations with Ali Amini. During the revolutionary crisis I had been in the habit of ringing Amini (a former prime minister) and Abdollah Entezam (a former foreign minister) to discuss my conversations with the Shah. The primary purpose of my telephone calls had been to find out whether there was a correspondence between what the Shah said to them and what he said to me; but in addition I had wanted to coordinate my own reactions with theirs, for these two men harbored no personal ambitions and were therefore in a position to contribute to the resolution of the crisis.

One day when the Shah had asked me for my honest opinion about his personal fortune (which had increasingly become an issue in public debates), I had replied that I believed he should openly bequeath his wealth to the nation if only to put an end to the debate that was causing enormous damage. When I reported this exchange to Amini, I first told him, with some amusement, about a mannerism I had frequently observed in the course of my conversations with the sovereign. Whenever he sat down the Shah was in the habit of crossing his legs and maintaining that same position for long periods, in a manner that was both dignified and relaxed. But when he seemed to find one of my questions irritating, he would show his discomfort by suddenly changing his posture, uncrossing his legs and crossing them the other way. It gradually dawned on me that the Shah performed this ritual when he was confronted with facts he did not wish to face. And that was exactly what he had done when I made my suggestions about his fortune: nervously recrossing his legs, he had assured me that he had already donated his fortune to the Pahlavi Foundation.

During the interrogation in which this document was discussed, the judge told me how Savak had used its telephone taps to prepare detailed reports about my views of the state of the country, reports which had reached the Shah through high-ranking officials. The judge was clearly baffled by what he had read in my file. He found it difficult to understand why the Shah had not taken steps against me when my analyses amounted to open criticism of his political views and when I had allowed myself to go so far as to make humorous remarks about the way he crossed and uncrossed his legs. I explained that the Shah had really had no other choice because, faced with the disturbing turn of events, he needed to listen to the views of people he had previously kept at a distance. I also told him that the Shah had had an amazing capacity for concealing his feelings, and that he should bear in mind the fact that my telephone conversations only served to confirm the general tenor of remarks I had made to the Shah's face, although at the palace I had obviously been a little more discreet.

The Savak recordings of my conversations with Amini proved particularly valuable for my defense when I eventually appeared before the revolutionary tribunal. My judges could see for themselves that I had maintained my independence under the former regime and that, even though I had been in constant contact with the court, I had never become its unquestioning servant.

In its final judgment which led to my acquittal, the tribunal thus specifically jettisoned the hypothesis that I had been in connivance with the court. It was not without irony that the indiscreet "eaves-dropping" of a regime reviled by the revolutionaries played a part in convincing the Islamic judges of my innocence.

At the end of my sessions with him, the examining judge acknowledged that my detention had been unjustified. He assured me that he would ask the procurator to release me immediately. When I took my leave of him on that day, I felt extremely glad that I had finally come before a competent and just person. He phoned me a few days later to tell me that my detention was at an end at last, that I was free to go, and that I should set about preparing my defense for the revolutionary tribunal, dismissing all the accusations made against me, explicit or otherwise. He advised me to write what was tantamount to an autobiography, because he was of the opinion that it would be useful, given the thick file Savak had on me, for my own views to be available to the court along with everyone else's. I was set free on September 28, 1983, and several months later, in March 1984, I appeared before Section 9 of the tribunal to have a final judgment passed on my case.

On the basis of the conclusions reached by Ansari, the tribunal—presided over by a cleric named Nazem-Zadeh—acquitted me on all charges. Most notably, I was entirely cleared of accusations of connivance with the former regime, of extracting material gains, and of maintaining any kind of political relationship with Bani-Sadr. The tribunal also lifted all the restrictions imposed on my reentry into academic life and granted me the right to claim five years' back pay for my post as university lecturer (for my salary had been frozen by the revolutionary committees).

Afterward I would meet Ansari from time to time. He was studying for a degree in law, and he used to ask me for advice about the books he should read. Whenever I gave him a book which had become difficult to obtain in the shops he would be deeply touched, and he always insisted on paying me. It was only when I offered him copies of my own works that he was prepared to accept them as gifts.

One of the issues that preoccupies a prisoner when he is freed is the question of who, apart from his family, played a part in trying to obtain his release. Out of prison at last, I began to learn, little by little, about the men and women both inside and outside my country who had been concerned about my fate and who had tried to intervene on my behalf with the Iranian authorities. Among many others were Claude Bourdet and his wife, whom I have known for more than thirty years, and Jacques Attali, whom I had grown to respect from the time when, having completed his studies in 1971, I entrusted him with some research work in his capacity as a UNESCO adviser. On my wife's request, all my friends' help was channeled through Amadou-Mahtar M'Bow, UNESCO's director general, who acted with great tact and determination.

The Quiet Courage of the Simple People

Possibly the most effective of all the pleas made on my behalf was that of Rassouli, the driver who had worked for me before the revolution. It was only two years after I had left prison, and then by the most unlikely chance, that I learned of his courageous and almost foolhardy deed, though he brought me flowers the day after I was released.

Rassouli had become one of the ardent supporters of the Islamic revolution on the staff of the Ministry of Higher Education, but when he heard of my imprisonment he had not hesitated to organize a petition to the revolutionary tribunal, requesting that I be released. It was signed by many members of the service personnel: drivers, messengers, watchmen, cleaners, secretaries.

The signatories had referred in the petition to my behavior toward the ministry's humblest employees and stressed that I had always acted in their interest, even when this had involved breaking administrative rules. They declared that they could not understand how a regime which claimed to be Islamic and popular could hold a person like me behind bars.

A few months later, when the country was in the grip of great tension and executions were a daily event at Evin, Rassouli received a strange and worrying telephone call late one evening: "This is Evin Prison. Are you indeed Rassouli?"

"Yes, sir."

"It was you, wasn't it, who sent a petition in favor of the cursed Naraghi?"

"Yes, sir," he replied in a steady voice.

"I suppose you're aware that pleading on behalf of a traitor is tantamount to being a traitor oneself?"

"Yes, sir."

"If you know that, why did you plead in Naraghi's favor?"

"Because neither I nor the other people who signed the petition believe that your prisoner is a traitor."

"In that case, you would presumably be prepared to come and testify to this effect before the tribunal."

"Yes, sir."

"The others would also come?"

"Yes, sir, the others would also come."

All of a sudden and totally unexpectedly, the man at the end of the line broke into laughter and announced to the bewildered Rassouli: "Put your mind at ease. Neither you nor your friends will be summoned to the tribunal, because we've reached the same conclusion as you. Your man has been a victim of ill-intentioned machinations. We've decided that he's innocent and he'll soon be released. You may reassure your friends. Good night."

Chronology

1901. Granting of the first concession by the Qajar king to D'Arcy, an English banker, for the exploitation of oil resources for sixty-six years.

1906. Establishment of a constitutional monarchy.

1926. End of the Qajar dynasty and the accession to the throne of Reza Shah Pahlavi.

1935. Persia becomes Iran, by royal decree, in all national and international correspondence.

August 25, 1941. Occupation of Iranian territory by British and Soviet troops.

September 17, 1941. Mohammad Reza Shah becomes Shah of Iran.

February 7, 1951. General Razmara, the prime minister, is assassinated by militant Islamists.

April 28, 1951. Mosaddeq becomes prime minister and nationalizes Iran's oil.

October 16, 1952. Break of diplomatic ties with Great Britain.

August 19, 1953. Anglo-American coup against Mosaddeq brings the Shah, who had left the country three days earlier, back to Iran.

1965. Hassan-Ali Mansour, the prime minister, is assassinated by the same Islamic movement that killed Razmara in 1951.

August 6, 1977. Amir-Abbas Hoveida resigns from the post of prime minister after thirteen years in office and is replaced by Jamshid Amouzegar.

October 23, 1977. Mostafa Khomeini, the son of Ayatollah Ruhollah Khomeini, dies in Najaf (Iraq) where his father is living in exile. The death gives rise to numerous demonstrations in Iran by the Ayatollah's sympathizers.

December 31, 1977. President Jimmy Carter and his wife are received by the Shah and Empress Farah at Niavaran Palace in Tehran. He describes Iran as "an island of stability in a turbulent ocean."

January 8, 1978. A large-circulation Tehran daily publishes slanderous articles about Ayatollah Khomeini, who is notably described as "gay."

January 9, 1978. Students at Qom seminary protest against the article and organize a demonstration which leads to several deaths.

February 18, 1978. To mark the fortieth day after the deaths of the Qom protesters, violent demonstrations take place in Tabriz. Reformist clerics, led by Shariatmadari (originally from Tabriz), enter the stage with protests against the regime. The American consul in Tabriz reports that the demonstrators had mostly been young unemployed people and that their violence had been a result of the nonreligious society in which they had been raised.

March–April 1978. The National Front is increasingly seen as the opposition group likely to come to power.

June 26, 1978. The Shah declares, "No one can overthrow me. I enjoy the support of a large majority of people, of all workers, and of 700,000 soldiers." The sovereign was referring to the fact that there had not yet been any demonstrations by workers or soldiers.

August 19, 1978. The Rex cinema in Abadan is burned down, leading to more than four hundred deaths. The opposition accuses government agents of having been behind the crime, and the event marks a new stage on the way to radicalization and violence. It will emerge later that militant Islamists were to blame.

August 1978. The CIA assures President Carter that Iran "is not in a revolutionary situation, nor even in a prerevolutionary situation."

September 7, 1978. Several thousand people gather in Jaleh Square in Tehran. Demonstrations being forbidden, soldiers open fire and dozens of people are killed. The date marks a decisive break in the dialogue between the regime and the opposition. It is also a time when the masses begin to enter the stage (the square is located in a working-class area of southern Tehran), ensuring the mastery of religious leaders over the movement.

October 6, 1978. Khomeini arrives in Paris after leaving Baghdad. From now on Khomeini directs the protests from Paris as the symbol and leader of the movement (which is far from being uniformly religious).

October 10, 1978. Demonstrations in more than forty towns. Strikes by thirty thousand workers at the Isfahan steel mill, strikes in Tabriz and Sarcheshmen. In the course of the month the demands become increasingly political (calling for the lifting of martial law, the release of political prisoners, and the dissolution of Savak).

October 11, 1978. President Carter reasserts his confidence in the Shah in a press conference in Washington.

October 18, 1978. Near total stoppage at Iran's largest oil refinery in Abadan. At the end of the month oil production drops to 1.5 million barrels per day, a little more than a quarter of the production level at the beginning of the events.

October 30, 1978. The chief of police in Mashad is killed by Fedayin.

November 5–6, 1978. The Sharif-Emami government resigns and is replaced by a cabinet including many military men and headed by General Azhari. Shutting of schools and universities, suspension of liberties, the arrest of Amir-Abbas Hoveida and General Nassiri, former head of Savak.

November 11, 1978. President Carter strongly criticizes the CIA for giving him erroneous reports about the Shah's popularity.

December 6, 7, 12, 1978. Carter states publicly for the first time that he is uncertain about the Shah's prospects of holding on to power.

December 29, 1978–January 6, 1979. Shapour Bakhtiar is appointed prime minister, heading a "constitutional government," after the Shah announces his impending departure for an indefinite length of time and the establishment of a regency council.

January 6, 1979. Arrival in Iran of General Huyser, deputy commander of American forces in Europe. He has been given the task of preparing a report about the state of the armed forces, of trying to reunify the army, and of ensuring the loyalty of its commanders to the Bakhtiar government.

January 16, 1979. The Shah's definitive departure for Egypt, then Morocco (February 15), the Bahamas (February 30), Mexico (June 10), New York (October 22), Panama (December 15), and Cairo (March 23, 1980), where he dies of cancer on July 27, 1980.

February 5, 1979. Khomeini appoints Bazargan (a very close friend of Bakhtiar) as prime minister of the revolutionary government.

February 11, 1979. Announcing its neutrality, the army abandons the Bakhtiar government, making way for the coming to power of the revolutionaries headed by Khomeini.

February 12, 1979. Shapour Bakhtiar steps down. Ayatollah Khomeini calls on the population to respect public order. Jimmy Carter recognizes the new Iranian regime and proposes "peaceful cooperation" with its leaders.

February 16, 1979. Execution, after a secret trial, of four generals, including General Nassiri, former chief of Savak. Congregation of the Fedayin at Tehran University and protests against censorship and Islamic television and against a government of bazaaris which does not meet the aspirations of workers.

February 18, 1979. Break of diplomatic ties with Israel. Yassir Arafat visits Tehran.

February 19, 1979. Creation of the Islamic Republic party (IRP) by people close to Khomeini: Mohammed Javad Bahonar, Mohammed Beheshti, Seyyed Abdolkarim Mousavi, Hashemi-Rafsanjani.

February 23, 1979. In response to a call by Fedayin, 100,000 demonstrators gather at Tehran University and propose a program of opposition to imperialism and support for a workers' government.

March 30, 31–April 1, 1979. On the 30th and 31st a referendum is held over the choice of regime (abolition of the monarchy and the establishment of an Islamic republic: 94 percent in favor). On the 1st, proclamation of an Islamic republic.

April 1, 1979. Execution, after a hasty trial, of Amir-Abbas Hoveida, the Shah's former prime minister.

July 19, 1979. Announcement of a partial fusion of the Revolutionary Council and the government, marked by the entry into government of a number of religious figures as well as Bani-Sadr.

November 4, 1979. Occupation of the American embassy in Tehran and the taking of about sixty hostages by a group of armed students who demand the extradition of the former Shah from the United States. Five black hostages are released on the 22nd.

November 6–18, 1979. On the 13th Iran calls for a meeting of the UN Security Council and offers to release the hostages if the Shah is tried by an international committee of enquiry; on the 14th the members of the Security Council decide that holding such a meeting would be pointless.

November 14, 1979. The United States decides to freeze Iran's official assets after an announcement by Iran about withdrawal of Iranian deposits from American banking institutions.

January 25, 1980. Bani-Sadr is elected president of the republic.

April 19, 1980. Execution, in Iraq, of Ayatollah Baqer-Sadr, head of the Shiite community, his sister, and eight clerics.

May 1, 1980. Separate demonstrations: one called by the authorities in front of the American embassy, a rival demonstration by groups from the Tudeh, Peykar (Marxist extreme left), Fedayin, and a gathering of Mojahedin which leads to harassment by hezbollahis.

September 22–23, 1980. On the 22nd the start of the Iran-Iraq War; Iraqi aerial attacks against Iranian military bases; on the 23rd Iraqi troops move into Iran.

November 11–23, 1980. On the 11th Kurt Waldheim, UN secretary general, gives Olof Palme the task of mediating the Iran-Iraq conflict. After visiting Tehran and Baghdad, Palme rules out the possibility of rapid resolution.

January 19, 1981. In Algiers, Warren Christopher, American assistant secretary of state, signs an agreement between Iran and the United States setting out ways and means of restoring the status quo prior to November 1979: commitment to noninterference, restitution of Iran's frozen assets and the Shah's fortune, cancellation of all litigation. The Algerian Central Bank is to act as the depository and financial guarantor. A "tribunal of Iran/US disputes" is to be established within three months to settle outstanding litigation.

January 20, 1981. Fifty-two American hostages are released and leave for Algiers, then Wiesbaden, then the United States. Statements issued by the foreign ministers of EEC countries on the lifting of sanctions against Iran. Each country is left to adopt its own position.

February 5, 1981. Announcement of an operation aimed at "liquidating once and for all" the insurrection in Kurdestan, the scene of violent confrontation.

February 12, 1981. According to Hojjat ol-Eslam Ali Ghoudoussi, procurator general, Islamic tribunals have examined 11,565 cases and condemned 2,600 people, 406 of them to capital punishment; there is no incidence of torture, only "Islamically sanctioned punishments."

June 21, 1981. After two days of debate the Parliament declares the dismissal of President Bani-Sadr by 177 votes to 1, with 1 abstention.

July 25, 1981. Raja'i is elected president of the republic.

August 5, 1981. François Mitterand asks French citizens living in Iran to leave the country; calls back for consultation Guy Georgy, the French ambassador to Tehran, who has been told to leave within three days by the Iranian Foreign Ministry.

August 30, 1981. Bomb explosion at the building where the cabinet meets, killing President Raja'i and Prime Minister Bahonar. Intensification during the entire period of violent attacks and executions, particularly of the Mojahedin.

September 9, 15, 1981. Confrontations between pasdars and the Mojahedin lead to several deaths in Tehran.

September 30, 1981. Top army commanders and the minister of defense are killed in an air crash on their way home from the front.

October 2, 1981. Presidential election: Hojjat ol-Eslam Khamene'i, leader of the IRP and sole candidate after the withdrawal of the three other IRP candidates, is elected with 96 percent of the votes.

November 8, 1981. Violent clashes in Bukhn between army regulars and pasdars and Kurdish autonomists.

February 8, 1982. Twenty-two Mojahedin leaders, including Musa Khiabani, the movement's military commander, are killed in an operation launched by the pasdars.

May 24, 1982. Iranian troops take Khorramshahr.

June 9, 1982. Iraq declares a unilateral cease-fire along the entire length of the front.

December 10, 1982. Election of eighty-three members to the Assembly of Experts, responsible for selecting a single or several successors to Imam Khomeini. The assembly will meet twice a year but will not act until after the Imam's death.

February 1983. Top leaders of the Tudeh (communist party) are arrested. Eighteen Soviet diplomats are to be expelled. The Islamic revolution no longer has any internal enemies.

Index

A NOTE ON THE AUTHOR

Ehsan Naraghi was born in Kasham, Iran, studied sociology at the University of Geneva, and received a Ph.D. from the Sorbonne. In 1958 he created the Institute for Social Research and Studies in Tehran, and in 1966 he undertook for the United Nations the first worldwide study of the migration of scientists and intellectuals from poorer to richer countries. He went to Paris in 1969 as director of the Youth Division of UNESCO, and in 1975 returned to Iran as head of the Institute for Educational and Scientific Research and Planning. Among his other books are *L'Orient et la crise de l'Occident* and *Enseignement et changements sociaux en Iran du VIIe au XXe siècle*, and a number of works in Persian. He now lives in Paris where he is special adviser to the director general of UNESCO.